THE BOARD

Behind Closed Doors
With the Directors of DFP, Inc.

By

James R. Ukropina

Cover Illustration

By

Baruch Inbar

ISBN: 1-4033-8254-9 (e-book)
ISBN: 1-4033-8255-7 (Paperback)
ISBN: 1-4033-8256-5 (Dustjacket)

Library of Congress Control Number: 2002094939

This book is printed on acid free paper.

Printed in the United States of America
Bloomington, IN

1stBooks - rev. 02/04/03

International food conglomerate DFP, Inc. has enjoyed stunning growth to become a darling of the stock market, thanks in part to the heroic efforts of its visionary and charismatic CEO, Mark Gregory. But the company's Board of Directors, led by corporate veteran George Hartfield, realizes that Gregory's passionate, often shoot-from-the-hip style and his tight control might not always be in the best interests of shareholders. The resulting clash of wills, strategies and values creates high drama that mirrors today's headlines.

For anyone who has ever wondered what goes on behind closed doors at America's largest companies, this book offers an insider's view as it chronicles the life of one corporate Board. An innovative blend of fiction and keenly observed fact, *The Board* weaves a compelling tale of crisis and intrigue as DFP's Directors and CEO Gregory together face such challenges as overseas corruption, accusations of sexual harassment, stunning market reversals and the ever-present threat of a hostile takeover.

In an era when boards of directors are increasingly held accountable for the actions of a few ambitious executives, *The Board* illustrates how integrity, cooperation and solid experience can trump the pressures of emotion or expediency. Ultimately, it is the reassuring saga of the 13 dedicated men and women who serve as DFP's directors. *The Board* should be read by casual readers seeking a lively introduction to this rarefied world, by students who will find a treasure trove of behind-the-scenes insights and certainly by anyone currently serving on a board of directors. Written by a distinguished veteran of Fortune 500 boardrooms, *The Board* is a blueprint for how to ensure that effective oversight reigns in corporate America.

Dedication

This book is dedicated to my family. They provided me with the time and support to engage in corporate governance activities and encouraged me to complete this book.

The Final Cast of Characters

(Year 16)

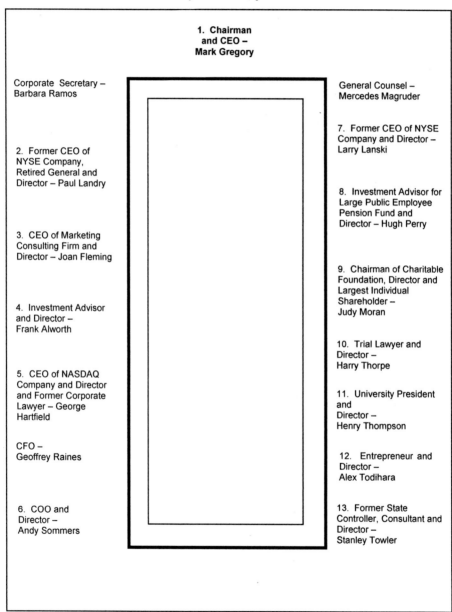

1. Chairman and CEO – Mark Gregory

Corporate Secretary – Barbara Ramos

General Counsel – Mercedes Magruder

7. Former CEO of NYSE Company and Director – Larry Lanski

2. Former CEO of NYSE Company, Retired General and Director – Paul Landry

8. Investment Advisor for Large Public Employee Pension Fund and Director – Hugh Perry

3. CEO of Marketing Consulting Firm and Director – Joan Fleming

9. Chairman of Charitable Foundation, Director and Largest Individual Shareholder – Judy Moran

4. Investment Advisor and Director – Frank Alworth

10. Trial Lawyer and Director – Harry Thorpe

5. CEO of NASDAQ Company and Director and Former Corporate Lawyer – George Hartfield

11. University President and Director – Henry Thompson

CFO – Geoffrey Raines

12. Entrepreneur and Director – Alex Todihara

6. COO and Director – Andy Sommers

13. Former State Controller, Consultant and Director – Stanley Towler

THE METAMORPHOSIS OF BOARD MEMBERSHIP: HISTORY OF DIRECTORS JOINING AND LEAVING THE BOARD OF DFP, INC.

Year of Operation of Company	Name of Director and Business Affiliation When Joining Board	Name of Director Resigning from Board
Year One	**Richard Collins** – Entrepreneur **Agnes Collins** – Spouse	
Year Two	**Dr. Henry Thompson** – University President **Alex Todihara** – Entrepreneur	**Agnes Collins**
Year Three	**David Nugent** – Supplier to DFP **Charles Frank** – Securities Firm Partner	
Year Four	**Mark Gregory** – New DFP CEO **Paul Landry** – Former CEO of NYSE company and Retired Air Force General **Hugh Perry** – Investment Advisor for Large Public Employee Pension Fund **Harry Thorpe** – Trial Lawyer	

Year Five	**George Hartfield** – CEO of NASDAQ company and Former Corporate Lawyer	
Year Six	**Judy Moran** – Former COO of Grillco **Stanley Towler** – Consultant and Former State Controller	**Charles Frank**
Year Seven	**Larry Lanski** – Former CEO of NYSE company	
Year Eight	**Robert Granger** – DFP COO	**David Nugent** **Richard Collins**
Year Nine	**Joan Fleming** – CEO of Marketing Consulting Firm **Frank Alworth** – Investment Advisor	
Year Ten		
Year Eleven		
Year Twelve		**Robert Granger**
Year Thirteen	**Andy Sommers** – DFP COO	
Year Fourteen		
Year Fifteen		
Year Sixteen		**Mark Gregory** **George Hartfield**

TABLE OF CONTENTS

Part II: TROUBLE

Part III: REBOUND

Part IV: CLOSING COMMENTARY

INTRODUCTION

"What goes on inside boardrooms?" "What are some of the difficult issues faced by directors?" This book responds to these questions and others that corporate board members receive from non-board members over and over again.

Thousands of books and articles have been written about corporate boards and corporate governance, and the current popularity of these topics is reflected by the increasing media coverage of this area, including a focus on recent corporate mega-failures. In addition, there are now annual director "colleges" at, among other places, Stanford, Harvard and Wharton. These colleges are designed to educate board members and prospective board members about the principles of good corporate board governance. But most materials about boards concentrate on how they *should or shouldn't* operate.

Why is this book different? It takes a new approach. It describes how many boards *do operate*, on a meeting-to-meeting basis, when reaching decisions concerning critical issues and matters that arise in the boardroom. It does so in a fictional setting that allows a certain amount of creative license in depicting more than the usual intensity in the relationships and issues involved. At the same time, this book is not an intense legal or business drama but instead, a fast-moving primer about how directors perform – or don't perform – their duties.

In most cases, each chapter covers a board or board committee meeting and leads off with a meeting agenda or, if emphasized, a specific agenda item; then a dialogue emerges with reflections from various board members. Finally, there is a disclosure document or epilogue depicting how the company informs its shareholders or employees about the board decision. In addition, there are "transition" sections or mock newspaper articles between chapters that briefly describe what has transpired over the period of time between board meetings.

In short, this book is a travelogue about what goes on behind boardroom doors. How one will react to this book will turn, somewhat, on how one views corporate leadership. A well-known shareholder activist, in a public address that I heard in person, once depicted all CEOs – and presumably a large number of directors, because many of them are current or former CEOs – "as liars, womanizers and cheats." I don't expect anyone with that mindset to read this book with an objective point of view.

On the other hand, a respected representative of a large, successful institutional investor advisory firm joined the board of a New York Stock Exchange company several years ago with a similar expectation of what he would encounter in his boardroom experience – his first with a large company board. When he retired from that company's board after five years of service, he told his colleagues – including this author – that he was extremely impressed with his boardroom experience because during his tenure his fellow directors had focused only on one issue: How to enhance shareholder value.

Many governance commentators place themselves between these two polar opposites – in their view, boards are usually marginally helpful or hurtful and CEOs aren't much better. In almost every instance, however, I have found my fellow directors' devotion to fiduciary duties and the CEOs' leadership roles have been exemplary and productive.

Much of the criticism that is lodged against directors – who serve the 90% of public companies that are in sound condition – appears to come from parties who have never served on boards and never will. Certain critics, while perhaps well-intentioned, are not well grounded in the difficult decisions that board members must make, often under emergency circumstances. Others, while more sophisticated, emphasize the negative, such as identifying the "worst" boards in the country and rarely identifying the "best."

What is my personal experience with board governance practices in recent years? Based upon that experience, in my opinion, most board members, CEOs and board chairmen of public companies do an effective job in representing shareholders' interests.

Some critics may say I am an apologist for directors of U.S. corporations. In fact, I am a "cheerleader" for U.S. boards because they have helped to build trillions of dollars of shareholder value. Certainly there are boards that do not merit cheers but rather a chorus of boos. The latter, however, is a very small universe compared to the former. Thus, if that is true, while vigilance for questionable corporate governance conduct is truly needed, excessive zeal could destroy a fragile framework for what has been over the past century the most productive economy in the world.

Notwithstanding the above remarks, I need to emphasize that, in my view, there is a critical need to continue to be vigilant about proposed corporate governance reforms, especially for some companies that have marginal practices in the area. Also, a warning is in order. If boards do not undertake to make appropriate changes in the governance area, look for shareholders to take the helm to a greater extent and place even more pressure on boards through shareholder proposals. These proposals, submitted by shareholders for inclusion in a company's annual meeting proxy statements through SEC Rule 14a-8, have gained much stronger support in recent years, with numerous proposals receiving in excess of 50 percent of the shareholder vote. While most of these proposals have to be precatory in nature (wishful and not mandatory) under applicable state law, reality soon may dictate that they become mandatory when such a high percentage of votes are cast in favor of them.

Regarding reforms, this year Congress approved the Sarbanes-Oxley Act, which provides for a multitude of reforms for board members and corporate officers. Many of these reforms were long overdue – more independent directors, for example – while others may be overdone. Only time will tell. Even so, you can't legislate integrity and it will be important for American business, if not critical, that officers and directors embrace the spirit of the Act along with the letter of the law. At this point, corporate America needs to embark on a mission to regain the confidence of investors, and sound governance will be a huge component of that mission.

At the same time, reform can be intoxicating because it is an exciting concept. However, successive reform programs could, in general, be incredibly destructive to the corporate segment of American capitalism, and, in particular, could make it truly difficult to recruit and retain strong directors. Whether substantial corporate governance reform is needed at this time may turn on whether recent corporate wrongdoings are largely aberrational in American industry or turn out to be systemic. I strongly expect that the former will be true, although the sheer number of corporate scandals uncovered in the early 21st century supports the principle that corporate wrongdoings are at least semi-systemic.

Good Governance and Directors

What is good governance? I'm not sure, but I believe that most good governance work is done by directors who concentrate on "big ticket" issues. Among the tasks a director should spend most of his or her time on are:

- Monitoring operating results with appropriate criticism and guidance when needed.
- Becoming involved in strategic issues.
- Providing judgment, perspective and guidance to senior management when requested.
- Attracting and retaining corporate officers, with a focus on management development and succession planning and an emphasis on an orderly evolution of the staffing of the CEO position. (In May 2002, the Business Roundtable opined that the "selection, compensation and evaluation of a well-qualified and ethical CEO is the single most important function of the board.")
- Setting base salaries and incentive compensation.

- Monitoring industry trends and competitors, especially for change and technological advancement.
- Reviewing and critiquing financial reporting practices with appropriate reliance on financial officers and independent audit firms.
- Developing an awareness of and promoting the appropriate legal and ethical standards for a corporation and providing oversight to determine if those standards are being met.
- Encouraging an open approach by management, with adequate and early disclosure of good and bad news, plus seeking management's support in supplying independent expert advice and counsel when board members need assistance to perform their fiduciary duties.

A part of good governance is that the CEO-Chairman not only listens to, but also hears, what the directors say. In this book, our CEO, Mark Gregory, tries to listen, but, in a few instances, his emotions get in the way and he becomes hardheaded. As you will learn later in this book, time can run out for the hardheaded CEO.

Each director can also bring his or her own expertise to the Board and should provide it when called upon by management, or when management should, but doesn't ask for it. Knowing when to "speak up" effectively in a boardroom when not asked to do so is an art, not a science, but it is an important trait for a strong director.

I have found that the best boards are those that provide independent constructive advice to management while operating as a "team" with members of management. At the same time, much criticism has been advanced by some corporate activists (a few of whom represent rather zealous philosophies) about the need for directors who are totally "independent" from management. The extreme positions taken may be best exemplified by a recent argument that if a board's good work helps cause the price of the stock to increase with board members' stock options correspondingly increasing in value, board members can become overpaid and lose their independence. Certainly if the value of original grants are excessive, that's one thing, but for boards to be disqualified as not shareholder oriented when they have helped to increase shareholder value is twisted logic indeed. While having a substantial majority of independent directors on a board is absolutely essential – and now part of stock exchange rules — certain yardsticks that are advocated for relationships destroying independence can be incredibly rigorous and, in this author's opinion, somewhat misguided. Few senior corporate executives or senior leaders of other institutions serve on boards of large companies for the compensatory return or because they can obtain new business for their own employer or their company. Other directors, who may appear to have few, if any, ties to management may, in fact, be more heavily dependent on directors' fees for much of their annual compensation. This latter group may appear to be independent but in practice can be far less so than the first group.

In trying to achieve good governance, most strong boards in the United States have adopted a set of comprehensive governance guidelines that help them meet special needs. They cover such matters as the appropriate size of the board, the mix of "inside" and "outside" directors, and how directors should address executive compensation. By now, there are probably well over a thousand sets of such guidelines for publicly held companies, but there is still a remarkable lack of congruence among them — arguably a good outcome, since most boards and companies have vastly different needs. A sample set of "mid-stream" guidelines is included in Chapter 10 of this book. Such guidelines will become even more prominent if current reform proposals are adopted which would make these guidelines mandatory for listed companies.

In order to evaluate U.S. boards, it is worthwhile to compare them to boards in other countries. From my experience, boards in the United States operate far differently than boards in other parts of the world. Boards in other countries often operate on a more pro forma or ministerial basis than ours. There are many reasons for that difference, including that, in some parts of the world, there are two-tiered boards. One tier includes employees or members of labor unions, and the other includes the types of persons one finds on U.S. boards. For various reasons, including, I believe, suspicion by board members of one another, these foreign boards seem to become less deeply involved in operating and financial issues than do U.S. boards. In still other parts of the world, particularly in some parts of the Far East, boards, in form, may seem to resemble U.S. boards; but, in substance, the chief executive officer does not seek much advice from board members because many of them are "insiders" and are so heavily affiliated with management that they do not truly provide a fresh perspective.

While the system of corporate governance in the United States is imperfect, most commentators continue to believe it is the best system in the world to govern corporate entities. In part, this book is designed to help validate that position.

James R. Ukropina
Los Angeles, CA
November, 2002

ACKNOWLEDGEMENTS

There are certain persons whom I would like to thank and acknowledge in connection with writing this book.

First and foremost I wish to acknowledge the incredibly helpful assistance of Tim Robinson. Tim, a former Washington Post editor and columnist, as well as the former top editor for the country's two largest independent legal publications, has brought a journalistic approach to this book and has managed to overcome much of my lawyer-like tendencies to overuse legal jargon.

With Tim's help, I have tried to create some memorable characters inside the boardroom. At the same time, we've provided behind-the-scenes information about the dynamics of how boards of major corporations carry out their functions. In addition, I would like to thank Tim's wife and business partner, Jan Andrew, for her guidance in how to market and distribute this book. Thanks also to Tim's screenwriting partner, Bob Close, for reviewing drafts of the book. Bob's background as a business executive brought additional perspective to the project.

Many of my current and former colleagues from my various board affiliations also have encouraged me to prepare this book. Most of them believe that a book like this one has not been written previously for a number of reasons. We all concluded that to their knowledge confidentiality restrictions were a large part of the problem and that most directors do not have the time to assemble this type of material. On the other hand, now that I am semi-retired from my law practice, all of them encouraged me to write such a book. I'm glad they did, since the journey alone – even with a fictional board – was well worth it.

One of the most thoughtful and encouraging of these parties was Norm Augustine, the former Chief Executive Officer of Lockheed Martin, and a colleague of mine on the current Lockheed Martin board. Norm has written four books and numerous corporate governance articles, most of them the best of their kind. He provided me with many excellent ideas and topics for this book and submitted extensive and creative comments on a final draft of the book. Not being embarrassed to accept help, I used them all, including a list of "warning signs" for directors which is included at the end of this book.

I also was fortunate enough to receive additional and comprehensive comments from Pat Hobin and Evelyn Mak, two distinguished corporate lawyers. This book is far better off by reason of their incisive comments.

Substantial comments came from Max Messmer, the Chief Executive Officer of Robert Half International and a former partner of mine at the law firm with which we have been affiliated, O'Melveny & Myers LLP. I also received some very thoughtful comments about the book outline from an associate of Max Messmer's, Reesa Staten, the Vice President of Corporate Communications at Robert Half International. In addition, John Lillie, my life-long friend and the former Chief Executive Officer of Leslie Salt, Lucky Stores and American President Lines, carefully reviewed the outline for and a final draft of this book and gave me the opportunity to quote substantially in *The Board* from remarks he made to the board of directors of Lucky Stores at a time when that board faced a critical decision about how its members should respond to the second of two successive hostile tender offers.

Another helpful commentator concerning my book outline has been Richard Koppes, now a prominent lawyer in private practice in Sacramento, but who, in his earlier life, was the General Counsel and, for a time, the Chief Executive Officer of the California Public Employee Retirement System (now the world's largest public employee retirement fund). When Rich was at CalPERS, we participated extensively in the early stages of corporate governance debates. Because he was such a constructive force, we were able to develop an amicable "Second Compact" on corporate governance that helped institutional investors and corporations resolve a number of difficult, early debates about how corporate governance should be carried out in a manner that was both effective for corporate management and satisfactory to major corporate investors. Rich was a pioneer in the corporate governance field and continues to be one of its foremost authorities. He is the ideal corporate activist: tough-minded, knowledgeable, fair and constructive.

I also want to thank Joe Grundfest, a former SEC Commissioner and now the W. A. Franke Professor of Law and Business at Stanford Law School, where he is one of the outstanding experts in the field of corporate governance as well as in class action litigation. Joe pioneered one of the first directors' colleges, and I have had the opportunity to be a speaker or panelist at a number of the sessions there. He gave me some excellent comments when I first started to write this book. In addition, Simon Lorne, a former SEC General Counsel and now a partner at a large Los Angeles law firm, reviewed my outline and Si encouraged me to move forward. He is the author of *A Director's Handbook of Cases*, and I encourage those who are interested in the legal aspects of corporate governance to read his excellent book.

Attorneys at the O'Melveny law firm, for which I am now Of Counsel, helped me considerably. One of my former partners, a good friend and now General Counsel of the Automobile Club of Southern California, Avery Brown, reviewed the book extensively and gave me numerous useful, substantive and stylistic comments. (Avery may have missed his calling when he didn't continue with his initial instincts to become a professional writer.) I also wish to thank others at the firm with whom I have worked over the years on corporate governance counseling and issues, including the late Jim Cross and Graham Sterling, as well as Bart Beek, Ken Bishop, Rick Boehmer, A. B. Culvahouse, Kent Graham, Jack Hardy, Tom Leary, Jim Levin, Ted McAniff, Fred McLane, Chuck Niemeth, John Power, Gary Singer, Diana Walker and many more. Still others at O'Melveny & Myers who reviewed drafts for me and provided useful thoughts and critiques were Bart Aikens and Leslie Culhane. Members of my family also weighed in, including my sister, Jo-an, and my three sons, Mike, Mark and David.

While I was in business and faced some truly difficult operating and governance issues, much of the helpful legal advice I received was provided by Doug Kranwinkle (formerly an O'Melveny partner and now an Executive Vice President and General Counsel at a large telecommunications company). His advice not only was substantively sound from the standpoint of legal doctrine but also grounded in good judgment and perspective. All CEOs should have such able assistance from their legal counsel. Doug also reviewed a draft of this book and offered words of encouragement.

Two good friends, Phil Irwin, a former O'Melveny partner, and Phil's wife, Sandra Irwin, a corporate and trial lawyer and an aspiring novelist, also provided many good thoughts and encouragement. Sandra did a strong job of reminding me how directors need to handle issues dealing with directors with diverse interests.

One group of attorneys from whom I have learned a lot are legal counsel with whom I have worked in my capacity as a board member. These include both "inside" and "outside" counsel. Of the outside variety, I include John Spiegel and Jim Lower, both of Los Angeles, and Ernie Yarnevich in Kansas City. The "insiders" go back to the late Russ Freeman and the late Joe Twomey, and then on to Bill Vinson, Carol Marshall, and now Frank Menaker, Dave Carmichael, Michael Cahill, and Rich Sommers.

One of my closest and most rewarding professional associations with a general counsel was with Michael Roster, the general counsel of Stanford University when I was a trustee and a member of the legal committee of the board. Mike is now general counsel of a large NYSE company and the head of the country's largest association of general counsel.

The staff at O'Melveny & Myers has been particularly helpful in preparing multiple drafts of this book. The staff members who have been active include my two assistants, JoAnne Hooper and Norma Scalise, and many of those in our Text

Editing department who spent long hours over word processors and proofreading this material. I want to thank Mee-Lee Szeto for her help on a number of graphic presentations for and layouts in the book, as well as others in that department, and, especially, Erik Hansen, for his proofreading and extensive editorial commentary.

By the way, whoever said writing a book is an easy task is nuts! Fortunately, Norm Augustine gave me adequate warning, but it still proved even more formidable – and happily more fun – than I imagined.

Part I

GROWTH

James R. Ukropina

CHAPTER 1

INSIDE THE BOARDROOM

Looking Back and Recalling the Challenges of a Decade of Board Service

(First Quarter of Year 16 of DFP's Operations)

George Hartfield got off the elevator at DFP's four-story corporate headquarters on its suburban campus in the rolling Dakota hills and saw Barbara Ramos leaning against the wall, waiting for him.   Barbara's job as DFP's Corporate Secretary included more than 20 specific and complex duties. One of them was to make sure that the Board of Directors' meetings ran smoothly.   She prided herself, rightfully so, in George's mind, with doing her important job with dignity, poise and efficiency.

"George!" she said. "I heard you would be here a little early. Any problem?"

"No, B.R. (the name by which she was known to her colleagues), I just wanted to look at today's agenda to be sure we're taking all the steps we should after our last difficult and rather contentious meeting – especially about the continuation of directors' and officers' indemnification insurance*, since I expect a few big-time lawsuits may be coming our way. Also, you can't always count on business colleagues to help you out when you're sued.   Remember how our good friend Roger Spayder, in a similar setting a few years ago, pulled the rug out

---

* A glossary of terms, explaining the meaning of this term and about 200 others, appears at the end of this book.

from underneath some of his own partners and cut off their indemnification funds for their litigation defense?"

He paused. "And, in any event, I guess I also wanted to spend some quiet time in the Boardroom before my last meeting."

He looked sheepishly at B.R. "I'm allowed to be a little sentimental, aren't I?"

"Of course," she said, smiling. "Hope you don't mind, but I told Mark you were coming in early. He'd like a few minutes alone with you, too."

The past few weeks had been particularly tense ones between George – as DFP's unofficial "Lead Director" – and DFP's charismatic Chairman and Chief Executive Officer, Mark Gregory. He was glad he'd have some time with Mark before today's meeting got under way.

As B.R. and George started walking down the hall toward the Boardroom, she handed him a folder. "I want to show you something before the meeting starts," she said. George opened the folder and saw it contained a proposed resolution expressing the Board's appreciation for his 10-plus years of service as a Board member, during which time he had served not only as the Lead Director but also in several other key roles.

"George! I'd swear you're blushing." Knowing George as well as she did, B.R. wasn't surprised that he'd be embarrassed by the attention. George, himself the Chairman and CEO of a large company, was a force to be reckoned with when he deemed it necessary to step in and provide decisive leadership to the Board or advice to Mark, but he also could show humility.

"Well, I…" He *was* blushing.

"It was Mark's idea and all of the others wanted to join in. You deserve all that praise, and so much more for what you've done for our shareholders," B.R. added as she opened the door to the Boardroom. "I'll go tell Mark you're here."

Sitting alone at the Board table, George looked around the imposing Boardroom and recalled some of the tough issues he and the other Directors had faced here: layoffs; volatile sales and earnings; harassment charges against executive personnel; proxy contests; bribery allegations; environmental crises; a hostile takeover bid; and so many more.

Though he had been in the Boardroom scores of times before, its emptiness made it seem even larger than usual. The walls, done in a dark walnut, made the room appear striking – almost haunting. But then George grinned as he remembered the early days of DFP, when the Board sat around a small table in a cramped office area overlooking the Company's first manufacturing plant. Governance practices then were a little crude, but there were more jokes and it was more fun. The entire world had become far more serious.

Hanging on the wall in this momentarily very quiet elaborate chamber were oil paintings of corporate facilities and of DFP's founder, Richard Collins. Richard didn't look like a happy man in the portrait, but, if he still had been living, he would have been ecstatic. His heirs had made tens of millions of dollars from the appreciation in DFP stock since Richard's simple kitchen-appliance idea had grown into the $3-billion-revenue global conglomerate it was today.

The Boardroom now had all of the most up-to-date communications bells and whistles, including ultrasensitive microphones and conference call devices. Its newest high-tech pride and joy was a large, inverted pyramidal screen that dropped from the ceiling. Videos, films and graphics could be shown on the pyramid's four sides.

The imposing rectangular table at which George sat was more than 15 feet across. It dominated the room, which was 75 feet long and more than 30 feet wide. As he looked down and saw his reflection in the highly polished tabletop, George remembered that even something as simple sounding as the selection of a Boardroom table had caused a minor conflict between Mark and the Company's founder.

Mark had told George that when he first discussed a new conference table, he had suggested to Collins that they buy a round one. The founder of DFP was puzzled. To Richard, Board members acted best as "rubber stamps," there for appearances for the most part. Besides, a well-compensated Board seat was a nice way to reward his friends.

"A round table for the Directors? Why in the world would you want to do that?" Collins asked.

Mark told George he had replied, "Well, I actually like input from Board members because I find their perspective and judgment useful. I look for help and ideas from Directors about new strategies, product development, streamlining our operations and providing a broader set of good ideas than those I can obtain from my day-to-day colleagues.

"I know you regarded them as interlopers for the most part, Rich, but in my view, you missed a lot of good advice. A round table will facilitate interaction, insure better communication, and, best of all, insure that no one needs to sit at the end of the table."

Even though Collins had been about to resign as Board Chairman, he still liked things done his way – and Mark didn't feel the shape of the table was worth fighting over. So, instead of having a round table, DFP went with the traditional long rectangle at which George now sat – a beautiful piece of furniture made by Sam Maloof, a world-famous California wood craftsman. Though beautiful and sturdy, the table had to be refinished every few years. because some Directors were sloppy or careless with pens and other writing instruments. Also, at one Board meeting, one of the Directors – Hugh Perry, a lively and outspoken money manager for the Dakota State Teachers Retirement System, one of the Company's largest shareholders – became excited and inadvertently knocked over and broke a glass carafe, deeply gouging the table. The DFP corporate maintenance group tried to fix the gash but it was still there – one of the few physical mementos of a rare difficult and argumentative Board meeting. But, it had led to a lighter moment – a "resolution" adopted at one Board meeting assigning Hugh a permanent, fixed seat: the one with a deep gash in front of it.

While the Board table was the room's clear focus, there were smaller tables around the edge of the room where members of the corporate staff and outside advisors and consultants could sit during meetings. And, thanks to a resourceful regional manager in Tehran, the beige carpet underneath the Board table was surrounded by Persian rugs with bold geometric patterns that he had shipped to headquarters just before Iranian soldiers invaded his office.

On one side of the Boardroom was a table with an antique silver service, along with coffee, tea and juice to help the Directors through lengthy meetings. The silver service had been willed to DFP by a grateful former employee when she died shortly after cashing in some of her early stock options. Light snacks were available – but not the big spread that once tempted the Directors. The CEO, who, like most U.S. CEOs also acted as the Board Chairman, had cut back on the more lavish offerings because they induced sleep, always a hazard during lengthy financial presentations.

A small office with a telephone was off to one side of the Boardroom. Mark discouraged Directors from taking calls during meetings, but some of them were still active CEOs and had to leave the Boardroom occasionally for emergencies. It was rumored that one of the early and more insecure Directors, never having a true emergency, liked to have calls placed to him by his secretary during a few Board meetings each year to remind his colleagues of his importance. That Director was pushed off the Board before he reached 70, the mandatory retirement age for DFP Directors.

The room was dimly lit, which seemed unusual to most of the Directors – but that was Mark Gregory's style. He thought it made the room a better place to reflect on difficult issues. Nonetheless, at least once a year, one of the Directors would go to the door and turn up the rheostat to shed more light on the deliberations, especially when fine print was involved. Another Director, a flamboyant trial lawyer named Harry

7

Thorpe, was somewhat of a prankster and liked to fool around with the Boardroom lights. Once, after a recess had gone on for what he thought was far too long, Harry turned the rheostat for the light up and down, up and down, up and down – as if to suggest it was time to get on with the meeting, much like it was time to get ready for Act Two of a play.

Spread strategically across the Board table were large, gray speakerphones, each of which looked like a sprawling praying mantis. They were used during the course of routine, regularly scheduled Board meetings for any Director who could not attend. As the Board became larger in number, it seemed that at least one Director was absent from each meeting, but he or she could still participate by telephone. From time to time, in addition to the Directors' voices, the speakerphones would broadcast dogs barking in the background, or babies crying (you knew that Director was staying at home with his grandchildren). Once, out of the speakerphone on the table came the unforgettable and incredibly loud sound of a Director snoring. Apparently he had become bored with the Board after listening to and participating in more than five hours of deliberations. After all, he was halfway around the world on a business trip and the clock already had struck midnight there before the meeting even started.

There was one exception to the phone call-in policy: the CEO no longer permitted them during emergency or specially called Board meetings that addressed sensitive agenda items, such as a proposed acquisition offer for a target company containing a premium bid, a difficult personnel issue, a new financing or certain regulatory or tax disputes. And, there was a good reason for that policy: Years earlier, one former Director, David Nugent, had been told on a speakerphone call that the Company was about ready to make a highly confidential 50 percent premium bid for Ajax Cooking Utensils, Inc. (ACU). David's secretary, Rebecca Dark, immediately phoned her broker and purchased some "calls" on ACU stock with an exercise price well below the effective purchase price. The SEC caught her, but that was the end of conference calls for sensitive agenda items except in extraordinary circumstances. In future cases, management and Board members used semi-creative code words, such as "Tango" for a target acquisition company in Argentina. Unfortunately, most of the hastily conceived code words were easily decipherable by the most amateur cryptographer.

M ark Gregory had come quietly into the Boardroom while George was reminiscing. He walked over to George, shook his hand and sat beside him at the table. "You look like 'The Thinker,' George – we're not used to seeing you this quiet in here."

"I'll miss our meetings, and I'll even miss this room," George said. "But, it's time for new blood."

There was an awkward pause before George continued. "I hope you realize, Mark, that our Board had to take the action it took…"

Mark cut him off. "George, we've discussed it ad nauseum. Let's leave it at that. The Company and its shareholders are in great shape – and wouldn't be in that position without you."

B.R. came into the room, giving George and Mark the opening they needed to lighten the mood. B.R. was well-liked by everyone – remarkable, she would joke, since she was a trial lawyer by training. She had worked her way up through the Company's corporate law department and then served as a human resources executive before being promoted to her current position. Along the way, she married a lawyer in the local district attorney's office and they had a 2-year-old daughter. Family photos lined her desk. A tall, attractive brunette who maintained a professional manner at all times, she had a lot of patience – and a good sense of humor that came in handy when she needed to deal with Directors' last-minute travel and logistical arrangements before and after each Board meeting. She liked those challenges and actually thought that the reasonable "care and feeding" of Directors was an important part of her job and of others in the corporate office. Directors needed to be focused on corporate policy and not airline guides, she figured. When she started, however, airline guides weren't her strength; she once almost sent a director to Stanford University instead of Stamford, Connecticut.

"Well, B.R., did you set aside enough time to read each and every word in the resolutions today?" George teased. It had become a standing but fun joke between them that in her first Board session as Corporate Secretary, she painstakingly read aloud about the first 50 words in one resolution, in all their legalistic minutiae, before the Chairman cut her off. George kindly had taken her aside after the meeting to tell her the laborious reading of each resolution wasn't necessary because the Directors already had read them in the traditional package of materials sent to each Director before a meeting. She had been mortified by her faux pas, but she appreciated. George's discreet handling of it helped seal their friendship.

"Well, there's *one* resolution I might forget to mention to the Board if you're not nicer to me today!" B.R. smirked, pointing to the folder containing the resolution of appreciation for George's service.

As George and Mark shifted to small talk, B.R. went around the room to make sure everything was set up properly for the meeting. Place cards were in front of each chair – Hugh's in front of the gash in the table, of course. Though there was no "official" seating chart, Directors seemed to get accustomed to a particular seat and, often, when their place card was put elsewhere, they would move it back to where they thought it should be.

A tall stack of documents was also on the table in front of each chair. Atop the stack was a revised agenda for the Board meeting. Typically a few last-minute agenda items developed and would need to be added. There also were a set of recent articles and securities analysts' reports about the Company, and a series of corporate documents relating to matters that would be dealt with during the course of the meeting, such as the final form of routine registration statements to be filed with the SEC and signed by Directors. The stack could reach nearly a foot high at times.

Finally, there was an envelope in the Board notebook for each Director containing a check in the amount of $1,500, representing the attendance fee for the Board meeting. In some cases, additional checks were enclosed in the envelope for committee meetings attended by the Director earlier that day or the prior afternoon. Directors were spending twice as much time now in numerous committee meetings as they were in full Board meetings – and often, it was in the committee meetings where the real Board work was done. Of course, the meeting fees reflected only a small portion of the Directors' total compensation, much of it in stock, because the actual meetings were only a portion of the Directors' work. Most of their time was spent reviewing lengthy and complex documents and reports and thinking about upcoming Board decisions.

Satisfied that all the documents were in order, B.R. took her seat at the table as the other Directors began to arrive. She liked this Board a lot. It was particularly strong – thanks to Mark and George's belief in having a solid group of corporate advisors. In addition to Hugh, Harry, George and Mark, the Board's other nine members were:

- Frank Alworth, a financial consultant and investment advisor to the Dakota Foundation.
- Joan Fleming, CEO of her own highly successful marketing and consulting firm.
- Paul Landry, a retired Air Force General and also a former CEO of a Fortune 500 company active in heavy manufacturing.
- Larry Lanski, a former CEO of a New York Stock Exchange company in the telecommunications industry.
- Judy Moran, the former owner of a company that had been acquired by DFP, and now the Company's largest individual shareholder.
- Andy Sommers, the Company's Chief Operating Officer.

- Dr. Henry Thompson, President of Dakota State University.
- Alex Todihara, an entrepreneur and independent investor.
- Stanley Towler, a former Dakota State Controller and political consultant.

As the Directors drifted in, Barbara remembered having read through corporate minutes and internal Board reports from early in the Company's history. In them, she had noted that some of the initial Directors had stark weaknesses – some so severe that they needed to be addressed through suggested early retirement or resignation. She was glad they were no longer around. The current high quality of the Board members was just what the events of the previous months had required.

After all, DFP had been through a lot in the 10-plus years since George had joined the Board. That's why she had decided to include in today's package a news article that had been written about the Company 10 years earlier. She pulled out a copy and handed it to George.

"Remember this? I included it in the Board materials 10 years ago as well."

George smiled as he looked at the article and showed it to Mark. "I sure do–and I remember it seemed as if we were about to embark on a long, hard journey at the time. Who could have known just how tough it would be? Mark, remember when you read it for the first time?"

"I sure do! Was that really a decade ago?"

A CORPORATE SECRETARY MAKES THE MINUTES OF
THE LAST BOARD MEETING A LITTLE TOO DETAILED

"<u>No</u>! shouted Mr. Bixby, slamming his fist down on the table. The floor shook, the walls trembled. Mr. Watson turned ashen. 'Y-y-you m-m-mean w-w-we…' The words wouldn't come out. He seemed to choke on each syllable."

Source: The New Yorker Collection

CHAPTER 2

DAKOTA BUSINESS JOURNAL TRACES DFP'S EARLY HISTORY
Collins to Gregory to Grillco
(Ten Years Earlier—First Quarter of Year 6)

Mark was sitting in his office holding a copy of the Dakota Business Journal's Sunday magazine when his private line rang. Before picking up the phone, he jotted down one last comment in the margin of the article that he had been reading. Then, he took a look at the caller ID and smiled.

"George, I figured that would be you!" Mark said as he lifted the receiver.

"What did you think about the article?" George asked, trying not to sound too eager. "Should we unleash our libel lawyers on them?" Mark could imagine George grinning as he made the remark – overall, the article had been quite flattering to DFP. But, Mark also knew George had been more than a little worried about the CEO cooperating as much as he had during the preparation of the piece – and especially in allowing the reporter to see some internal documents about the early history of the company. However, DFP's Corporate Communications VP had assured them that this was the right time strategically to have such an article appear in the business media. The pending Grillco deal had raised a lot of questions about DFP's aggressive growth pattern, and this kind of historical article would put it in a context that both the public and investors could understand.

"Well, like anyone who's had his ups and downs in the media, there are a few nits I would pick," Mark said, looking down as the heavily marked-up copy on the desk. "But, after all, we can't control the article once we decide to go down this path. Oh – and I'm not sure Rich is going to be flattered by how it portrays him and the founding of the Company."

"Frankly, Mark, I think it's one of the fairer articles of its kind that I've seen," George said, to the CEO's surprise. George was not a fan of the media. "And Rich always has been the type of guy who thinks any publicity is good publicity."

"I was impressed that the reporter took her time to really understand the material – and it's certainly long enough to tell any outsider all they'd ever need to know about the Company."

"Both of us learned a long time ago to take our media coverage with a grain of salt," Mark said, "but we do have to remember that it reflects how the community and others perceive us."

"Speaking of that – I was wondering, George, what you'd think about my including it with the agenda material for tomorrow's Board meeting? Some of the Directors are bound to have seen it, but the out-of-town folks might not have."

"Good idea, Mark – actually, I was calling to suggest just that. It would be a good reminder to them of just how far we've come as a Company, and as a Board."

Mark could hear George's other line ringing.

"Sorry, Mark – gotta go! See you tomorrow."

Mark punched another button on his telephone. "B.R., could you make sure that the Dakota Business Journal article on us is included in tomorrow's Board package? Thanks!"

James R. Ukropina

From the Dakota Business Journal's Sunday Magazine:

'Pop' Quiz:
What's the Next Step for Dakota's Fastest-Growing Company?

By Maria Bartels
Dakota Business Journal Staff Writer

By now, everyone in the Dakota business community probably knows the story. But, for those of you who've been asleep the past three years, here's the recap.

Richard "Rich" Collins, former Dakota-State-football-star-turned-salesman-turned-entrepreneur-and-inveterate-tinkerer, was riding the moderate success of a small specialty food company based on importing high-end coffee makers from Italy and making tweaks to them. Those tweaks made them attractive to coffee fanatics who purchased them through a cleverly written mail-order catalogue – or through Collins' extremely early and equally clever Internet site.

But one night, he walked through his kitchen just as his wife Agnes finished microwaving some popcorn for their kids. He took a taste, and it just wasn't as good as what he'd remembered having as a kid. So, he went out to the proverbial garage – in his case, the one attached to their modest house on Pine Street in Dakota City.

The result: A one-step, back-to-the-future popcorn popper that resulted in freshly-popped local Dakota corn, buttered and salted to taste, that became a must-have in the state's movie theaters, cafeterias and ballparks. Refining the home version of the popper and touting it on infomercials a few months later, Rich Collins became a late-night TV superstar. The machine took every "foodie" award available for best new product, and its sales set new direct-marketing records.

Every PopMasterPlus he sold went out with a coffee sample that, according to the label, "is a gift from us – use it in your current coffeemaker, or, better yet, try it in our CoffeeMasterPlus, and really see how good coffee can taste!" Of course, the special offer included for the higher-priced Coffee-MasterPlus proved irresistible to many who had thought they just wanted a PopMasterPlus. As the orders poured in for both products, Rich's nickname truly applied, and Dakota Food Products was born. Shortly after incorporation, Collins concluded "Dakota Food Products" was too big a mouthful for customers and others so he changed the corporate name to DFP. He also created a rectangular logo in blue and white (his college colors) with "D" in the upper left hand corner, "F" below and in the center and "P" below in the bottom right hand corner. Before he made those changes, he dressed casually and posed as a music agent to purchase the name rights for DFP from a local Dakota rock group that had incorporated, "Danny, Frank and Pauline, LLC, "and used the trade name DFP."

Adult Supervision

Like many entrepreneurial companies that grew too fast, DFP soon found itself in need of adult supervision, and that experienced management came in the form of its current CEO, Mark Gregory. Joining the Company about two years ago, he pushed it toward the larger kitchen-appliance mainstream with some small, but key acquisitions and soon put together an investor group to purchase the Company from Collins. After that, he made small and successful acquisitions of companies making other kitchen appliances, as well as a few food producers and marketers.

All of the smaller acquisitions have been profitable, as Gregory is known to have a great "sniffer" for undervalued companies. He's also reported to be a superb negotiator, lacing his negotiating tactics with good humor and down-home stories his "Daddy" told him during his childhood in the Kentucky mountains. In one deal, he reportedly told the prospective seller that when the deal closed, he would serenade the seller and his wife with his guitar after dinner in a private room at the ritziest restaurant in New York City. That was the clincher, as the seller's wife was already attracted to Gregory and his offer, and reportedly told her husband that he'd better not lose the deal.

"Mark's deal-making savvy is really something," one of his more cautious business partners told the Business Journal. "He's a deal genius, which is good, but he's also somewhat of a deal 'junkie' – always on the lookout for the next one, which can be bad. Not that he's made a mistake – yet."

Under Gregory, the acquisition strategy – which was approved by the Board after two full days of debate at a Board retreat – moved DFP from manufacturing equipment for home use to equipment for restaurant use. And the home version of the PopMasterPlus, like many fad kitchen appliances that wind up on eBay, soon became a DFP relic.

At that retreat, Gregory had also proven that he was a good listener. He paid close attention to a speech by Collins that, according to one of those in attendance, helped guide him into the strategy he took to grow the company.

"You watch," Collins had said, according to that person's notes. "People are living longer, and they don't want to cook at home anymore. We should hit the restaurant market – make standard and specialty equipment for the fish places, the steak houses, barbeque and chicken outlets.

"But let me tell you where the action is going to be – and damn it, I'll bet you two cases of Dom Perignon champagne that I'm right. It's going to be with the ethnic restaurants. Let me name just a few that are starting to emerge: Armenian, Indian, Japanese, Korean, Lebanese, Salvadoran, Serbian and Thai. Then, of course, we have all the old standbys – Chinese, Italian and Mexican. And here's something else: many of the restaurant owners are recent immigrants, and they won't be able to pay cash up front for their major equipment. We can set up a finance company, charge them reasonable interest, and make a fortune. Most immigrants are hard workers and pay their bills, so it will be a profitable, low-risk business for us."

In fact, it has been. And it has continued to allow DFP to continue its acquisition fever.

Now, though, DFP faces its largest challenge yet with the pending acquisition of GrillCo, which manufactures and distributes a high-performing counter-top electric grill called Grillit, endorsed by a former boxing champion. Will this be the acquisition that could take DFP into yet another amazing growth spurt? Or will it be Gregory's folly? Perhaps a look back at the Company's history can help provide the answer.

Rich's Way – or Else

Even in its early days, the Company that became DFP would never have been described as a "mom and pop" operation. That's because it was always clear that only one person was in charge: the hard-charging but debonair Rich Collins.

Described by both friends and foes alike as a "my way or the highway" leader, he was full of the aggressive self-confidence that combined with his physical skills to earn him all-conference honors as a middle linebacker at Dakota State. Whenever anyone would complain or try to rein him in, he'd shrug and say, "I only play the way my coach taught me: full speed ahead with an all-out blitz." Near the end of his business career, Collins can be seen around town as a well-dressed man with custom suits from Savile Row but, in the last analysis, he still appears to most as a burly but highly tailored linebacker.

As he nears the end of his term as a DFP Board member, Collins believes the Company wouldn't be where it is today without him.

"Hell," he said, during an interview in his new 10,000-square-foot house on his 400-acre ranch in the Dakota foothills, "those guys know I'm more of an 'idea' guy than a button-down type – all those rules, regulations, they're not meant for me."

19

But, he added with a wink, "I agree with how Mark's running the Company now – and I especially like how my stock price keeps moving up."

When asked if it was true that he provided each of the early members of his Board of Directors with a small rubber "Aye" stamp with his initials on it after they were appointed, Collins just laughed – but also winked again.

Playing by the Rules

Based upon interviews with corporate insiders and public corporate records provided to the Dakota Business Journal, the real story of the Company's earlier days is a little more structured than Collins suggests. It was obvious that after the strong sales of the PopMasterPlus, Collins' innovative invention, and his marketing savvy that simultaneously boosted the sale of the much-higher-profit-margin CoffeeMasterPlus, he would have to at least play by some of the usual rules and regulations. A victim of his immense success, Collins could no longer run the operation as if it was his candy store.

According to John Eisenberg, a local attorney, Collins hired Dakota City's largest corporate law firm, Eisenberg & Watson, to help him take the first steps, holding a meeting of "dummy incorporators" to document and confirm the creation of the Company. Two young lawyers at the firm had signed the Certificate of Incorporation, which were then filed with the Secretary of State's office in Dakota, creating the new corporate entity. They met with Collins to lateral the corporate governance proceedings to him and to his wife, the only shareholders at the time. At the first Board of Directors meeting, they ratified all the incorporation steps already taken, and then authorized the usual matters: The election of corporate officers, opening of bank accounts, adopting Bylaws, and the like. (The law firm agreed to be paid in stock rather than cash for some of its fees, and its partners always regarded that as one of its best "legal" decisions.)

Collins then asked a friend, Dakota State University President Henry R. Thompson, to join him as a shareholder and a new Board member; Agnes Collins resigned from the Board a few days later. Dr. Thompson invested $45,000 in the Company's stock and Collins invested $450,000, and their shareholdings were proportionate to those investments for some time. Next, they needed some additional capital to meet the rising demand for the manufacture of a new generation of the CoffeeMasterPlus as well as the PopMasterPlus.

Eisenberg was given consent by Collins, his client, to provide information for this story. According to the lawyer, another of Collins' friends, entrepreneur and independent investor Alex Todihara, was able to extend credit to the Company through some convertible promissory notes to finance the purchase of much-needed equipment, and also to have enough working capital to get the Company started in earnest. Two months later, he too was named to the Board.

Todihara brought a lot of ability to the Boardroom. After spending his youth in Japan, he became an honors graduate from MIT in electrical engineering. He founded and sold a small electrical components business before going to Harvard to earn his MBA. From there, he started to buy, sell, and finance companies, and his batting average for success was sensational. He also had patience for businessmen like Collins, who he regarded as brash but brilliant.

Eisenberg acted as corporate secretary for the early board meetings. He said Collins, Thompson, and Todihara concluded that the quality of their products would be the most important benchmark for their success – particularly if they could produce them on a timely and cost-effective basis.

Within 90 days, the Company was up and running; Collins, Todihara, and Thompson met for the first time as a real Board of a now viable Company. Plans were made to allow selective investment in the Company and a list of prospective investors was drawn up for a private placement of the DFP common stock. Twenty-five individuals agreed to sign on as investors, but Collins remained the majority shareholder.

Though the Board only met four times a year during the first few years of DFP's operations, Collins still privately seemed to think of board meetings as an impediment to speedy action. When the Directors did assert themselves, according to more than one insider, Collins would just tell them that he was the one running the Company and they would be better seen but not heard. Nonetheless, on critical issues the Board members would insist on being heard, and, in one instance, they outvoted him.

At that meeting, Henry Thompson, who was a very formal academic and did not underestimate his own intellect, reminded Todihara and Collins, that in board meetings he was always to be addressed as Dr. Thompson "because I have a Ph.D. in biology – and don't you forget it!" (Thompson, who by all standards was a versatile academic, also reminded them that he had a master's degree in business with an emphasis on accounting and finance.)

The Board added more members after the Company approached First Dakota Bank for a $750,000 line of credit to finance future growth. While bank officials reportedly had no issue with the loan request based on the Company's financial and operating history, they felt the Board needed more mature members to provide the necessary oversight to Collins' sometimes quirky, unfocused behavior.

Collins, by now resigned to the fact that his Company had outgrown his style, agreed – though he apparently wanted to make sure that the new members would see his side of the issues when necessary. After numerous interviews with Collins and the other Board members, two new Board members were chosen: David Nugent, CEO of one of the Company's key suppliers, and the President of the local Rotary Club to which Collins had belonged for years; and local stockbroker Charles Frank of Frank Brothers, who had been a big supporter of the Company since Day One, as well as the broker for many of the area's well-heeled citizens – including Collins.

While the Company's early results were encouraging, they were below the expectations of his investors. So, Collins decided to shift gears and focus on his strong point: marketing. He sought celebrity help and found out that TV cooking guru Mary Higgins liked DFP's products – which now included a stir-fry pan and a food processor – and she agreed to endorse them in exchange for a small cash fee and some shares of stock of the Company.

Then, Collins noticed that DFP's television infomercials received their highest response in the Southeastern United States, leading to exceptionally strong sales there. To maximize that regional market, he signed an endorsement contract with retired NASCAR driver Champ Hutler. Thanks to the efforts of Hutler – a colorful, back-slapping, good ol' boy – the Company's products became wildly popular with the audience of the biggest U.S. spectator sport. They particularly liked a space-age beer cooler that

required little energy but kept a six-pack cool for two days.

Although Collins was thriving as a marketer for his Company, the Board decided improvement was needed in two key areas: strategic management and cost-effective manufacturing. Costs in the latter were starting to skyrocket, and too much overtime pay was needed to keep up with orders, particularly for "Champ's Ice Chest." But the decision related to the former – strategic management – would lead to the hiring of Mark Gregory as CEO, and, in turn, to a reduced role for Collins.

New Life on the Board

When Gregory was presented to Collins as the potential future Chief Executive Officer of DFP, little did Collins expect that eventually he would face a proposal from Gregory to buy out all of the shares of DFP stock held by Collins and his family.

Actually, Collins was more than ready for the proposal, he now says. He had reached a burnout stage with DFP, and admittedly was running out of energy to push forward with DFP's ambitious growth plan. And he says he thought Gregory was a good man for the job.

Gregory had just left Spayder Enterprises three years earlier, formed a good-sized leverage buyout company and had acquired Asher Electronics, an electronics company that supplied components for the missile and space industry. Asher had prospered under Gregory's leadership, and he finally sold his interest to one of the large aerospace companies for a giant profit. He reached an agreement to buy out Collins' DFP interest by acquiring 51 percent of that interest on the front end in a cash transaction and the last 49 percent over the next two years under a so-called "earnout" contract.

As a part of the deal, Collins agreed to let Gregory have immediate control of the Board. So Gregory then added three new Directors: Retired Air Force Gen. Paul Landry, who also had been a CEO of a Fortune 500 company; Harry Thorpe, a well-known and colorful trial lawyer in the Dakota area, and Hugh Perry, a money manager for Dakota's largest public employee pension fund, which, in turn, was a joint investor with Gregory in taking control of DFP.

Even now, Gregory looks back on those appointments with pride. "These are three smart guys who brought diverse backgrounds to the Board and have a collegial approach to Board proceedings, while maintaining their independence," he said. But the Board appointment of which many believe he is the proudest came a few months ago.

That was when Gregory also asked George Hartfield to join the Board. Hartfield is in his mid-50s and had been the managing partner of one of the state's largest law firms before becoming Chairman and CEO of a Nasdaq-traded oil and gas exploration company. Known as an excellent manager and a first-rate attorney, Hartfield has been a leader in the legal community and clearly brought a touch of class to the Boardroom – plus, on the personal side, Hartfield was an old friend of Gregory's father.

On the more practical side, Gregory knew Hartfield's presence in the Boardroom would assist the Company in obtaining new financing for expansion from the investment community.

Mark Gregory's Impact

At first glance, Mark Gregory might have been an unlikely candidate to become DFP's first outside CEO. Gregory was as tightly focused as Collins could be unfocused. His time with Roger Spayder, the state's most notorious – but highly successful – corporate raider, had hardened him.

But, at second, third and fourth glance, the Board realized it had found its man. Gregory, an extremely handsome and charismatic leader, had graduated from Claremont McKenna College with a degree in economics and had worked a few years as an analyst with one of the major strategic consulting firms. (And the terms "handsome and charismatic" aren't just empty flattery; even now, Gregory is teased by his peers about having worked his way through college by appearing in television commercials for a major clothing chain and singing ballads accompanied by his guitar to admiring young crowds – especially women – in local clubs. At 6'4" and 220 pounds, Gregory looks as if he could resume that lifestyle any time he wanted.)

From there, he received his MBA at Stanford Business School and went to work immediately for Spayder in his offices in midtown Manhattan. "Spayder the Raider" – as he is called by friends and enemies alike – had made an enormous amount of money taking over underpriced companies using brutally aggressive tactics.

While on Spayder's staff, Gregory had made some good decisions about potential takeover candidates and how they should be priced and pursued. But, the word was growing in the business community that Gregory was the "good guy" to Spayder's "bad guy" – and it wasn't an act, it was the way Gregory preferred to conduct business. Any successful negotiation, Gregory says to this day, should be a win–win for both sides.

Needless to say, the rumors got back to Spayder that Gregory seemed to be polishing Spayder's rough edges – and Spayder wasn't happy about it. Then came the coup de grace – Wall Street started to say that Gregory was not only shrewder than Spayder, but also even smarter. He was known as immensely intelligent, a quick study and a person who made quick but excellent intuitive decisions. Enough said. Spayder unceremoniously fired Gregory – the only setback in Gregory's rising career and a huge disappointment to Gregory because Spayder had assured Gregory he was his protégé and successor.

Though an ultimate Type A personality, Gregory said he weathered the storm well. After all, his reputation was solidly intact and actually had grown because of his quiet opposition to Spayder's tactics. He spent some time with his young children. He then accumulated substantial wealth through his LBO ventures, including the Asher Electronics deal. After that success, many headhunters and investors contacted him – but

he thought the best and most challenging call came from the search firm retained by DFP to find a new CEO.

The biggest drawback to becoming DFP's Chief Executive Officer and ultimately its controlling shareholder, Gregory recalled, was that the new job would again mean spending less time with his wife Melynda and their three children. Like any young business superstar, he admits to continually struggling to balance his work life with his family life, but credits his wife – herself a former corporate lawyer – with understanding his time demands and supporting his decision.

And, of course, there was Collins to contend with.

"I knew the stories, and I knew Rich, and they didn't bother me at all, after what I'd been through," Gregory said, though refusing to discuss his time with Spayder. "Rich is a genius in many ways – and I've told him that time and time again – but at this point he should focus on his creative strengths. He has, and he's been a huge supporter of mine since I've been here."

Collins agreed. "Mark's been fair in every dealing I've had with him. No complaint there."

Nor should there be any complaint on Collins' part. In what all seem to agree was a very friendly buyout, Gregory soon put together the investment group and purchased Collins' interest in DFP. The deal made Collins extremely wealthy and kept him on as the Company's "creative guru" and one of three television spokesmen for a three-year period.

And, there has been no complaint from Gregory either. Outside observers marvel at how well the Company has been run by him over the past few years, and even its lowest-level employees are outspoken in their support for his spectacular growth record and his ability to take the Company public through a highly successful initial public offering.

The Grillco Deal

Still, concern remains about Gregory's latest acquisition plan, if only because it is the largest he's yet attempted. Moran's

Grillco is a Company valued at $50 million, but the counter-top electric grill market is becoming increasingly crowded.

Plus, Grillco's owners, Jeff and Judy Moran, are said to have placed an essential condition on the purchase of their Company: they want to be named to the Board of Directors of the combined companies.

"As you know," Gregory said in an interview, "I can't get into the details of our discussions with Grillco. However, I believe it is a strong Company and is an excellent fit with ours."

And, is the addition of new Board members an issue?

"I've come to know and like Jeff and Judy extremely well," Gregory replied. "I think they have built an excellent business or else we wouldn't be wanting to acquire it. Other than that, this is a matter that is before the Board – so I can't discuss it further."

The Morans did not return telephone calls seeking their comments. However, others familiar with Grillco's position said their need for Board representation was "obvious."

27

"DFP is now worth $150 million. It's buying Grillco for $50 million in DFP stock. That is such an obviously large potential shareholder position in DFP that the Grillco directors would be negligent in their duties if they didn't seek such representation," said one source. "I'm sure the DFP Board members will understand that."

Another source said there were many plusses for DFP in the deal above and beyond the entry into the counter-top grill market. "Grillco has a first-rate manufacturing facility that can be adapted easily for DFP's needs," she said, "plus it owns nearby real estate for continued expansion of that facility."

But the questions remain: will it be too much too fast for DFP to absorb Grillco, and possibly adversely affect the chemistry of the current Board? Or is it the right move at the right time – and does it set the stage for the continued growth of Mark Gregory's grand vision?

The DFP Board meeting is scheduled for tomorrow.

#   #   #

A financial snapshot of the Company:

Note: The chart below – like others in this book – reflects the sales of DFP for a particular operating quarter, in this instance the first quarter of the Company's sixth year in business, as well as net income, earnings-per-share and cash flow per share for the same period. It also compares the first-quarter results of the sixth year with the first-quarter results of its fifth year in business, and shows variance data for the most recent quarter as compared to the DFP's plan for that quarter. Finally, the chart reflects DFP's stock price performance versus an index consisting of recent stock prices for peer group companies, as well as an important balance sheet ratio reflecting DFP's level of indebtedness versus its equity capital. This data, along with a booklet about 80-100 pages long with more voluminous financial information, was provided to the Board every month so that its members could monitor DFP's operating results, financial condition and relative stock price performance. Depending on DFP's recent operating performance, this information could be the subject of lengthy or brief discussion at each Board meeting. (For a large, multi-division corporation, comparative operating data also is provided to the directors for each major division, subsidiary or segment of the business.)

DFP INC.
COMPARATIVE QUARTERLY RESULTS
($000)
(First Quarter of Year Six)

	Most Recent Qtr.	% Variance from Comp Qtr.	% Variance From Plan
Sales	40,000	+3	+5
Net Income	4,400	+4	+5
Earnings/Share	.07	+5	+6
Cash Flow/Share	.09	+6	-4
Stock Price versus Peer Index	+6%	-	-
Debt/Equity Ratio	20%	-	-

CHAPTER 3

A 'ROUTINE' MEETING

When the Plate Is Full

(Second Quarter of Year 6)

Agenda for Board Meeting

1. *Approval of minutes*
2. *Review of first quarter results – CFO*
3. *Operating Report – CEO*
4. *Report on financial condition of DFP and consideration of proposed debt offering – CFO*
5. *Review and authorization of proposed code of ethics, including policies concerning conflicts of interest, insider trading and prohibition on payments to government officials – General Counsel*
6. *Declaration of cash dividend – CFO*
7. *Authorization of amendment to Bylaws, including change in authorized number of Directors – General Counsel*
8. *Annual Meeting matters – General Counsel*
   a. *Authorization of time and place of meeting*
   b. *Approval of proposed proxy statement*
   c. *Review and approval of Annual Report to Shareholders*
   d. *Review and approval of SEC report on Form 10-K, including acceptance of recommendation of Audit Committee for inclusion of financial statements and 10-K report*
9. *Review of proposed acquisition of Grillco – CEO*
   a. *Proposed purchase price*

  b. *Terms and conditions of acquisition*
  c. *Possible additional Board seats for two principals or their representatives*
  d. *Recommendation of management*
  e. *Review by legal counsel of legal issues involved in acquisition*
  f. *Presentation by investment banking firm, including fairness opinion with respect to transaction*
  g. *Presentation by CFO on tax aspects and financial reporting aspects of acquisition*
  h. *Discussion of need for confidentiality – General Counsel*
  i. *Potential Board approval of proposed transaction*
 10. *Other business*
 11. *Adjournment*

"It looks like this stack gets higher and higher every meeting," Paul Landry said to no one in particular as he sat down at the Board table and eyed the documents in front of him, including financial statements containing the strong operating results from the first quarter.

Before the meeting he and the other Directors had received their usual wealth of material, including financial statements for DFP's most recent quarter; financial statements for the year to date; a recent report on employee recruitment and turnover; credit ratings for DFP's debt securities; shareholder profiles, and more. On top of that, the pending Grillco deal meant there had been additional and voluminous material to review, including a description of Grillco's operations, a description of the management team, financial statements, investment banker reports, a report by a private investigation firm on any history of litigation, regulatory enforcement agency involvement or integrity issues, a review of Grillco's financial projections, and a summary of interviews with Grillco's customers, vendors and related parties. As he thumbed through the new stack, Gen.

Landry noted that much of it supplemented the previous documents.

"Enjoying your reading, General? What did you think of Sunday's article in the *Business Journal*?" CEO Mark Gregory said amiably as he entered the room and took his seat at the head of the table.

Landry looked up and exaggeratedly rolled his eyes as he gestured at all of the documents. "So much material, so little time!"

"Well, a better reason than ever to get started a little early," Mark said with a friendly smile. "We have a lot to get done!"

"Mark, before we dig into the formal agenda," Charles Frank brusquely interrupted, "why don't we get into the most important matter first? The Grillco deal may be a good one, but if the Morans have to join this Board, I think we ought to kill it!"

Some of the Directors looked at each other and nodded. However, others, especially the more sophisticated George Hartfield and Alex Todihara, were growing a little weary of Charlie's lack of diplomacy in the Boardroom. But they and other Directors had discussed the Grillco deal among themselves in emails and phone calls earlier in the week, and knew that today's meeting would be more contentious than usual. Compared to the "routine" matters before them in the first part of the meeting, the potential debate about the merits of the Grillco acquisition was likely to present a significant challenge – not only in terms of the appropriate action, but also in terms of the Board's longstanding collegial relationship with Mark.

"I echo Charlie's comments," Dr. Thompson said. "It's not that I'm against growth – or even the Grillco purchase. I'm just more concerned about Jeff and Judy trying to force their way onto the Board this way – and I'm a little bit peeved that you haven't involved us early enough in the process."

"I agree," Harry Thorpe added. "It seems like we're becoming an afterthought on some of these matters."

Mark – who prided himself on his ability to hear such rumblings and not be caught unaware – knew he would have to counter such concerns during the meeting. But first things first.

"I understand your concerns, but I still think we have a lot of other important matters to address," Mark said. "Let's stick with the agenda for now." He called for the approval of the minutes of the previous meeting.

"Aye!" the Board replied.

Then, the CFO, Geoffrey Raines, was asked to review DFP's first-quarter operating results. He thought they had been great.

Agenda Item 2: Review of first quarter results – CFO

"Geoff, that's a spectacular set of results," Gen. Landry said after the CFO had finished. "I commend you, Mark and the management team for them." After pausing a moment, he added: "I noticed, however, that a couple of DFP's operating divisions did not achieve plan. What do you think the Street's reaction will be?"

"Our overall earnings per share will be well ahead of Street expectations," Geoff responded. "We also have conditioned the market to the probability that a few of our divisions won't be as strong as they have been in the past, but other divisions more than make up for the shortfall. I expect, however, that if our refrigeration products don't start to pick up a bit there will be increased pressure for us to sell that division and reinvest the sale proceeds elsewhere."

Harry nodded, but had another question for the CFO. "Geoff, when you announce the results, do you intend to forecast the operating results for the upcoming quarter and for the year?"

"Unfortunately, we're at that point – because SEC regulations almost require it. Of course, we're hedging those forecasts with the usual caveats about the economy and customer demand. Currently, we're forecasting 30 cents per share for the year."

Alex looked up from the draft earnings report he had been reading. "Are these projections necessary? It seems to me we put ourselves way out on a limb by making them." Some of the others nodded in agreement and Todihara added: "Even though this business is a little easier to project than some, I still have heartburn thinking about our relational exposure with our investor groups – and even potential legal exposure if we're wrong."

Mercedes Magruder, who always attended the Board meetings at Mark's request, leaned forward. As the Company's General Counsel, she was keenly aware of Todihara's concerns. Mark looked at her, a commanding presence sitting at the other end of the table, and then motioned for her to speak.

"In preparing our projections, let me assure you that we draft them carefully and rely on some safe harbor provisions of the federal securities laws," Mercedes said. "If properly followed, they should permit us to avoid any liability if they turn out to be off-target. Among other things, we're listing a number of risk factors we think are appropriate qualifications to achieving the projections, including references to assumptions about interest rates, economic conditions, capital expenditures and the like. We added a new risk factor concerning the importance of avoiding a long strike with one of our key labor unions. It now appears that the strike is about a 50-50 proposition."

"Be sure you cover all the risk factors and don't put down too few," George Hartfield said. "I also think you should look at the comparable risk factor disclosure sections of your competitors' SEC filings to be sure that we're picking up all the industry dynamics that we should in these materials."

At that point, Mark stood and walked to a lectern at the front of the room.

Agenda Item 3: Operating Report – CEO

"Given the fullness of the agenda, we should move quickly to the operating report. While Geoff has provided you with the operating results and the numbers, I want to provide you with my usual list of the five 'high points' and the five 'low points' from last quarter." He reeled off a number of recent successes: The landing of large new contracts with international customers, including customers in China, Brazil and Norway; the development of two new exciting products; the efforts of the Company and a trade association to head off some adverse federal legislation in the OSHA area; the recent escalating stock price for the Company's common stock; and the recruitment of a new head for one of DFP's divisions pirated away from one of DFP's principal competitors.

He followed with the quarter's disappointments: The Company's recently lost bid for some attractive new business with a state agency in the Northeastern United States; a highly publicized lawsuit brought by a disgruntled senior employee for unlawful termination, which, among other matters, alleged what appeared to be unfounded sexual harassment claims; a pending piece of state legislation that would require more than $5 million of new emission control equipment for the plant's principal operating facility in Dakota; a lawsuit brought by one of the Company's major customers for breach of contract for failure to deliver specially ordered goods on a timely basis; and the discovery of some accounting fraud in a small division, which fortunately had been uncovered before it found its way into the Company's consolidated financial statements released to shareholders.

Mark saved the best for last. He announced that, in addition to the Grillco acquisition, the controlling shareholders of one of the best medium-sized companies in the industry, Coffee Brew King Inc., had approached him with an offer to merge with DFP on a friendly basis, with an advantageous exchange ratio for the Company in a swap of stock of the two companies. Mark said this development was the product of his salesmanship with the principals of that company that spanned over the past five years through social occasions and industry conferences. For various reasons, the merger might not happen and could not be seriously negotiated for another year. The pricing formula for the deal already was locked in, as Mark was worried about the pricing running away from him. Coffee Brew King, he learned, was the exclusive manufacturer of coffee makers, coffee cups and coffee bags sold by an emerging company headquartered in Seattle. Its founders envisioned that the Seattle company soon would have coffee houses on street corners around the globe, and Coffee Brew King would continue to be its principal vendor.

After a brief discussion of the potential merger, the CFO returned to the podium.

Agenda Item 4: Report on financial condition of Company and consideration of proposed debt offering – CFO

Raines said the Company's current debt-to-equity ratio was extremely conservative, and, accordingly, the Company's credit rating was high. In view of the recent interest rate decline, he recommended that the finance committee of the Board consider a $75 million debt offering, which might either be a straight debt or a convertible debenture offering.

Various Directors chimed in. Was the debt offering needed? Was the timing right? The CFO responded that while the Company did not have an immediate need for the debt proceeds, they certainly could be applied within the next two years. Plus, the after-tax interest cost would not be particularly heavy in the near term. Further, the debt offering could be used, in part, to retire previously issued debt securities that carried a higher interest rate; he noted, however, that there would be a penalty payment under the relevant bond indenture for the early call of that debt.

The Chairman asked for the "sense" of the Board and, without a vote, a consensus emerged that the Finance Committee, working with the CFO, should explore an offering of not less than $75 million but not more than $100 million. The CFO said he was pleased, because the Company had a longstanding, but perhaps overly conservative position on the level of its debt. This policy meant that its ability to achieve higher marks for "return on equity" results were more difficult since its "E" in the "ROE" formula constituted a much higher percentage of its capital than for most of its competitors. The new $100 million of debt ultimately would bring its debt/equity ratio more into conformity with most of the other companies in the industry.

Which investment banking firm should be the underwriter for the debt offering? While some of the Directors had suggestions based on recent experiences with various firms, it was the consensus of the management group and the Board that they should stick with their traditional investment banking firm, Andrews & Molinari. After all, A&M had brought some interesting acquisition ideas to them over the past few years.

Agenda Item 5: Review and authorization of proposed code of ethics, including policies concerning conflicts of interest, insider trading and prohibition on payments to government officials.

Mark had asked Mercedes, as General Counsel, to take the lead on the discussion of an updated Code of Ethics. She explained that the Board hadn't reviewed the Company's Code of Ethics for some years and it was appropriate that a new code be adopted.

"I know all of you have received a draft of the Code of Ethics, but I'd like to summarize its essential provisions," she said. Noting that while conflicts of interest or related party transactions, as covered in state corporate law statutes, were not flatly prohibited, any material conflicts of interest transactions would have to be approved by a majority of disinterested Directors or a majority of shareholders after a full disclosure to them of both the facts surrounding the potential conflict transaction and the advantages and disadvantages to the Company. While she said she typically was not comfortable in bringing such matters to the Board, it was possible that an officer or a Director in the future could bring a first-rate investment opportunity to the Company in which he or she was participating and wanted to give the Company the first chance to invest, if its management and Board concluded such a move was in the best interest of the shareholders. She reminded the Board that, in its infancy, DFP had joint-ventured an acquisition with Alex Todihara and it had proven to be one of DFP's most successful deals.

After discussing conflicts transactions and how certain companies had recently been embarrassed and even sued because of such matters, the General Counsel moved to the duty of confidentiality and prohibitions on insider trading in DFP's stock. She reminded the Directors that they had to keep confidential all sensitive information that was discussed in the Boardroom. To do otherwise could kill an important deal or make another far more expensive. She also explained that officers, Directors and anyone with access to material inside information about DFP could not trade in the Company's stock without the risk of incurring potential legal liability – both civil and criminal – and incredibly bad publicity for that person and the Company. Accordingly, she noted that the Code's insider trading provisions required that any party subject to the insider trading provisions needed to call the Office of the General Counsel first, in order to obtain permission to trade in the Company's securities. She told the Directors that not only traditional insiders, but also anyone to whom they delivered inside information, could be regarded as insiders under the federal securities laws. Importantly, if one of their "tipees" traded on the basis of such information, a Director could be the one held liable for the use of that information.

"I know I'm not telling you anything that you don't already know on some level, but Directors and officers should take great pains to avoid even the appearance of trading on inside information," she said. "Once it is alleged that a Director knew something that others didn't, it is very difficult after a questionable trade to prove a negative such as, 'I didn't know about the pending bullish earnings announcement.'"

She also reminded the Directors that the Company had adopted a so-called "window period" trading policy, whereby the DFP Directors could not trade in the Company's securities until a quarterly or year-end earnings press release had been on the Street for about three days, and then the Board (and others who ordinarily had inside information) could trade for the next three weeks. There could be exceptions to the window periods because special information may not have been disclosed in the earnings release, and a total "freeze" would be placed on officers, Directors and other insiders from trading in the Company securities (for example, if negotiations were underway for a merger but they weren't concluded by the time of the release and premature disclosure could kill the deal).

She described other materials in the Code, including those relating to confidentiality, moonlighting and similar issues. The final matter she discussed was the prohibition on payments to government officials, because the Company had entered into a number of major markets in Europe and Asia where government bureaucrats often sought such payments from aggressive bidders for government contracts. More than once, Company representatives had been approached by government officials in lesser developed countries requesting that a "bribe" be paid in exchange for delivering a favorable contract to the Company. Up to now, the Company had been able to successfully withstand such requests, but, she said, pressure was growing on some divisional officers to make such payments. In a very few situations, she explained, foreign payments are lawful under the U.S. Foreign Corrupt Practices Act, if they are payments made to ministerial officials for ministerial service. Mercedes explained that payments to customs officers or harbormasters for moving perishable goods, for example, might very well be lawful under the federal legislation but, even so, under the DFP Code of Ethics, couldn't be made without approval by her office. For pragmatic reasons, she and Mark had approved some small payments so DFP's officers could move perishable goods off of the docks. Without such payments, in many countries people and goods could be stalled for weeks.

"If we're always 'goody two shoes,' won't our foreign competitors run all over us?" Alex interjected.

Mark immediately responded. "As far as I'm concerned, integrity has to be the hallmark of this Company." He paused for effect. "That integrity must start at the top, and that includes the Board. I'm not willing to push the envelope and I hope none of you are either. We might get some business in the short term that way, but that approach will always come back to haunt us.

"Having been active in the foreign markets, I can assure you that once you start to pay bribes to obtain or retain work, the requests for them never stop. Obviously, some minor 'grease payments' may be required to do our day-by-day business, but we can only make those as sanctioned by our federal law – and there are relatively few such payments specially permitted, like payments for obtaining permits, visas, police protection, utility service and the loading and unloading of cargo.

"Let me give you a personal example: I found myself getting off a plane in a remote airport, and then stuck in a customs office in Southeast Asia. The customs officer essentially told me that if I paid him $100, I could get through customs that day."

A few of the Directors smiled. They had been in similar situations.

"If I chose not to make the payment," Mark continued, "I'd have to wait for 24 hours before I entered the country. When I complained to the local police, the customs officer increased his request to $200 and I paid it. That kind of payment, as Mercedes mentioned, is legitimate since you are really paying for a ministerial act that the government official is required to carry out under any reasonable circumstances.

"I'd like to make some concluding comments. If we're going to be competitive in this era, we have to be aggressive and really fight hard for our market position. At the same time, our corporate culture has to embrace an ethical code on a day-to-day basis. If we don't do that in our international operations, the new code will just gather dust and be a totally ineffective tool. I have asked Mercedes to serve as our Chief Ethics Officer and conduct some practical seminars on ethical issues to show how we can be ethical and still be profitable, tough competitors."

After extended discussion on the Code of Ethics – particularly whether it was sweeping enough in light of increasing media coverage about the alleged erosion of business ethics – the Board unanimously voiced its approval. George suggested that the Code of Ethics should be publicized and included as an exhibit to the Company's annual report; Mark said that was an excellent idea and asked B.R. to arrange for the revision of the annual report, which was being worked on in the galley proof stage at DFP's financial printing firm, S.S. Downing & Co.

Agenda Item 6: Declaration of cash dividend

The cash dividend currently was being paid at a rate of $.02 per share per quarter, which amounted to hundreds of thousands of dollars in dividend payments a year. There was a brief discussion about whether the dividend rate should be increased, but the CFO explained that dividend policies essentially had become very restrictive in U.S. industry and that few companies paid large dividends any longer. He said the Company had the capacity to pay higher dividends, but that he and the senior management didn't think that was a good use of corporate funds. Further, if the dividend rate got too high and operations were to slip, the Company would have to either cut its dividend or terminate it, which was a very difficult undertaking.

"I think we should stop paying the dividend altogether," said David Nugent. "The only parties that care about these dividends now are retirees and I'm not sure we need to worry much about them. Of course, there may be a few retired Company officers and employees who also are concerned about the dividend, but I think it's a lousy use of our corporate funds because they're not tax deductible to the corporation and are taxed at ordinary income tax rates when received by individual shareholders. In my company, we never pay dividends. Mark, I think you're stuck in some ancient practices that you ought to reconsider."

"You know, Dave, you and I have discussed this issue for a long, long time. As you know, some investors focus on dividend-bearing securities. Also, a dividend yield can help set a floor on the price of a stock. While a relatively small group of our shareholders depends on our dividend, I wish to remind you that a key local charitable foundation – one of our largest shareholders – puts a lot of emphasis on the receipt of our dividend. Unless you want to alienate the Dakota Foundation, one of our major shareholders, which we helped start, we're going to continue to pay our dividends just like we have in the past."

Gen. Landry had heard this discussion before. "Let's get on with it," he said. "I move that the dividend, as proposed, be approved.'

"Second the motion."

"Any discussion? Hearing none, all those in favor, please say 'aye.'"

The Directors all voted in favor of the motion – even Nugent, who said he was doing so with some reluctance, adding that he didn't want to have his reluctance recorded in the minutes. "I don't want my dissent to embarrass some of you financial wizards!" he barked, taking some of the Directors by surprise with his little attempt at humor.

Agenda Item 7: Authorization of amendment to Bylaws, including change in authorized number of Directors

Mercedes had been asked to lead this discussion as well. It was fairly straightforward: Amend the Company's Bylaws to change the authorized number of Directors from 11 to 13. She reminded the Board that the average size of Boards with a revenue base similar to the Company's ranged from about 11 to 14, adding that the Nominating Committee was about to recommend two new Directors to the Board. Without discussion, the Bylaw amendment was adopted.

Agenda Item 8: Annual Meeting matters

The matters ranged from authorizing the time and place of the annual meeting of shareholders to approving the proposed proxy statement and other annual documents that had been carefully reviewed by the Board prior to the meeting.

"Just a minute," Gen. Landry interjected. "After we had all those weird people show up at last year's annual meeting, I suggest we no longer meet here in Dakota City, but, instead, go to a remote city in the northern part of Dakota and have an annual meeting starting at 6 a.m.!"

"After last year's annual meeting," Mark said, "I'd rather meet in Zanzibar, but I don't think we could get away with that. This year we have a more streamlined agenda in place and some procedures in mind that will cut off unnecessary discussion by corporate gadflies, a few strident disgruntled employees and the usual shareholder who, for the sixth time, will ask about when we're going to increase the dividend."

George was somewhat concerned about what he had just heard. "Look, Mark, an annual meeting of shareholders is just that, a meeting for our shareholders. While it may be a little frustrating at times to listen to speeches and complaints, it seems to me that's your job and you should have a little more patience. If you try to cut them off prematurely, some of your regular and friendly shareholders might switch sides. Your best bet is to grin and bear it. I've learned that when the CEO does that, after a while a lot of members of the audience will help him move the meeting along with their informal commentary, and later, their motions to adjourn."

Dr. Thompson agreed. "Annual meetings can be difficult, but they do provide a good forum for shareholders to sound off and for us to hear from people we might not ordinarily hear from."

Corporate Secretary Barbara Ramos spoke up. "You should understand that whenever I receive shareholder comments that I think are important for the Board, I pass them along to you. You could see more of them, of course, but I don't send them all because many are repetitive or based on personal vendettas. Trust me, you don't want to go there."

Next on the agenda was the Annual Report to Shareholders, as well as the proposed Form 10-K report to be filed with the Securities and Exchange Commission. Along with it came a 20-minute report from the Audit Committee, which, among other things, set forth the committee's recommendation to include the financial statements in the 10-K report.

The Board members knew this was a particularly important segment of the meeting, especially in light of recent litigation about misleading corporate financial reporting – and because of the increased workload being demanded from Audit Committee members. The Committee had taken more than four hours in its recent meeting to go over DFP's year-end financial statements with the CFO, the Company's internal auditors and the Company's external auditors. They reviewed footnotes, financial statements and the Management Discussion and Analysis section in the 10-K report. One Audit Committee member said that by the time he finished with his review and the discussion he had spent more than 10 hours reviewing materials and raising questions with various members of the audit team. He then went on to say that over the course of a year, including his travel time, he had spent about five to six full workweeks on DFP Board matters – and far more than that if he counted the time he spent analyzing and thinking about DFP's issues.

Another Director had privately complained to Mark that he was thinking of resigning as a member of the Audit Committee because his evolving legal duties seemed almost to the point where shareholder activists expected an audit committee to conduct its own audit of the auditors. Taking that approach, he proclaimed, not only was incredibly time consuming, but also cost-prohibitive. In effect, it seemed some shareholder activists wanted a "fraud audit," which would take at least three times as long and four times as costly as a traditional audit.

Mark noticed that the Board meeting already had passed the two-hour mark, and he knew it would take three more hours

– at least. He had decided months ago that it made sense to build in an official recess from time to time during a lengthy Board meeting, because otherwise Directors would begin to move in and out of the meeting, disrupting the group's focused attention on critical corporate matters.

"I think this is a good time for a break," Mark said. "Agenda Item 9 is going to take a while, I believe. Let's recess the meeting for 15 minutes and reconvene then."

Some of the Directors went out of the Boardroom to listen to their voicemail messages and a few of the more tech-savvy Directors took out their laptop computers and Blackberries to check their e-mails.

CHAPTER 4

MEETING RECONVENES FOR
GRILLCO DEBATE
Do the Morans Have the Right Stuff?

Agenda Item 9: Review of proposed acquisition of Grillco

"It's time to look at the Grillco deal," Mark said after the Directors had all returned. "I want to remind all of you that this deal is consistent with the strategic plan we labored over at our offsite conference earlier this year – especially since Grillco's operations fit so nicely with our core business. You'll recall we had our sights set on a substantial, mature and well-managed company, with products that are complementary to our product line. We also concluded that any acquisition must have a projected rate of return of somewhere between 15-18 percent after tax – and, actually, the Grillco projections are at the high end of that range.

"With respect to the background materials we gave to you before the meeting, I want to review them briefly. Fortunately, Grillco has audited financial statements for the past few years that you've had the opportunity to review, plus the company's unaudited statements for the first two quarters of Grillco's fiscal year.

"You'll note that both its revenues and earnings are on an upswing, and Grillco continues to develop new products with high profit margins. Grillco also has information systems that will work with ours, as well as compatible compensation and fringe benefit plans."

He paused for emphasis and looked around the room before continuing. "By the way, our auditors tell us that Grillco's audited financial statements appear to be conservatively prepared, with large reserves for some potential new warranty claims and potential operating contingencies. Thus, I see little or no risk of our having to restate Grillco's prior years' earnings after we acquire them because of any financial reporting gymnastics. We all know companies that haven't been so lucky. Our friends down the road acquired a company last year and then had to take a big writedown because of a lack of diligence concerning financial data. It's now embroiled in a lot of shareholder litigation that alleges the board and officers were grossly neglectful.

"We've also had the opportunity to review a report from our investment banker concerning how our proposed price relates to comparable transactions, and the banker is prepared to give the Board a fairness opinion, a copy of which you also have in front of you. Also, the Grillco management team has been evaluated and is described in your materials. It's clear that, in addition to the Morans, there's a solid group of senior executives who are still relatively young. But, I know some of you still have heartburn about the apparent aggressiveness of the Morans in trying to gain some seats on the Board."

Several of the Directors nodded as Mark continued. "What I'd like to do, then, is take this discussion in two parts. First, let's look at the terms and conditions of the deal, and then let's look at the governance issues involved in bringing the Morans onto the Board."

At that point, DFP's outside legal counsel – including an M&A lawyer, a tax expert and an antitrust specialist – and an investment banker, James Andrews of the firm of Andrews & Molinari, joined the meeting. The room took on a new air of seriousness.

Raines, the CFO, presented the terms of the deal, including the $50 million proposed purchase price, which, according to

Raines, included a relatively large "strategic premium." So, the deal would probably be dilutive to the Company's earnings to the extent of 6 percent or 7 percent of its earnings per share over each of the next few years. On the other hand, Raines explained, the terms and conditions of the deal were extremely good and DFP had a lot of post-closing protection in the event any Grillco contingent liabilities were to develop following the closing (such as a lawsuit that might be filed against Grillco that wasn't disclosed to DFP). The Morans, who assured the CEO that Grillco was a clean operation, had agreed to a two-year post-closing indemnification or hold harmless provision for undisclosed liabilities, subject to some carve-outs for certain small, routine liabilities. Also, the Morans had agreed to a material adverse change, or MAC, clause in the deal. Under this clause, DFP could walk away from or terminate the deal if Grillco's business started to sour significantly between the date of signing and the proposed closing date. Such provisions made DFP management feel quite good about the quality of Grillco.

Andrews, the investment banker, was pleased that the proposed acquisition would be done entirely for stock. He said that this feature would permit some favorable financial reporting consequences and that he expected the Street, upon hearing the announcement, to trade DFP stock down by less than 5 percent. He did say that a few securities analysts might attempt to throw cold water on the deal but, with his usual confidence, he said he didn't expect the opinions "of such simpletons" to be widely followed.

Andrews had made a number of appearances before the Board, and he told the Board that the deal was a reasonable one. He explained that the pricing had been based on a review of comparable transactions in the industry and that the post-closing indemnification by the sellers gave DFP relatively little deal risk. Andrews, who was one of the more pleasant and casual bankers who visited the Board, said A&M was prepared to deliver a fairness opinion under which his firm would opine that the transaction was fair from a financial perspective.

But the savvy Directors, doing proper diligence to fulfill their duty of care, peppered Andrews with questions. They asked him what kind of assumptions he had used about the growth of Grillco and what he saw as the principal deal risks. Andrews had prepared for this. He said he saw relatively few risks – although he admitted that one important patent for Grillco was expiring and it covered one of Grillco's significant products. He also said there was some growing competition with respect to one Grillco division but that overall he regarded the Morans as terrific operators with a reputation for high integrity. He conceded they were tough-minded and had somewhat abrasive personalities, but he thought they would be good additions to the Board and the Street would see it that way.

Raines and the outside tax counsel, Stephanie Sterling, took about thirty minutes to cover the financial reporting aspects and tax issues involved in the proposed deal. The tax lawyer explained there were some favorable tax consequences for the rather complex deal structured for DFP that would cause the Company's overall tax rate to decline as a result of the deal.

Throughout her presentation, Sterling cited numerous Internal Revenue Code sections and regulations that few could understand. She did say she promised a probability of 90 percent success rate with the tax outcome and that a large part of her firm's fee was based on that contingency. She had the audacity to turn to the CFO and remind him to book an accounting reserve for the certain fee payment to her law firm which would be made, she predicted, in about five years after the statute of limitations had run and tax audits were completed and DFP could realize its tax deduction without further IRS risk. The CFO found little to smile about, as he expected the deductions only would be approved after endless tax audits, and even some potential litigation with the IRS. Fortunately, thought Raines, her contingent fee will be calculated after carving out defense costs.

At that point, Mercedes thought the Board members needed a jolt from their tax lecture. She reminded them that the deal had not yet been publicly announced and if the Board approved it the Directors should not discuss it with anyone. They could only do so once there had been a press release about the proposed transaction and the market had digested the release.

As the details rocketed around the table, so did the questions. Dr. Thompson asked whether the CEO would pick the Grillco acquisition over the Coffee Brew King one he had discussed earlier in the meeting. The CEO refused to pick the better alternative but said they both made sense for shareholders. Some of the Directors felt that this answer was evasive but most of them understood that he truly believed both deals could make sense for the shareholders. Charles Frank asked whether shareholder approval would be probable for the Grillco deal, and the General Counsel replied that they had already analyzed the shareholder-voting constituency. The conclusion: The vote would be easily obtained.

"Look, we're all pretty much agreed – I think – that this is a good deal," Harry finally said. "But let's get down to basics: Do both Jeff and Judy belong on the Board? Do they have the Right Stuff?"

He looked at Dr. Thompson. They had tacitly agreed to be silent when this issue first arose, so they could listen carefully to what the others said.

Gen. Landry and Alex said they knew both of the Morans and – while they respected them both – they found Jeff a particularly difficult personality. A significant discussion followed about whether the Morans could be team players on the Board, especially since they would be, when taken together, the holders of the largest percentage of the Company's outstanding stock.

Hugh proposed that he meet with the Morans, since he knew them, to discuss their interest in the Board and to explain to them a possible compromise to their condition that they both be added to the DFP Board: Perhaps one of them – preferably Judy – could come on the Board and the remaining Moran – be it Jeff or Judy – could select a professional, such as a money manager, to represent their interest. He said he wanted to share with the Board the names of five or six candidates whom he felt might be good candidates to be a proxy for Jeff Moran. All the Directors thought this approach was a good idea but conditioned their approval on Hugh working out a reasonable compromise on the board membership issue. Mark did express some concern that one prospect, a money manager, might have a conflict of interest because he would know more about DFP's stock than perhaps he or his firm should. Nonetheless, he said he was prepared to go along with the idea.

Without being asked for a further opinion, Andrews, the investment banker for the deal, reminded the Board that it was highly probable that if DFP did not move forward with its bid that a competing company would do so. He urged all due speed.

"Ha," Alex thought to himself. "I'll bet he's far more concerned about his firm's commission for the deal – let's see, what would that be? $300,000? – than for our shareholders." Of course, directors often wondered about the irony of the fairness opinions from bankers who should be objective and reliable. In some cases, however, their fee arrangements were designed so that if there was no deal, there would be no fee. In those cases, one wondered about justifiable reliance on such an opinion, although in recent years, fees were being restructured so they weren't all contingent. Also, more and more bankers were not delivering opinions where they found the fairness hill far too steep.

The deal was unanimously approved. The General Counsel – always thinking ahead, if somewhat presumptuously – distributed a draft press release prepared by the corporate communications staff that announced the Board's approval of the deal. The DFP Board members tinkered with the press release a bit, falling victim to "drafting by committee," which often leads to "paralysis by committee." Finally the press release was approved. That afternoon, it was agreed Mark would call the Morans and the press release would be issued to Wall Street and others.

"For the signing of a big deal like this one," Mark said, "I think we will need to have a special meeting so we can approve the final merger contract. Inevitably, it will contain some material changes from the deal as it is currently laid out in the letter of intent. B.R., what date looks good?"

B.R. opened her appointment book to look at the various corporate events coming up, and suggested a date within 30 days. Some of the Directors thought that was a little too quick; Mercedes agreed, saying it would probably be better to push it out a little further, in case complications arose in signing a contract.

"Okay, we can call an emergency session if any unforeseen items come up that require earlier action," Mark said. "B.R. will give you the exact date and time later.

"Gentlemen – and ladies, of course – I think we've had a very successful meeting. Is there anything else before we adjourn?"

Agenda Item 10: Other business.

"Yes, I have something I'd like to bring before the Board," George said.

George had listened carefully throughout the meeting, making detailed notes to himself and voting affirmatively to every request. But, more importantly in some ways, he was curious about how the CEO, Mark, the son of his old friend, Tom Gregory, was dealing with these difficult issues.

George had been quite impressed with Mark's management of the Company since his arrival. Mark had brought a refreshing breath of organization and energy to DFP and had been able to handle effectively the day-to-day senior management issues while also being able to look at the big picture. But George had some concerns with Mark's sometimes-brusque handling of the Board and his apparent insistence, in private, that, in the final analysis, he should be the person calling the shots – whatever the situation.

As George saw it, Mark had to be the captain of the ship – but he didn't always seem to realize that he should listen to his advisors before making an important change of course. George believed in giving the CEO a lot of running room and a strong presumption of rectitude, but he also felt the Board should have an opportunity to help him navigate if he got too far off course. It was as if Mark didn't know that in the minds of many of the Directors the Grillco deal pushed the envelope – some saw it as too pricey and the Morans as less-than-perfect partners with whom they would now have to work closely, even taking at least one of them onto the Board.

"Before we break up," George said to Mark, "let me make a suggestion. With our Board expanding, I think we need some formal corporate governance guidelines outlining how we should interact with you and the rest of the management team. You'll recall, I mentioned this idea at the end of our last Board meeting."

Though holding himself in check emotionally, Mark felt a little ambushed by George's raising such an important matter under "Other Business." But he was kicking himself for not taking on the guidelines issue shortly after that meeting – maybe he wasn't listening closely enough, he thought to himself.

"Well, we have traditional Bylaws and a few guidelines," he said. "What kinds of matters are you talking about?"

"Yes, I agree our Bylaws are strong. But these guidelines would complement them in areas such as the qualifications we look for in new Board members, Board committee operations, the size and timing of transactions to be brought before the Board and the like."

Dr. Thompson nodded. "I voted in favor of the Grillco purchase, but I still think you moved a little too fast and too far before getting the Board involved," he said.

"I agree," Harry said. "As a Board, we don't want to slow you down, but we do want to be able to offer our advice as early as possible. That's why we asked George to draft these guidelines – he's had more experience being on the boards of fast-growing companies than any of us."

George, who was sitting close to B.R., gave copies of his proposed guidelines to her to distribute to those around the table. Rich Collins rolled his eyes as he looked through them.

"Looks like more bureaucracy to me," Collins said with a smile. "But I'm not going to be on this Board much longer anyway."

George had anticipated Collins' reaction. "Rich, as you know, sometimes bureaucracy serves a purpose – especially where shareholders are concerned. These guidelines also will help protect us, and the Company you created, in many ways.

"And, Mark – these won't hinder your ability to make fast decisions," George asserted. "I think in the long run it will be better for all of us if we have a few more informal rules on these sorts of issues. Also, this draft is hardly a long form set of guidelines nor as rigorous for management as many of them. For example, they don't call for periodic executive sessions of the Board without management present. Our next version probably should cover that issue and other related matters so the Board may, from time to time, act a little more independently."

"Since I haven't had a chance to review them yet, can we deal with them offline?" Mark asked. "I'd like Mercedes and B.R. to take a look at them, of course."

"Of course," George said. "We can ratify them easily by signing a unanimous written consent whenever we've all finished reviewing them."

"Very well," Mark said, almost too stiffly.

Agenda Item 11: Adjournment

"Now that's taken care of," Mark continued, "is there any other business?"

The Directors were silent. Some shook their heads.

"That ends our official agenda. But I want to take a moment to personally thank all of you for being so helpful to me today, on so many levels. As we continue to grow and prosper, we're going to face many issues that may test our personal friendships and our working relationships, but I think it's important that we work together effectively – and we've proven yet again today that, with a little patience and thoughtfulness, we can do that."

The meeting was adjourned.

Later that afternoon, the DFP Corporate Communications Office issued a press release that began:

DFP, INC.
DFP Plaza
1417 Main Street
Dakota City, Dakota 98765

DAKOTA CITY — DFP, Inc., today announced that its Board of Directors unanimously approved the acquisition of Grillco, a Dakota City company that manufactures the popular "Grillit" counter-top electric grill. The transaction is subject to the approval of DFP shareholders and a review by regulatory agencies, including an anti-trust review under the Hart-Scott-Rodino Act. That review may take between 30 to 60 days depending on whether the Federal Trade Commission requests additional information after the initial filing of an application. In any event, the current schedule contemplates a closing in the late fall.

"I am pleased to announce that we have signed a Letter of Intent and that we expect this excellent company founded by Jeff and Judy Moran to become part of the DFP family later in the Fall," said DFP CEO Mark Gregory. "It will take us to the next stage of becoming a broad-based kitchen-appliance Company and fully complement our line of products."

Mr. Gregory did not announce the purchase price, saying the details would be worked out over the next few weeks, and that a suitable additional press release would be issued at that time.

Once the deal is complete, the DFP Board will expand by two members, Mr. Gregory added. "We are pleased to have Judy Moran joining the Board, and look forward to the significant contribution she will make. And, we have asked Jeff and Judy to take the lead in helping us select another Director who will bring a new area of expertise to the Board."

Contact: Dawn Drury, DFP Vice President of Corporate Communications, 555-627-4276.

The DFP-Grillco deal closed four months later, under the basic terms discussed at the second quarter Board meeting.

James R. Ukropina

***A few weeks later, the Board adopted the following
guidelines:***

DFP CORPORATE GOVERNANCE GUIDELINES

1. *Board Qualifications.* At least three-quarters of the members of the Board of Directors (the "Board") shall be independent. An independent Director means a person who: (a) has never been an employee of the Company or any of its subsidiaries; (b) has not had, during the past two years, any interest in any material transaction, or any business or financial relationship, with the Company or an affiliate of the Company (other than service as a Director); and (c) is not a relative of an executive officer or Director of the Company.

2. *Audit Committee.* There shall be an Audit Committee of the Board, consisting entirely of independent Directors, which shall oversee the Company's financial reporting process and internal controls, review compliance with laws and accounting standards, recommend the appointment of public accountants, and provide a direct channel of communication to the Board for public accountants, internal auditors and finance officers.

3. *Nominating Committee.* There shall be a Nominating Committee of the Board, consisting of a majority of independent Directors, which shall be responsible for the evaluation and nomination of Board members.

4. *Compensation Committee.* There shall be a Compensation Committee of the Board, consisting entirely of independent Directors, which shall be responsible for (a) ensuring that senior management will be accountable to the Board through the effective application of compensation policies, and (b) monitoring the effectiveness of both senior management and the Board (including committees thereof). The Compensation Committee shall establish compensation policies applicable to the Company's executive officers.

5. *Transactions Committee.* There shall be a Transactions Committee of the Board, consisting entirely of independent Directors, which shall be responsible for reviewing all related-party transactions involving the Company, and considering and making recommendations to the full Board with respect to all proposals involving (a) a change in control, or (b) the purchase or sale of assets constituting more than 5 percent of the Company's total assets.

From the Dakota Business Journal:

Argonaut Announces Price Cuts

DAKOTA CITY – Kitchen appliance maker Argonaut today announced a 15 percent price cut in its best-selling appliance, the BBQNow! counter-top electric grill.

Coming on the heels of DFP's acquisition of Grillco, Argonaut's chief competitor, the move is the latest attempt by Argonaut to maintain its market share in the popular counter-top grill space. Since that acquisition, Argonaut has clearly been trying to position itself as a struggling David against DFP's Goliath.

The price cuts took some merchants by surprise. "These products – both the Grillit and the BBQNow! – are extremely popular with consumers, who already consider them reasonably priced," said the owner of Wilhelm-Sumners, a popular cookware chain. "They seem to fly off our shelves."

The price cuts will be accompanied by an aggressive advertising campaign that directly compares the features and specifications of each appliance, an Argonaut spokesperson said.

James R. Ukropina

"I'm J. Calhoun Langdon who achieved, at the age of 37, the presidency of Alpha Plastics; 12 directorships; multi-multi millionaire and one day it hit me to discover what it was all about. Now, I want to pursue this meaning and become one of the best damn gurus in the business."

Source: Wall Street Journal

CHAPTER 5

LOOKING FOR THE BALANCE

Family Life Matters, Too

(Third Quarter of Year 6)

Agenda for Board Meeting

1. *Approval of Minutes*
2. *Quarterly Financial Results – CFO*
3. *Operating Challenges – CEO and COO*
4. *OSHA Claims*
5. *Response to Competitive Assault*
6. *Other Business*

Agenda Item 5: Response to Competitive Assault

George regarded Mark as an outstanding leader, manager, merchant and marketer on many levels. Ordinarily, thought George, Mark had a level head and was rarely emotional or impulsive. This Board meeting had been different, though: From the start of the session, Mark had appeared angry, and now he was recommending a set of tactics that didn't seem to make any sense. Even the title of the agenda item seemed unnecessarily warlike.

"I have to tell you that our competitor, Argonaut, is attempting to bury us. It's cut its price to the bone, and we're losing market share!" Mark fumed. "If they want a price war, I think we should retaliate in kind."

Most of the Directors had never seen Mark so livid. After all, the Argonaut approach wasn't unheard-of in such situations.

"Wait just a minute, Mark," said Alex, as other Directors nodded sagely in agreement with Todihara's request for further deliberations. "It seems to me that Argonaut has a strong balance sheet with plenty of cash. Retaliatory price cuts will only lead to a never-ending downward price spiral for some time. Ask yourself, Mark: Can Argonaut, as a matter of good business practice, continue to sell its products at far below its cost for any appreciable period of time?"

"As far as I'm concerned, they never should have started these rapacious tactics in the first place, but I doubt they could continue for too long," replied Mark, somewhat petulantly. "On the other hand, I think some of their senior managers are bad apples and they might just try to bury us with an irrational plan."

Judy Moran – who from her first days on the Board had become an outspoken, freethinking Director – took great pride in Grillit, the product that had sealed the Grillco-DFP deal. "Mark, we looked at some of these issues a while back. It was clear to us at that time that the Grillit has many more bells and whistles than Argonaut has on its appliance. And their pricing on this product never seemed to be as important as for many other products. Are you sure their price cuts are what's causing us to lose market share? Or is it just that Argonaut is engaged in a more aggressive, costly and necessarily short-lived marketing campaign?"

Stanley Towler spoke up. A former Dakota State Controller and political consultant, he was the newest addition to the Board, brought on with Jeff and Judy's approval after the Grillco-DFP merger. The Board viewed him as an important person to help lead the Company through increasingly complex political minefields as it grew. "Look at it this way, Mark, I understand that in the past few years Argonaut and DFP have lawfully collaborated on some product safety ideas that have earned us some awards up at the state capital, and helped both of us. Why are you taking this so personally?"

"I'm sorry if you think I'm taking it personally. I'm not. It's just that this is such a bad business practice on their part that they could bring us down," Mark said.

"It's up to *all* of us to make sure they don't," Towler said firmly. "We don't know what's going on over there, and we have to remain focused on our response. Argonaut may be in a tough position in connection with its own operations. Anyway, I doubt this price-cutting will last too long, and I think we can withstand it. Plus, we should consider staying on relatively good footing with the Argonaut executives and work our way through this with a more aggressive marketing campaign. You know, they're not bad guys – I run into them at the Club a lot."

"DFP already had the best marketing program in the industry," Alex added. "And we've just added a new, more effective website to our marketing mix. Don't forget: Our recent infomercials have been successful in pushing our slow-moving products. Maybe we should just pay more attention to that approach."

George had listened carefully and now felt it was time to speak. "Mark, as you may have gleaned by now, we think retaliatory pricing isn't the way to go. Instead, it seems to most of us that it makes more sense to increase your marketing budget for the Grillit. We need to differentiate our products more and let the customer decide which is the best buy based on our quality."

As a former CEO himself, George didn't want to interject the Board into day-to-day decisions that should be made by the CEO. "On the other hand, this is largely an operating question," George added. "For this type of matter, we think it's important to leave this issue to your best judgment. After listening to us, what are your thoughts?"

"Well," said Mark, "I'm still quite angry about Argonaut, but after listening to your comments about some of the issues, you've convinced me that further price cuts might not do much for our market share. So, maybe our strongest countermeasure would be to increase our marketing budget. We actually have a surplus in that part of our budget right now, and this may be just the right time to deploy it. Champ Hutler, our NASCAR hero, called and said he's got some extra time to help us. Argonaut turned him down as a race car sponsor years ago, so he says he's more than ready to go to war!"

The Board seemed relieved as Mark continued: "You know, I owe you all a vote of thanks for your input. I guess my emotions were getting the best of me here."

"Well, Mark, you haven't had to go head-to-head with Argonaut the way we have in the past," Judy playfully interjected. "You'll get used to it."

"I don't know if I'll ever get used to it, but if all of you agree that I should continue a civil relationship with those idiots over at Argonaut, I'll do my best."

When the meeting concluded, George thought it was time for a heart-to-heart talk with Mark. As they walked over to a previously scheduled lunch at the Fargo Club, they began sharing small talk – mainly about Dakota State's new football coach and how the team would do next year. After they had finished their lunch – a hamburger with fries for Mark and a romaine, roasted beet and orange salad for George – they ordered coffee. Anyone looking at them from across the room might have thought they were related, perhaps uncle-nephew; George was an impeccably dressed and well-tanned man with gray hair whose physique reflected his love for tennis and golf, and Mark's designer suit and tie were only a cut above George's.

"Mark, do you have another 30 minutes? There are a couple of matters I'd like to discuss with you on a very personal level. Since I've been a friend of your father's for so long, I hope you don't mind me taking this liberty."

"George, I always have time for you – and I know how much Dad appreciates your interest in my career. You always raise important issues and provide good suggestions for me and the rest of the management team." But Mark also had a feeling about what George wanted to discuss. "I'm sorry I kind of 'lit up' at the Board meeting today, but I'm getting frustrated at our inability to deal with competitors as effectively as I'd like."

"Mark, the feeling is mutual: You're an outstanding manager and an extremely creative businessman. On the other hand, you haven't had the opportunity to deal with this Board of Directors very long. I hope you don't think it's impertinent of me, but I'd like to give you some off-the-record advice about how your Board can play an ongoing, important role that should benefit you."

"George, you know I..."

"Just listen to me, please. God, I wish someone had sat me down years ago and forced me to listen to a talk like this."

George knew he would be telling Mark a lot that the CEO already knew; still, he felt it was time for a light refresher course. He began.

You might say that the concept of a Board of Directors goes way back in history – even King Arthur sought advice from his Knights of the Roundtable. Looking back, it seems to me that the Roundtable board probably was one of the most clear-thinking and effective boards of all time. It had one strategic objective and it certainly was carried out, at least according to what I now know about those times. As I recall, the objective was simple: "It's clear the climate must be perfect for all the year in Camelot." Too bad it's not that easy today.

When companies started to develop here in the United States, boards of directors were relatively small and often a rubber stamp for the president or the chief executive officer. Even after World War II, many boards were so-called "rocking-chair boards." The board meeting often started promptly at 10 a.m. and routine matters were discussed. Then the meeting ended exactly at noon, just in time for a cocktail hour and lunch – regardless of how far board deliberations had progressed.

That didn't really begin to change drastically until the 1970s when shareholder activists emerged. They really started shaking up boards that, up until then, largely consisted of "good old boys." Board membership started to reflect more diversity as women and representatives of ethnic groups – including African-Americans, Hispanics and Asians, among others – were added.

Then directors were faced with some serious litigation that exposed them to substantial liability. In one of those cases, *Van Gorkom* in Delaware, a board was found negligent in setting a sale price for a company in a negotiated acquisition. While that case ultimately was settled, it sent chills up and down the spines of many directors. Delaware responded with a favorable statutory approach whereby directors of Delaware corporations could only be held monetarily liable if they were grossly neglectful or engaged in conflict of interests transactions and self-dealing. So, in dealing with ordinary course transactions without conflicts, ordinarily, directors should be off the hook for monetary liability unless there are special circumstances. That's what we lawyers call an exculpatory statute.

Even so, directors remained nervous. They became even more so when institutional investors took larger and larger stock positions in a number of companies. In fact, those investors caused significant changes in the senior management at then-troubled companies like General Motors and American Express. At about the same time, most boards began to become more disciplined and diligent. Most focused on attempting to do all they could to enhance shareholder value.

Even that wasn't enough. A number of institutional investors still weren't satisfied. In the late 1980s and throughout the 1990s, representatives of a number of public employee pension funds (which, in turn, owned large chunks of U.S. equities) insisted that corporate governance practices become more independent from senior management and more professional. A number of pioneers in the field helped formulate corporate governance guidelines similar to and far more comprehensive than those we recently adopted. There were even some conciliatory "compacts" between private industry and the public employee funds concerning what constituted appropriate corporate governance practice. On top of all that activity, boards started to have a majority of independent directors and appeared more responsive to shareholder interests.

I'm giving you all this basic background because I want to explain how I have seen boards perform and how they can help CEOs like you. We all start with the idea that we first have to do what the law requires and, as we have discussed previously, we have to act with due care, loyalty to shareholders, and in good faith. Even more importantly for you, most good directors believe they should only advise you extensively in the case of a crisis, when formulating policy and strategy, and when working on important management development and compensation matters. As far as your decisions on operating matters, unless operating results reflect a large disparity from the business plan or your budget, most of us like to follow the principle of "NIFO": Nose In, Fingers Out of the corporate tent!

As I see it, one of our major roles is to be supportive of you as our CEO, especially when you seek our perspective and judgment. In some cases, we may have to offer constructive criticism, as others and I have done from time to time. But that's our job; I encourage you to listen carefully, since that is the best way for you to learn.

As my college football coach said, "When the coach stops yelling at you, it's time to start worrying." In other words, we may come down a little hard on you at times but we are only trying to do so from the perspective of what is best for the shareholders and, incidentally, for you.

Mark had listened politely all along, nodding in the appropriate places. It was all good advice, and he didn't mind hearing it again from George. But George wasn't through. He looked around the now-empty dining room to make sure again that no one could overhear their discussion but then he lowered his voice anyway.

"Mark, there's one other matter I'm particularly concerned about."

Mark looked puzzled.

"I realize it appears to have little to do directly with your corporate life, but you'd be surprised." George shifted uncomfortably and continued. "How are things at home? When was the last time you took a vacation with your family?"

Mark bowed his head briefly before looking up to answer.

"Frankly, George, I had to skip vacation over the holidays and only had a short vacation with my family last summer. Melynda is becoming impatient, and I have to say I really can't blame her." He paused, wondering how much detail George wanted to hear. George motioned for him to go on.

"Last month, I had to miss a special performance by our 9-year-old son in the school play in order to attend an industry conference. I had planned to attend the play but my plane arrived too late to make it. Another time, my 7-year-old hit a home run in a softball game and I arrived just as her game was ending. She asked me if I had seen her hit. I had to tell her 'no.' That hurt her a lot, and I have to say it hurt me as well."

"Mark, let me tell you something," George said. "Those kinds of moments come around a very few times in life. Only you can be at those events and only you can take a vacation with your family.

"Recently, the Board members and I have become concerned about these 80-hour weeks you're putting in. While we admire your efforts, we think they're starting to become counterproductive for you and the rest of us. We could be wrong, but we think you're far too uptight, and that you're not seeing the forest for the trees. The Grillit situation is a good example."

Mark bristled a little when he heard that the Board was paying so much attention to his personal life, but in his heart he knew it was the right thing for them to do.

"From time to time," George continued, "you seem too immersed and too intense with respect to corporate issues – like you were today. We want to encourage you to spend more time with your family and delegate more of the day-to-day managerial tasks you now take on."

"But..." Mark tried to interrupt. George held up his hand.

"Mark, I believe you're becoming far too involved in minutiae, and you need to become involved at a higher level in the management process. You need to spend more time on strategy and less time worrying about what's going on in the trenches. Leave the day-to-day stuff to others. Start to delegate more."

"George, how do you expect me to manage if I don't know everything that's going on? I'm a hands-on manager! That's the way I've made my way up the ladder, and I'm not sure I can change now."

"Mark, I can't tell you to change your style altogether, and I realize you're a hands-on manager, but there's nothing wrong if you feel a little exposed or vulnerable from time to time as long as you have a good management team behind you. If you don't change and DFP continues to grow, after a while, though, you'll find that your management style is going to drag you down; you'll lose your perspective and judgment. Those are the qualities that we're really paying you for. If you have to beef up your management team – and I think that may be a real need at this stage of the Company's growth – then you should do so. If you delegate effectively, you'll free up a lot of time for important, big picture issues. At the same time, you'll have to monitor those assignments. How much monitoring is needed – that's an art and not a science."

George's voice took on a more soothing tone. "Mark, face it: You're too valuable to us to have a heart attack or family problems. Both can be avoided with a little more balance on your part. We also notice that, like most of us, you may have put on a few extra pounds. Though that may not seem like a problem now, I can assure you it will be soon."

"George, what is this, my annual physical exam?!"

"No, Mark, I'm just trying to get you to stand back and see how this business is affecting you from a lot of different perspectives. One of my jobs as a Director is to be sure that you don't lose sight of what is important, both as a businessman and as a person. I had to learn the hard way.

"Your father probably never told you this, but before I was married to Helen I was married to Ingrid, a young woman I met in business school. She was terrific, but I lost sight of our relationship and she unceremoniously and, without much warning, divorced me before I knew what had happened."

Mark smiled sympathetically. It was as if George had listened in on the argument he and Melynda had just the last weekend.

"I suspect Melynda and you aren't near that threshold yet – but I warn you that if you don't pay more attention to your family, you're apt to encounter problems that will be really difficult to deal with. Your kids are at an age when they need more attention from you."

"Okay, George. I hear you. I'll schedule some time off."

"I knew you'd say that, but we wanted to make sure you actually did it," George said, smiling. "So, as a bonus for your hard work – and to cut that work off for a short while – the Board and I have arranged for you and your entire family to take a long weekend at the end of this month and go to the Lake Country and stay at my home."

"Really generous, George, and I'll take you up on it soon. But I have a retreat planned to go over strategic planning with our division managers that weekend."

"That's what I mean, Mark. Sometimes you seem to think the Company can't run without your input every minute. I've done something that's incredibly presumptuous. I've talked to your COO, and he agreed to take full responsibility for that retreat," George said, surprising Mark again. "I had to truly pry it out of him, but he also agrees that all of you have been spending far too much time dealing with this recent price-cutting episode and that you could use some time off."

Mark knew there was no escape, and, frankly, he looked forward to having a chance to unwind. "Maybe you have been a little presumptuous, George," he said with a slight grin, "but, in fact, I appreciate your candor and the Board's concerns. Melynda, the kids and I look forward to the time together."

George signaled the waiter, who brought over the check and placed it on the table. Mark reached for it, but George beat him to it.

Two months later, Mark sent the following handwritten note to George:

Dear George,

I want to thank you for our talk at the Fargo Club. I have to be honest with you, though. At first, I was somewhat perturbed that you and the Board had delved into my personal life. But, upon reflection, I knew you were right.

I have agreed to spend a long weekend at least every month with my family, and Melynda and I already are planning a lengthy summer vacation, with the kids in Hawaii.

At the next Board meeting, you're going to see less of me – at least when it comes to my weight. I've started a regular physical exercise routine every other morning (and, no more hamburgers and fries for lunch). Again, you were right: My stamina, judgment and creative thinking have improved considerably.

Your interest in my personal well-being couldn't have come at a better time, and I'll be eternally grateful. You knew I was headed for trouble, even though I didn't.

Sincerely,
Mark

A financial snapshot of the Company:

DFP INC.
COMPARATIVE QUARTERLY RESULTS
($000)
(First Quarter of Year 7)

	Most Recent Qtr.	% Variance from Comp Qtr.	% Variance From Plan
Sales	200,000	+1	-3
Net Income	16,000	-2	-2
Earnings/Share	.21	-2	-2
Cash Flow/Share	.19	-5	-4
Stock Price versus Peer Index	-3%	-	-
Debt/Equity Ratio	60%	-	-

71

CHAPTER 6

AN ALMOST ROUTINE BOARD MEETING
Spayder Lurks in the Wings
(First Quarter of Year 7)

Agenda for Board Meeting

1. *Approval of minutes*
2. *Operating Report – CEO*
3. *Quarterly Financial Results (quarterly results vs. plan; quarter vs. prior year comparable quarter; comparison year-to-date results vs. prior year) – COO*
4. *New Foreign Market for Products – COO*
5. *Potential Debt Financing – CFO*
6. *Other Business – Special Matter*

Heavily laden with financial matters, the agenda suggested the DFP Board meeting would be routine. Although most of the meetings *were* relatively routine, the last item on this agenda, was in fact quite extraordinary. Mark, knowing it would be controversial, had saved a good deal of time at the end of the meeting to address it.

The meeting opened with a positive report from the CEO about recent DFP operating results. The tone of the report struck George as more positive than the actual operating results warranted. Two of the Company's five divisions were struggling in the weak economy and their respective market shares had declined. Three other divisions, however, remained robust and the CEO made an aggressive projection for the Company as a whole for a prosperous fourth quarter.

Most CEOs, as did Mark, thought a certain amount of optimism was required both internally, in order to provide a solid foundation for good leadership, and externally, where it was needed to present a strong public image for the Company's products. Mark often agonized about how his legal counsel warned him excessively to be less bullish and to be more equivocal and cautious. He trusted his legal department, which had now grown to 20 lawyers, but he was frustrated because he felt most of them didn't fully understand how the business world worked. For example, if the lawyers had their way, all the Company advertisements would have the following text allocation: 10 percent marketing message and 90 percent dull – and largely unenforceable – disclaimers.

Nonetheless, Mercedes, an extremely able General Counsel who had come from a large law firm in Minneapolis, had kept him and the Company out of trouble. Though he had some discomfort with her traditional conservatism, most of the time he was pleased with the balanced restraint Mercedes imposed on his financial projections to the Board, the shareholders and the Street. Long ago, she had become a valued member of the DFP Senior Operations Committee.

Mark recognized that Mercedes and DFP's outside counsel had done an admirable job in reshaping the Company's projection practices now that it had to comply with SEC regulations regarding full and even-handed disclosure. These rules had added additional restraints on what could be shared confidentially with securities analysts without concurrent disclosure to the public. They were among the reasons that she wanted to make sure that Mark be very careful in his language.

Though Mark appreciated Mercedes' candor, at the same time he sometimes wished she were a little less assertive in Board meetings. Recently, he had mentioned to the Board that the Company was looking at a major acquisition, and if it were to succeed, the combined new enterprise would become the dominant player in the industry. She immediately warned him, in front of all the other Directors, that he should never use the term "dominant" in an acquisition or merger setting because it was a loaded one. She indicated that in her experience, antitrust regulators loved to seize on the use of the term "dominant" when challenging alleged anticompetitive mergers.

At that meeting, Alex had looked up with a grin. "Say, Mercedes, how about 'semi-dominant?' Will that work?"

Mercedes didn't laugh.

"Can't you take a joke, Mercedes?"

"Not that one, it's too expensive. And B.R., leave that little exchange out of the minutes." The Corporate Secretary nodded. George wrote a note to Dr. Thompson, who was sitting next to him. "Henry, chalk one up for Mercedes."

DFP's Chief Operating Officer, Robert Granger, went to the lectern to present the traditional report covering DFP's prior quarter's operations. Although Bob was competent and ambitious, he had turned out to be a disappointment to Mark because of his inability to be a "strategist" – a weakness that was bothering Mark more and more and one that he had discussed with George.

George thought of that conversation as Bob slowly and systematically went through the numbers. It was clear that while Mark had hoped to put together a good management succession plan, Bob wasn't a realistic candidate to succeed him – at least in the near term. Granger had been pirated away from a competing company and brought with him many solid managerial skills; but, his bag of tricks didn't seem to include seeing prospects for new business and creative new products over the long term or finding a way to see around corners.

As Bob spoke, Mark remembered thinking he had made a great choice when Granger was first brought on board. Prior to joining DFP, Bob had served as the head of a large operating division of Langor Products as well as the treasurer of another publicly held corporation, HVI Dynamics. Before that, he had been the vice president of corporate development at a smaller company in the Midwest. But it turned out that, even with all that operating experience behind him, Bob had retained too much "staff mentality" in his blood.

Even with his flaws, though, Bob still was the best internal candidate to succeed Mark if Mark resigned or retired. (Like many CEOs, Mark never thought of a need for a new CEO because of an unexpected illness or death, since, in the near term, he saw himself as nearly invincible.)

Since the Board still had gained little confidence in the COO as a prospective CEO, Mark knew he would have to spend more time trying to develop Granger's skills, and, if successful, then spend time with Hartfield and other members of the Board to persuade them of the COO's strengths. This approach might work and could afford the COO more time to grow in the job.

Mark was somewhat troubled by another feature of Granger's style. From time to time, two Directors, David Nugent and Judy Moran, would go directly to Granger, without letting Mark know, and ask the COO questions about DFP. In a few cases, they expressed concerns about Mark's management decisions. Most of the time, it seemed, Granger "remembered" to tell Mark about these incidents but Mark learned that occasionally Granger would forget. Not good enough for me, thought Mark. How can I manage effectively if a few of my Directors go downhill into the chain of command and I don't know about it?

The Board meeting had gone on for nearly three hours when Mark turned to the last item on the agenda, "Other Business – Special Matter." As he started to talk, he noticed that some of the Board members looked about ready to nod off because of the number-laden agenda and the near-failure of the air conditioning system. He knew what he had to say would bring them to attention quickly.

"As some of you know," Mark began, "Roger Spayder has been purchasing a substantial amount of the Company stock. I received a letter from him yesterday that I wanted to share with you." He passed out the brief letter and watched its contents sink in to each Director as they read it. Spayder was requesting seats on the Company's Board, and the letter proposed that, at a minimum, he be added immediately to the

Company's slate for the Board of Directors at the Company's next annual meeting.

While Spayder's letter to the CEO was diplomatic on its face, it took little effort to read between the lines. If Spayder didn't get his way, he might begin a hostile proxy contest with management and the Board. His letter also made it clear that Spayder already had acquired 4.9 percent of DFP's outstanding stock, just under the trigger level for filing a Section 13(d) disclosure statement with the SEC. He also stated that he was prepared to acquire additional shares if necessary to gain a foothold in the Boardroom.

While many of the Directors were surprised, a few of them thought to themselves that Spayder actually could be a "shot in the arm" for the Company. Spayder had a good deal of successful experience in manufacturing operations, an area in which the Directors thought the management group at the Company needed some help. (Gen. Landry even scribbled a note that he passed surreptitiously to Harry: "Spayder's an SOB, but a darn good businessman!")

"Let me make it abundantly clear," Mark resumed. "I flatly oppose Spayder being added to this Board. After this meeting, I plan to write him a nasty letter and, at the very least, tell him to 'buzz off' – with an even stronger message to follow."

George looked around the room and pondered the conundrum in which he and the other Directors found themselves. Despite Mark's dislike of Spayder – and all of them knew about the past bad blood between the two – they owed a duty of loyalty to DFP's shareholders because, while Mark didn't respect Spayder, the self-styled corporate raider actually might increase shareholder value. At the same time, George thought to himself: "We want to try to follow our usual presumption of loyalty to senior management, but even so, Mark is overreacting to Spayder's letter."

But what bothered George even more was that Mark had not previewed this matter with most, if any, of the Directors prior to the Board meeting. Even if Mark had just gotten the letter late yesterday, he still could have briefed them in phone calls. After all, Spayder owned about 5 percent of DFP's stock; except for the shares owned by Judy Moran and Mark, that was one of the largest blocks of stock outstanding, especially compared to the relatively meager stock holdings of most of the other Directors. This time George felt Mark was misreading the Board.

Stan asked to be recognized. "I know Spayder; he is a little 'prickly,' but he's an extremely bright guy. He'd bring a lot of operating skills that we don't currently have on the Board. He's been deeply involved in our type of operations and is financially astute."

"But does he have the reputation for integrity that this Company is built upon?" Mark asked. "That's the real question."

Suddenly, Judy spoke up. No one realized she knew Spayder, much less that they had relatively extensive business dealings. "I must tell you that I've known Roger for a while, and recently he approached me to buy the Moran family block of stock at a premium," she said, to the surprise of others on the Board. "I asked him what he planned to do with our shares and he said he'd probably use it to initiate a takeover of the Company."

As she spoke, Mark furrowed his brow. Shouldn't she have told him this earlier?

But Judy wasn't through. "He then indicated that once he had control, he planned to ask for new Directors – except, of course, for me – and he would take DFP in new directions to enhance shareholder value. When I pushed him on how he planned to do that, though, he had absolutely no answer other than to say that there was great potential for increased profits and cash flow." She noticed Mark's worried look. "But, he didn't win me over. While I think Roger's very bright, I also think he's a 'shark' – and I wouldn't favor having him on this Board even if he does bring some strong qualities with him."

"Let's be fair, Judy," said Stan. "Spayder didn't say anything that other securities analysts haven't also been saying. All of them think there is untapped value in this Company – but, like

Spayder, they never have concrete suggestions on how to realize on it. In my view, you are confusing Spayder's aggressive personality with a lack of integrity. I don't think the two necessarily go together. Plus, a little aggressiveness never hurt a well-managed company."

Tempers ebbed and flowed for the next thirty minutes. Finally, George turned to Mark. "Okay, Mark, it's your turn. You've heard various views about Spayder. We all know that you detest him but, as fiduciaries, we have to look at this matter carefully. What is your proposal?"

Taking it all in, Mark had concluded that the Board clearly didn't share his view of the potential havoc Spayder might wreak as a Board member – some, it seemed, actually would welcome him! So, Mark put forth a possible compromise.

"I propose we include Spayder's name in our proxy statement as a self-nominated candidate for the Board," Mark said, to the surprise of some of the others. "We'll emphasize that he is self-nominated and that we recommend the current incumbent slate, without the addition of Spayder, as best for shareholders."

In the extensive discussion that followed, Mercedes suggested this approach: "We put a reference to Spayder's nomination in the 'classified ads' section of the Proxy Statement. Knowing his reputation, I doubt very much that this will satisfy him, of course. DFP doesn't have cumulative voting, so in order to elect himself to the Board, he'll have to obtain the vote of the holders of the majority of the quorum at the Annual Meeting. That is probably unlikely – although he might be able to call a Special Meeting of Shareholders at a later time and attempt to elect himself with an expanded slate."

"My view," said Judy, "is that Spayder is getting more than he deserves. He's getting some space in our Proxy Statement; if he wants to conduct a proxy contest over this matter, he's entitled to do so. As you recall, a lot of our stock is owned by our employees and some foundations. I doubt very much that they will be comfortable with Spayder as a Board member. So I think we have a good chance to be successful here, unless he attempts to go out into the market and buy some large blocks of stock. So long as we can command enough votes for a majority of the quorum represented at the meeting, we'll win.

"In this instance, I am firmly in Mark's camp and think we should go with his proposal. Also, you all should understand that if Spayder steps up and conducts an aggressive proxy contest, we will have no alternative but to go along with him or go public in a big way and oppose his candidacy. That may be expensive but, again, in my judgment, it will be an investment worth making."

It was becoming clear that Mark's proposed solution would satisfy the majority of the Board. George, glad that Mark had come up with the plan himself, formally moved that, "we nominate the incumbent slate of Directors for re-election at the upcoming annual meeting and that, in the Company's Proxy Statement, we disclose that Spayder is seeking a position on our Board. I further propose that the Proxy Statement and the proxy card provide a box for our shareholders, who so wish, can cast their vote for Spayder."

"Second the motion," said Judy.

"Is there any discussion?" Mark asked. There was none. "Let me just say that if Spayder is ultimately elected to this Board and performs in the same manner as he has in the past, I don't know what I will do. Having worked closely with him for many years, I have serious questions about his demeanor and his ethics. Remember, he unceremoniously canned me when he concluded that I was getting too much credit for putting together his good deals.

"On the other hand, for now I have to be guided by the majority of the Board – and I think my compromise position is the best one under the circumstances. All in favor?"

The vote was unanimously in favor of the motion.

A few days after the Board meeting, Spayder decided that having his name in the DFP proxy statement as a potential candidate wasn't enough. He promised to "campaign" for his Board seat in a proxy contest and turn up the heat with his own "fight letter" to the DFP shareholders, without consulting his own legal counsel. The letter, which was sent on Spayder's personal and opulently adorned letterhead, read:

To My Fellow DFP Shareholders:

I have had a successful career as an entrepreneur and businessman and have acquired many companies, as well as large blocks of stock in underperforming companies. Recently, I acquired 4.9 percent of DFP, and I'm considering acquiring even more shares because I believe DFP has a lot of untapped upside potential.

As some of you know, I've had extensive business dealings with your Chief Executive Officer, Mark Gregory. While I respect him, I'm afraid he spends more time driving fast cars and consuming vintage Chardonnays than he does on managing your company. With stronger management at DFP last year, its earnings could have improved dramatically.

I'm asking for a seat on your Board of Directors and one or two seats for friends of mine who are equally capable in making businesses work the way they should. Should I become a substantial influence in the Boardroom, I will continue to work with Mark Gregory to develop the Company – although, as far as I'm concerned, he would be "on probation" until I am satisfied that he is getting the job done. If you agree with my program, please sign the blue proxy card and return it to me in the enclosed envelope. Thank you for your anticipated cooperation and foresight in seeing this tremendous potential opportunity for you as a DFP investor.

A vote for me is a vote for better corporate governance and better corporate management.

Very truly yours,

Roger Spayder, Chairman
Spayder Enterprises

Two days later, an e-mail memorandum was distributed among officers and DFP employees who owned DFP stock. Written by one of the veteran, plain-speaking supervisors at one of DFP's principal manufacturing facilities, it read:

To My Fellow Shareholders:

By now, most of you have received Roger Spayder's letter in which, as usual, he toots his own horn and talks about improving management and operations. Most of what he has to say could be boiled down to one word: it starts with a "B" and ends with "T". For any of us who have followed his career – and I am a battle-scarred veteran of one of the companies he took over – we all know that he is one brutal SOB in how he manages and handles people. While he has had some success in improving stock prices, usually he does so by dramatically reducing the labor force, cutting compensation to the bone, and seeking more effort for less hourly pay. Most importantly, after driving out most of the shareholders from a company with tender offers using junk bonds, he then liquidates the company at a later date at a much higher profit than any of the former shareholders enjoyed.

If any of you want to talk with me directly about my experiences with Mr. Spayder, I can be reached at extension 4292. In the interim, I suggest you sign the green proxy card sent to you by DFP's management and return it to them, to preserve the character and integrity of DFP. Until then, the best thing I can say about Roger Spayder is that he lives up to his nickname, "Spayder the Raider!" With fear and loathing for Roger Spayder, I am,

Very truly yours,

John Henry Jackson

Spayder lost the election, but the final results were much closer than Mark and other Board members had expected. Nonetheless, after the Annual Meeting of Shareholders, Mark called George and gloated about his victory over his former nemesis.

George asked if Spayder had said anything to Mark after the election.

"Yeah, he did," Mark responded. "He said, 'I'm not going away, Mark, and I may see you next year. In the meantime, get the DFP stock price up to where it belongs!'"

Fortunately, DFP moved into a robust operating period and continued to grow. It had an uneventful public offering of its common stock (its second) after a fairly routine Board discussion, at which there was little disagreement over the offering price and the offering process.

Spayder sold most of his shares when DFP stock took an upward swing; shortly thereafter, he called Mark, who wasn't in his office. Spayder left a message about the sale of his shares, and then – as a final thought – he said: "Just remember, Mark, like General MacArthur said, I shall return."

Benefiting from new products as well as from strong and positive media attention, DFP was now becoming a leader in its field – not only in the United States but also in the worldwide food appliance industry.

CHAPTER 7

THE PAY'S THE THING

A Compensation Committee Meeting

(*First Quarter of Year 7*)

Partial Agenda for Committee Meeting

1. *Consideration of bonuses for the senior executives for their performance in the prior operating year.*

2. *Consideration of a three-year employment agreement for the CEO.*

L arry Lanski, the Chairman of the Board's Compensation Committee, called the meeting to order.
Though fairly new to the Compensation Committee, Lanski was seen by many as an excellent choice to replace George Hartfield as Chairman of the Committee that dealt with the often sensitive, sometimes contentious, issues that faced the compensation panel – and in general, he was thought to be a strong addition to the Board. A former CEO of a New York Stock Exchange Company, Larry had come aboard after the rather awkward "resignation" of Charles Frank. (Frank, the local stockbroker who was among the last Board members added during the end of founder Collins' influence, had proven to be an embarrassment. He treated the Board's members and their friends and families as little more than a potential client list for his brokerage firm and seemed much more interested in getting their business than in preparing for and participating in Board

sessions. Several members had complained about his activities informally to the Corporate Secretary, and B.R. had brought it to Mark's attention. Mark called Frank into his office and presented him with a letter of resignation, which he reluctantly signed. Lanski joined the Board soon after.)

Joining Lanski around the small conference table were fellow committee members Gen. Landry, Judy, and Hugh. Mark was also present, mainly to answer questions the Committee members might have during the first agenda item.

"A solid year in my judgment! It reminds me of a well-carried out bombing run over Vietnam," Gen. Landry said. To Judy, he added, "You're too young to recall that I led one of the first flights over Hanoi." To all, he continued, "As I see it, most of the Company's business units met plan goals and the two that didn't had good reasons for their plan variances."

"That may be," said Hugh, the money manager for the state teachers' fund, "but, as you'll recall, DFP's incentive plan is largely formulaic – with only about 20 percent discretion in the total award payment for us and the Board to deviate from the formula results, but only on a negative basis. Keep in mind that the rules about deductibility of high level compensation under the Internal Revenue Code prohibit upward adjustments based upon non-formulaic or subjective factors. If these units don't meet plan goals, officer bonuses are either reduced or disappear. After all, the shareholders, many of whom I represent as an investment advisor, only benefit if operating results are strong and meet Street expectations."

Frowning, Judy responded in her usual direct fashion. "So, what if the Company doesn't meet Street expectations? That's an incredibly stupid way to run a business or a railroad!"

"May be," said Larry, "but that's the way DFP's incentive plan works. Until we change it, that's the way we should administer it – unless you have a problem with that, Judy."

"I was just making an observation – a good one, I might add," said Judy. "But let's get on with our business or we'll be here all night."

The Committee then reviewed various recommendations for annual short-term cash bonuses, as submitted by management, covering the 10 most senior officer and staff members in the Company.

Lanski reported that he had met with Mark and discussed Mark's evaluation on how the senior officers had performed in the past year. All of the corporate officers, Larry said, had met most of their consolidated "target objectives" in terms of revenues, net income, market share and return on equity. Therefore, Mark had recommended that all but one receive a bonus equal to about 90 percent of the bonus that would have been paid if the ultimate "stretch" target results had been achieved. (As an example, Larry said that one of the principal targets had been a return on equity of about 12 percent; 11 percent ROE had been attained, so a haircut of about 10 percent was in order.) If the bonuses were approved, according to DFP's outside compensation consultants, each would be at about the median for compensation for corporations in the Company's peer group. In the case of one of the officers, however, a stiff reduction had been recommended in how the bonus formula would apply to him.

Judy turned to Mark. "Why should Randy Patterson's bonus be reduced?"

"Well, a couple of reasons: First, I don't think he was enough of a team player." Mark replied. He cited two instances in which Patterson had "gone around end" by trying to lobby two Directors outside the Boardroom for one of his favorite deals, which was subject to Board approval. While the Directors had found his views on the deal worthwhile, they were embarrassed, and reported the incidents back to Mark; they knew that the CEO had instructed all corporate officers, including Randy, not to approach Directors on important issues without clearing the contact with Mark first. "As some of you know, that ticked me off!"

"In the Air Force, he would have known better than to ignore the chain of command," said Gen. Landry. "I move that we support the recommendation."

"Second," said Hugh quickly.

"What's the second reason?" Judy asked. Frankly, she thought, the incidents showed that Randy had "guts" to go around the boss.

"In general," Mark said, "he has some work habits that need to be addressed. Although he gets his work done, it often requires extensive follow-up and re-thinking by the rest of us. He's a bright guy, but he really needs to get some focus and deal with those issues."

After further discussion – in which the General and Mark argued it was best to send Randy the message that if he didn't shape up, he might be due for a demotion or even termination – Judy finally assented. "If you're all so upset, I'll go along – but you're all too darn uptight!" (Judy also made a note to herself: maybe I should get to know Patterson. He might have some interesting insights about the Company.)

At that point, Lanski asked Mark to leave the meeting so the Committee members could have a candid discussion about the CEO's bonus, as well as the COO's, and begin the discussion about a proposed three-year employment agreement for Mark. Mark seemed to be slightly irritated about being asked to leave – on the basis that there should be little left for discussion – but Lanski insisted that he do so.

When the door closed, Larry said, "I wish Mark could be a little more sensitive about our need for candid discussion and unqualified consideration of how he and others ought to be paid. He needs a little more experience on how boards and their committees operate."

"Well, he's done a good job this year," Gen. Landry said. "I think we ought to pay him not only the formula amount but at least 10 percent over that."

"I'm disinclined to do that," said Larry. "Although Mark has had a solid operating year, I thought the way he handled the Spayder matter was not all that it should have been. Spayder probably will start a proxy contest next year – and while we'll probably win, it's going to cost DFP a lot of money. If Mark had only sat down with Spayder on a more open-minded basis, he might have avoided the conflict in the first place."

"That's a good point," Judy said. "At the same time, overall he is one of the best CEOs I know – bright, tough-minded, shareholder-oriented, a team player and, deep down, a terrific human being. He also is incredibly creative. Ten bigtime new products last year – twice as many as any of our competitors!"

"Mark is a first-rate operator," Gen. Landry agreed. "If we pay him his bonus at the target level, it will be equal to 100 percent of his base salary. As I said, I believe we should have a 'kicker' and pay him 110 percent of his salary. In addition to the bonus, of course, he is receiving stock options. So we have to be careful that we continue to take into account the economic equivalent value of the stock options we grant so that his total package doesn't exceed the total package of other, comparable CEOs. By way of illustration, some of you may recall the value of a stock option can be calculated under various formulas – such as the Black-Scholes formula – by taking the market capitalization of an option and for many industrial companies, dividing by about three. For example, if we grant a 100,000-share option at $12 per share, it has a market cap of $1.2 million and, under some assumptions, an economic value of about $400,000."

"That's an important point, General," said Larry. "We need to keep in mind what the total package is, in terms of aggregate compensation, taking into account Mark's stock incentive plans and all of his other benefits. We'll have one of our consultants come in over the next few months and run those numbers. Also, I want to remind you that it is important that we have in mind the total amount paid to the entire senior executive group. We can't pay the group too much, in the aggregate, and often compensation committees forget to calculate the total payout to the top management team. We need to be careful in that regard as well as being sure the differences in compensation levels for our senior officers are right and don't produce divisiveness.

"Speaking of stock options," Larry continued, "later today we're going to talk to Mark about his proposed stock option grant. We all may think it's generous, but one of Mark's quirks is to always insist that any grant he gets is as large as some grant received by one of the CEOs he's close to. This time, I've done some research on what others are paid, especially in this area. I think he expects to nail us by comparing this option grant with one made to his buddy at Stillman Communications, but I'm ready for him."

Ultimately, the Committee decided that Mark should not only receive his target bonus but also an additional 10 percent. At the same time, he should receive a strong message to moderate his behavior with regard to how he approached major potential investors such as Spayder. Lanski said he would deliver the message about the bonus to Mark.

The Committee meeting recessed briefly and Lanski left to talk with Mark.

Mark wondered what was taking so long! Nearly an hour had passed! He had gone down the hall to his office to return some phone calls while the Committee discussed his compensation, but he thought it would only take 20 minutes or so. He was surprised when his assistant rang and said Larry Lanski would like to come in to see him, as he expected to return directly to the Committee meeting.

"Is there a problem, Larry?" Mark asked as he motioned for Lanski to sit down.

"Not really – I think you'll be quite pleased with where we're headed. But there is one issue that we wanted brought to your attention before making the final decision," Lanski said. "It's not a compensation matter – it's more a matter of style and judgment."

"And that would be…?

"It's no secret that your handling of the Spayder matter could come back to haunt us, and we wanted to make sure you understood the potential consequences."

"If you're talking about my personal knowledge of how Spayder conducts business, that's extremely relevant! I'd be lax if I didn't bring that to the Board. But, I hear you. In the future, I'll consult personally with a senior Director or two, and probably Mercedes as well, before expressing any strong opinions about Spayder – or any other shareholder, for that matter."

Outwardly, Mark handled Lanski's concerns calmly. Inwardly, he took the message about demonstrating more moderation in his management style with mixed emotions. Given his resentment toward Spayder and his inside knowledge of Spayder's foul business tactics, Mark thought, the Board was being incredibly "soft" on Spayder. But there was no need to elaborate on that now.

"Mark, I'm glad to hear you're willing to involve senior Directors in dealings with Spayder in the future – and the Board will probably follow your future recommendations regarding him," Larry said. "Don't underestimate us. We know he's not the most ethical guy in the world, but we all hope to avoid a costly proxy fight next year. We don't want to get into a lot of mudslinging, and don't want to see you or anyone else use corporate funds to win a personal rather than a corporate battle."

"Point taken, Larry."

Lanski stood up. "Mark, please come with me – we want to tell you what our thoughts are on your comp package."

Every time Mark had been in a compensation discussion with the Committee, he was reminded of how difficult this topic was to discuss from either side of the table. Whether the position being discussed was stock clerk or CEO, the person whose compensation was at issue never seemed to think it was enough and the person in charge of it always seemed to think it was too much – or certainly, just right. It was a fine line, and Mark certainly planned on being a tough negotiator – as did the Board.

"Mark, we have approved the new proposed Equity Incentive Plan – subject, of course, to shareholder approval at the upcoming annual meeting. In doing so, we awarded you a large stock option, which you certainly should regard as a vote of confidence by us for your long-term value to DFP."

"Thanks," said Mark, "but I actually expected to receive more option shares. My buddy over at Stillman Communications, Lance Stillman, received a much larger stock option grant and a 50% higher salary. I must admit, I'm more than a little disappointed.

"Also, I'm only being compensated on a basis equal to CEOs in our industry who are at the median compensation level. I'm a damned good CEO – not a median CEO – and we've been getting good bottom-line results in a down market. And look at the products I've developed for DFP – various types of equipment that make mixers, tableware, glassware, dishes, bar supplies, cutlery, ranges, coolers, refrigerators, icemakers and blenders. We've also gone from being just a manufacturer to being a distributor and wholesaler."

Here we go again, Judy thought to herself – but he's right. He could run circles around most of those geezers who are the CEOs for our competitors. Before she could express her views, which – as usual – wouldn't be shared by all the others, Lanski spoke up. She was glad; it was best for a seasoned ex-CEO of Lanski's caliber to handle this.

"First, Mark, you've only been our CEO for a few years," Larry said. "Most of your counterparts have been running their companies for more than a decade. Further, the industry survey we use covers other companies that are mostly located in big cities where the cost of living and compensation are much higher than here in little Dakota City. As for the 75th percentile, all CEOs want to be there! If all of the boards did that every year, we would push industry compensation through the roof. Finally, Lance is in the telecommunications industry and CEOs in that industry are far more highly compensated than those in ours. Oh, and one other point: Your option, with a market capitalization of $3 million, has a Black-Scholes value of almost $1 million, and, in our humble opinion, you should be happy with it."

Looking around the room and judging the expressions of the others, Mark decided to fight this battle another time. Anyway, he was honest enough with himself to know that he was doing quite well for someone of his age and experience. "Let's not make a big deal of this," said Mark. "Let's file all of this away for some potential consideration of additional options next year or the year after."

"Very well, Mark. We'll keep that in mind. Now, if you could let us resume our confidential proceedings..." Lanski gestured towards the door and Mark left.

"I'm ready to approve his new employment agreement," Gen. Landry said. "Sure, from time to time Mark has sharp elbows when it comes to negotiating his compensation, but..."

"Let's be fair to Mark here," Judy interjected. "He also fought for relatively high compensation for his strong senior executives. He argued, often effectively, that it was important for DFP to be competitive in its compensation practices in order to keep its corporate 'stars.' Like it or not, the competitive market requires a company like DFP to pay a sizeable compensation package to its CEO or we'll lose him. Also, a guy with global managerial expertise, like Mark, isn't easily kept in a place like Dakota City. So a CEO package of well in excess of a million dollars is a must for us."

"I must say, Mark is always a hard charger in the executive comp area," Larry acknowledged. "He even pushed for liberalizing our established and heavily negotiated Compensation Committee targets or thresholds for award payouts. These were set by all of us rather carefully and cover our officer and employee participants under our three-year incentive plan. He maintains that for incentive plan administration mid-stream corrections of original benchmarks for payout are a good idea, even well into the plan performance period. For example, he might like to lower the target return on equity from the original benchmark set two years ago from 11 percent to 9 percent and have the 9 percent be retroactive two years back.

"As you know, we've done battle about that issue a number of times. I tell him that after the DFP stock declines in price, a lot of our shareholders also would like to turn in their stock for a lower purchase price. When I turned down his request, he usually concedes the issue but tells me he wants to revisit the issue again – and he does.

"Another issue he continues to raise, in a somewhat irritating manner, is that all of our stock options should be repriced with lower exercise prices. He wants stock options for our officers covering 400,000 shares with the current exercise price of $20 to be canceled, and, then, to be repriced for stock options for 200,000 shares at $10. In fairness, he excluded his own stock option from that proposal. But, I told him 'no way, Jose,' because of the adverse financial reporting consequences and investor relations problems. He became combative but persuasive because repricing is a tough issue when you think DFP could lose key officers and employees unless we took that step. Fortunately, shortly thereafter, our stock price went north and the issue went away. The point is Mark never lacks for aggressiveness when it comes to executive comp."

"Still," Judy said, "Mark is always tough-minded with himself and others when it comes to poor operating performance. We've seen him encourage a number of lesser-performing executives to leave the Company though, even then, he tries to allow the employee to leave with a certain amount of dignity. He always treats them fairly in terms of severance compensation and recommendations to prospective new employers. And I think we should keep him well compensated, because he's doing a great job!"

(That's one way of looking at it, thought Gen. Landry. It seems to me, though, that he provides severance payments that are too large because he's overly concerned about future lawsuits alleging unlawful termination. He remembered once receiving an e-mail from Mark that read: "Recommend a

$50,000 severance payment for Anne Croft, a three-year senior-level marketing department employee, who alleges she was harassed by one of our senior officers last month and has been discriminated against because of her race." The General had e-mailed back: "It's amazing how these tales of discrimination and harassment always seem to develop in the last few months of employment. I'll go along, but reluctantly. What a windfall for her!")

"Time out," said Hugh. "I manage money for retired teachers and they would find Mark's contract incredibly rich. Mark probably makes 40 times more than the average teacher. Shouldn't we get a reasonableness opinion from one of these good executive compensation firms before we approve it? We need to look at the competitiveness and reasonableness of his base salary, his bonus program and stock option grants, individually and taken together. We need a good firm to confirm that this package is in the ballpark for CEOs in peer companies and not a waste of corporate assets."

Larry jumped in. "Okay, Hugh, but I think you're starting to be like your clients – a nitpicker! Mark may do well versus the teachers but he gets paid chump change compared to movie stars and jocks. Of course, we can't control that. What we can do is finish this meeting and approve this contract for someone who is basically a first-rate CEO. I'm sure Mark will agree that the new agreement not be finalized until we get an opinion from the exec comp consulting folks over at the Mattingly firm. Is that okay?"

James R. Ukropina

Excerpt from the Compensation Committee Report in the DFP Proxy Statement:

The DFP Compensation Committee and the Board of Directors authorized a three-year employment agreement for Mark Gregory, the Chief Executive Officer of the Company. In so doing, it received the advice of Mattingly & Associates, a national compensation consulting firm. That firm delivered an opinion to the Board to the effect that the employment agreement contained traditional terms and conditions, was competitive, and, from a financial perspective, was reasonable for the Company's shareholders.

A financial snapshot of the Company:

DFP INC.
COMPARATIVE QUARTERLY RESULTS
($000)
(Third Quarter of Year 8)

	Most Recent Qtr.	% Variance from Comp Qtr.	% Variance From Plan
Sales	260,000	-3	-5
Net Income	19,000	-4	-6
Earnings/Share	.24	-4	-6
Cash Flow/Share	.22	-3	-7
Stock Price versus Peer Index	-8%	-	-
Debt/Equity Ratio	61%	-	-

CHAPTER 8

A PRESENTATION BY A "FAST-TRACKER"
Preparation, Preparation, Preparation
(Fourth Quarter of Year 8)

Partial Agenda for Board Meeting

Agenda Item No. 14: Proposed acquisition of Orbitron –
Cedric Paddington

I f any DFP Board meeting ever went poorly from the start, it
was this one. From time-to-time, several Directors had to
excuse themselves to deal with urgent issues related to their
other obligations. Mark had to take a brief recess to answer a
call from a Wall Street Journal reporter who was on deadline for
a profile of rising CEOs in the food industry, in which he was
being included. Somehow, to B.R.'s chagrin, a number of
major reports included in the Board Book were already
outdated versions that had to be replaced at the last minute.
So, conditions hadn't been ideal, and they were going to get
worse – very quickly.

Cedric Paddington had appeared before the Board before,
but only in a supporting role as a team participant in a larger
presentation. This was the first time he had taken the lead role
in making a presentation about a major deal. Paddington was
recognized as a fast-track young corporate officer who
appeared to be about ready for significant operating
responsibility, and he was there to talk about the proposed

acquisition of Orbitron, a deal that had been discussed briefly at the prior Board meeting.

The Orbitron deal represented a significant strategic change for DFP. Orbitron was not only an equipment maker, but also a food processor and grower, and was a top player in a number of its fields. Several Directors were uncomfortable with the deal, especially Judy, who continued to be a major DFP shareholder. She took Mark aside before the meeting and asked, "Where are your risk managers on this deal? We all know that after products you spread on your face, the next worst are products you put in your mouth. Mark, where's your head?!"

"Judy, Judy, Judy," Mark said, trying to imitate Cary Grant for a little humor, "haven't you heard of liability insurance? That cost is part of our profit projections and they're conservative. We even have projected escalating insurance premiums in the future because of more frivolous litigation to protect some guy who chokes when he doesn't chew his asparagus."

"Mark, I have a bad feeling about this deal. The controlling shareholders of Orbitron, the Orb family in Salinas, are bad apples. I'll support you because of your good track record for profitable deals. But, you'd better watch out. Don't get your glands into the deal, and," she said in a whisper in a sidebar conversation out of earshot from Paddington, "don't let that dealmonger Paddington push the deal too hard. Promise?"

Mark promised Judy he would be prudent, but the Board knew that he was enthusiastic about the deal. Still, most of its members were concerned that Paddington seemed to have done too much financial engineering in conceptualizing some exotic terms for the deal. Included, for example, was a suggestion that DFP issue some complex convertible subordinated debentures as the payment medium for the acquisition, making most of the interest tax deductible.

Before the meeting began, Larry had pulled Judy off to one side and said, "You know, I'm really worried about this – it's almost as if Paddington is more interested in having the deal described as the 'deal of the year' in some finance magazine than he is in achieving a solid business combination." So now, Lanski and the others looked skeptical as they turned their attention toward Paddington.

' Let me start out by saying that Orbitron is an extremely attractive company and it won't be easy for DFP to acquire it," Paddington said as he began his complex and colorful PowerPoint presentation, complete with animation. "We are going to have to pay a strategic premium that will be well over and above the typical premium that we would pay for a similar company with its cash flow and earnings stream at the usual price-earnings multiples."

Paddington moved through several slides relating to the target company, including its management, ownership profile, operating history, balance sheet and Paddington's projections concerning expected Orbitron profits for the next three years.

"Wait a second," said Larry, a sophisticated deal veteran. "Those three-year projections for Orbitron look more like a hockey stick than a realistic forecast. I know something about this company and I don't think highly of its management team – nor do I think highly of some of its directors. In fact, one of them cheats at golf!"

"Who doesn't?" Mark interjected, trying to lighten the mood a little. David Nugent laughed, but no one else did.

"I'm serious, Mark," Larry said. "I think there are a lot of 'red flags' here. Among other things, I'm worried about how Orbitron may have obtained some of its foreign business, particularly in four countries in the Far East where they seem to be winning a lot of government work. I just don't see how Orbitron could have been the low bidder. How do we know its officers didn't pay bribes to government officials in those countries?

"One of them is the 'reddest-flag' country I've heard of when it comes to needing bribes to buy government business. The last time a friend of mine was bidding there, he said the Minister of Finance told him just to add the amount of the bribe to the bid over and above its schedule of standard pricing, and they could recover it."

"We're looking into that," Paddington said. "And we can continue to do a lot of due diligence before we close the deal to assure ourselves that we are not taking on any contingent liabilities or bad actors."

Lanski wasn't satisfied. "Maybe so, but digging up the real dirt on these payments may not be easy. DFP has an excellent record in the foreign sector and we do a lot of business ourselves with our own government and with foreign governments in supplying bulk food and providing institutional kitchen and refrigeration equipment. We certainly don't want to be suspended from doing government work here or abroad or fined by reason of an acquisition that contains ugly skeletons in the closet or dirty linen."

Paddington realized it would take more than a slick PowerPoint presentation to sway this Board. He moved to the podium, and B.R. turned on the lights.

"Well, why don't we go ahead with a full discussion," Paddington began. "I'll tell you right now that we are recommending a large premium price for Orbitron – and we don't make that recommendation lightly. We know all of you will hold our feet to the fire in terms of achieving future operating results and we will have to achieve high profit levels to justify your decision."

Hugh spoke up first. "What is the return on investment that you project on average over the next three years? And, if we have to sell this company five years from now, what do you project to be its terminal or sale value?" Essentially, where's the beef?

Paddington stopped for a moment and collected himself. He hadn't anticipated these particular questions. He realized he hadn't made a thorough analysis of the projected return on investment. In addition, he hadn't thought much at all about terminal value. Nevertheless, he forged ahead. "The projected ROI is somewhere between 14 percent and 18 percent."

"Isn't that an awfully broad range?" asked Harry. "I'm a litigator and not much of a beancounter, but isn't the difference in dollars between the northern and southerly points of that range about hundreds of thousands of dollars per year, given our projected investment?"

"Yes, it is," Paddington replied rather timidly, "but we don't want to submit too tight of an ROI range and create unrealistic expectations. Also, our calculations use a variety of interest rate assumptions, discount rates, growth projections and the like. As we all know, at the end of the day, these projections are a big guessing game."

George, who had been reading over the financial projections, looked up swiftly when he heard the word "guessing."

"Let me ask another question," said Dr. Thompson. "I used to teach accounting and I'm not up on the current principles, but if I'm not mistaken, if we were to combine with the target company, we would have to set up a fairly large goodwill account. Under the new accounting rules, we wouldn't have to amortize that goodwill against earnings unless Orbitron started to slide downhill; but if it did, we would have to take a sizeable write-off on a non-tax deductible basis. What do you think our downside might be in terms of amortization of that goodwill?"

Paddington again didn't have a ready answer, and little beads of perspiration were appearing on his brow. It was sinking in to him that he should have prepared more thoroughly with respect to the ROI analysis and the financial reporting issues. Instead, he had spent most of his time trying to think of good reasons as to why using DFP convertible subordinated debentures made sense and why the Company should pay a premium. It was clear – he wasn't winning over the Board.

"At this point, it seems to me," said Harry, "that Cedric and you, Mark, need to do a lot more homework. We've asked a number of questions, and I don't think it would be a good idea for you or for us to move forward without those questions being answered more sensibly. I would insist that you narrow your estimated range of return on investment and get us some answers for our accounting and related questions so that we are certain that you're still enthusiastic about this deal before we follow your recommendation."

"That may make sense," said Mark, "but I don't think we should beat this project to death. As you know, I strongly support it – but I need a sense of the Board as to whether you are positive about it, so that if we bring you adequate answers you'll be supportive.

"If what you're really telling me is that this is a lousy deal on any grounds, then I'll pull it off the table and look for another one. But remember, if we take more than a month to get our act together on this matter, I assure you we'll lose this deal and someone else will make the acquisition."

Hearing that, George proposed a resolution. "I move that the Board express its sense of support for a potential deal for Orbitron, subject to further analysis of various financial, legal and tax matters as well as accounting matters. I also propose that we meet in two weeks in a special meeting within Mark's timeline so that the deal can be done – if it makes sense. Does anyone have a second to that motion?"

"Second," said Judy.

An active discussion followed in which it became clear that the vote wasn't going to be as decisive as it might be. Some Directors seemed enthusiastic, some seemed only acquiescent, and a few appeared to be ready to oppose the deal on any terms. The vote was split, with the majority in favor of George's resolution. The outcome was troubling to everyone since, after an appropriate level of discussion, most board votes are unanimous. In fact, some board chairmen may even defer or drop a proposal if they perceive it isn't going to receive unanimous support.

"Cedric, we've asked you a lot of questions and you didn't have the answers for many of them," George said after the vote. "While that's understandable in certain respects, I urge you to be sure we have specific answers to those questions. We also will be interested in seeing how you can narrow the projected ROI range. Is that okay?"

"That's fine," said Cedric. "In my view, enough information is here to justify moving forward, but I understand that you feel uncomfortable. I can assure you that by late tomorrow you will have from me, by fax or e-mail, the answers to all of the questions you have raised. I regret we didn't have all of those answers for you, but we just received much of the Orbitron data necessary to complete our analysis."

The meeting then adjourned. As the Directors filed out, Mark thought to himself that much of what had happened at the meeting was his problem and responsibility. Ordinarily, he had insisted that all corporate officers making a presentation to the Board have a dress rehearsal with him for a couple of hours on the day prior to the meeting. At those sessions, Mark would submit his own questions – and many of those questions would have been similar to those asked at this meeting – and Paddington would have been far better prepared for the many issues that he had to confront. Mark vowed to himself never to skip a "dress rehearsal" again.

At the same time, he vowed to drop some other meetings so he could keep enjoying a more balanced personal and family life. To accomplish this goal, he decided to hire an experienced corporate officer as a senior vice president who could "sub" for him at less important meetings, as well as assume some other duties that would save Mark a good deal of time. To compensate for the addition to payroll, he would eliminate a few redundant staff positions.

Harry was walking toward his car in the parking lot when Dr. Thompson came out of the building.

"Hold up a minute, Harry."

Thorpe waited for Dr. Thompson to come over to him.

"You know," said Dr. Thompson, "I'm convinced that Paddington wasn't even close to knowing the answers about the accounting issues or the return on investment analysis."

"I have to agree, Henry, and it worries me – a lot. A more mature person simply would have indicated that he hadn't yet run those calculations but would obtain the information for us and relay it shortly following the meeting."

"Harry, I'm seeing it more and more these days – even among our finest graduates, I'm afraid. Young people think they have to know all of the answers – and when they don't, they aren't honest enough to say so. They'd be better off if they just deferred their response!"

"Yes, I've noticed that as well," said Harry. "But we have to do everything we can to keep that from happening here. I'm going to talk to Mark about whether Paddington really should be on the DFP fast track."

Six weeks later, DFP issued a press release that began:

DAKOTA CITY – DFP announced today that it has entered into a merger agreement with Orbitron under which Orbitron will be acquired for a combination of cash and stock valued at about $50 million. Mark Gregory, DFP's Chief Executive Officer, said, "The Orbitron deal will be good for our Company and our shareholders, since it will result in a number of operating efficiencies without requiring any layoffs. We believe we paid top dollar for Orbitron. While it may have an immaterial dilutive impact on our near-term earnings per share, it is truly a unique company and has some of the most sought-after products in our industry."

"Even so," Mr. Gregory continued "We expect that our return on investment should be a reasonable one and that we will recover our investment in three or four years. Of course, we will have to wait and see, as a number of factors will predicate the ultimate results, but we strongly believe that it will be an outstanding deal for DFP."

One week later, Mark sent the following memorandum to his corporate staff:

I wish to announce that Cedric Paddington, our Vice President of Development, is leaving the Company to join a venture capital firm.

While we regret losing Cedric, he advised us that he wants to join a smaller firm with more entrepreneurial objectives. We thank him for his many contributions to the Company since his arrival here five years ago.

Mr. Paddington will be succeeded by Herman Fowler, who has been with us for more than 10 years in a variety of important operating and staff positions. In addition to serving as a Vice President of Development, Herman Fowler will also serve as my Chief of Staff.

"A billion is a thousand million? Why wasn't I informed of this?"

Source: The New Yorker Collection

CHAPTER 9

PEOPLE LIKE US?

A Meeting of the Nominating and Corporate Governance Committee

(Fourth Quarter of Year 8)

Agenda for Committee Meeting

1. *Review criteria for Board members.*

2. *Consider current Board members for potential re-election.*
   a. *Evaluate their performance during prior year.*
   b. *Prepare comments or critique for any Director to whom they are applicable.*
   c. *Authorize report to Board concerning review.*

3. *Review of alternatives with respect to vacancies on Board.*
   a. *Leave vacancies unfilled.*
   b. *Fill vacancies.*

4. *Consider candidates for vacant positions if applicable: Nominees who are self-nominated; nominees advanced by search firm retained by Committee; nominations from other Directors.*

5. *Nomination of incumbent Board members and others for potential election at upcoming annual meeting of shareholders.*

6. *Discussion of Corporate Governance Guidelines.*

This committee session was a particularly important one for DFP. A few weeks earlier, Richard Collins had given notice that he was resigning from the Board. Concurrently resigning was David Nugent, who was joining Collins on the Board of a newly formed publicly held company that was engaged in waste disposal operations. Collins joked with Board members that since he had established a food conglomerate, now it was time for him to find a place for the leftovers. (One Director thought to himself: "Right, Rich – but you're a leftover yourself from the Cro-Magnon era of corporate governance.")

At the final Board meeting Collins and Nugent attended, elaborate resolutions were passed concerning their outstanding Board service. The resolutions weren't read aloud, but they had been signed and placed in handsome plaques as gifts for the departing Directors. Rich had given Mark a private "heads up" about the two resignations a month before, so Mark was ready to add new Directors to the Board to replace them.

At a dinner the night before the Board and Committee meetings, Mark had given a humorous speech about the contributions of Rich Collins. He accurately reported that without Collins' creativity and drive in forming and promoting the Company more than a decade earlier, DFP never would have gotten where it was now. Collins, who by the end of the evening had consumed a few extra libations, said, "You know what, Mark? You're damn right!"

When the day was over, many of the Directors were personally sad to see Collins and Nugent move on. On the other hand, perhaps it was time for a change. The two departing Directors were "good guys," but it was time to recognize that it was the end of an era. It was time to consider their replacements and, inevitably, a new and more progressive approach to corporate governance.

Most of the remaining Directors sought new Directors who shared their goal – to help find ways for DFP to enhance shareholder value while working with the management group on an independent but collegial basis. Up until now, the Board had been split between the "Old Guard" and the "New Guard." Now, it was out with the old and in with the new.

"I call this meeting to order," said Dr. Thompson, whose original start-up investment of $45,000 in DFP was now worth more than $4 million. While he had sold off some of his DFP shares and made a huge profit, he continued to remain as the president of Dakota State University and was an active Board participant. "Unless there are any changes to the minutes of the previous meeting (he looked around at the other members – Alex, Paul and Harry – and none were indicated), they stand approved as submitted.

"At this point, I would like to revisit the criteria for selecting and retaining Board members. While the criteria we've been using are not too lengthy, I think we have found them suitable in the past – and for the most part, they have served us well. Our criteria include the following factors: Business or professional experience in leadership positions; experience in management with one or more large, complex organizations; intellectual capability, including the ability to be a quick study; character and integrity; ability to meet any special needs of the Company or the Board at the time (e.g., technological expertise); diversity of background; and an ability to work in a collegial manner. Any comments?"

"I'm still concerned about using diversity of background as one of our principal criteria," Todihara said. "While I think diversity, in and of itself, is healthy and extremely important, in my view we should find the best Directors to serve the interests of all our shareholders. By overemphasizing diversity, we could miss an extremely capable potential Director and take someone with lesser ability – simply because he or she provides diversity."

"I think this is a tough question," said Gen. Landry. "In my command in the Air Force, we made diversity a positive factor, and I think we should certainly consider it here. I wish to remind you that DFP serves many large and diverse consumer markets – and many of our customers are Hispanic and African-American."

"So?" Alex asked snidely. Gen. Landry continued without answering.

"I also wish to remind you we only have one woman on the Board and more than half our products are purchased by women. In my opinion, we would do ourselves a big service by having more Directors on the Board who are representative of our consumer profile."

"As chairman," said Dr. Thompson, "I would like to suggest the following: We omit any express reference to 'diverse background' from our formal Board selection criteria but, at the same time, keep that factor in mind as a long-term goal for the DFP Board. As we judge ourselves, we all know that some of our Directors already represent diversity and have been first rate – Judy may be, shall we say, just a little 'direct' at times, but she's a stellar Board member and the only woman on our Board. I, as an African-American, think I bring a different perspective to this Board – and I'm sure Alex, with your Japanese ancestry, you feel the same way on some level. There's no reason why we shouldn't be able to find another diverse candidate of our caliber if good candidates present themselves. Is that satisfactory to all of you?"

"Quite satisfactory to me," Gen. Landry said, "but before we leave this topic, let me tell you, some activists always seem to be picking a needless fight over diversity regardless of how diverse your demographics are for Directors, officers and employees.

"My friend Jon Jenkins, over at Jenkins Petroleum, received a form letter from Mark Long, the executive director of a large public pension fund in the East. It said something like this: 'Dear Mr. Jenkins: We looked at your new annual report and, in reviewing the photograph of your board members, noticed you have no women on your board and no persons of color. What are you going to do about it?' Jenkins, who is a little pithy in his style, wrote back: 'Dear Mr. Long: Received your letter critical of our board constituency. What are we going to do about it? We're going to suggest that you get a pair of good eyeglasses! This year, as a cost-cutting measure, there were no photos in our annual report, but we disclosed that our earnings rose by 30 percent. And, by the way, among the distinguished directors on our board are two women, an African-American and a Hispanic. Any other questions?'"

Everyone laughed as Dr. Thompson moved on to the next order of business. "We need to review the performance of our incumbent Board members over the past twelve months. You recall we've decided not to issue individual 'report cards,' but instead to review the consolidated performance of our Directors, as a group, over that period of time. We did so last year – with mostly good results – and I asked each of you to review last year's evaluations of those who remain on the Board to see if you had any changes to them. All three of you said you're satisfied with them, with the qualification that we need to make in-depth evaluations every 24 months. That will be our informal policy."

"That's entirely satisfactory to me," Harry said. "And while we're talking about the past year, I'd like to give you a pat on the back, Dr. Thompson. You had the unenviable task of telling one of our Directors that he hadn't been attending as many meetings as he should have, often came unprepared, and had taken far too many telephone calls during the course of the meetings to provide us with his undivided attention on important issues. He also told us the worst and most crude jokes I've ever heard."

"It wasn't pleasant," said Dr. Thompson, "But someone had to do the job." The Director, whose appointment to the Board had been urged by the CEO of a Company that had been acquired and agreed to by the Board with severe trepidation, never fit in. He was on the Board for less than a year; even now, three months after his resignation, it was as if he'd never even existed because his contributions – except for his jokes – had been virtually non-existent. ("A well-dressed cipher," another Director had called him.) It was a good reminder of the importance of the process of selecting a Director.

"But now," Dr. Thompson continued, "we can look at a more positive issue. We have two vacancies and four potential nominees – including a couple of exceptionally good candidates.

"Peter McMillan, a prominent architect, has been self-nominated, but actually he has quite good qualifications and owns a substantial number of shares of DFP stock. On the other hand, he has no public company Board experience and I doubt he would hit the ground running at a time when we need that.

"Ken Morrow, whom you all know, is pretty darn close to our CEO from a personal perspective and he has really strong manufacturing experience. While he is otherwise qualified, I'm not sure he'd be as independent and as objective as we all would like.

"Joan Fleming, on the other hand, was found by one of our executive recruiting firms and she appears to meet all of our criteria, with one possible exception. She runs her own successful marketing firm in Atlanta, and is its CEO. She has received national recognition for her marketing programs for her clients, but her one problem is that she hasn't served on a corporate board. She has served on a number of non-profit boards, including on some boards for extremely large charitable groups, but I'm not sure how that experience will translate to the corporate sector. I don't want to downplay her abilities, though – she graduated in the top 10 percent of her MBA class at Duke's Fuqua Business School.

"The fourth candidate is one I personally nominated – Frank Alworth. I've known him for decades. He's one of the top money managers in the country and a senior partner in his firm, located right here in Dakota City. He also says he has the time to serve on this Board. Like Joan, he has limited corporate board experience.

"With that, I'd like to have a brief discussion about each of these candidates. First, I assume you read the extensive material prepared by our corporate staff on the backgrounds of each of the prospects." The other members nodded. "Since I chair this Committee and because I thought it was important, I met personally with each of them. With respect to their personal qualities, I believe they all would make good directors."

Alex, holding up a document entitled "Criteria for Board Membership," said, "We've spent a lot of time developing these criteria and I think we should apply them. A critical criterion is whether there are any special needs for DFP's Board at this time. In my view, we have at least a couple. In losing Rich Collins and David Nugent, we lost two Directors who had lots of familiarity with the operations of this Company, and, of course, in Rich, we had one of our most important members with respect to creativity and marketing. Accordingly, I think we might want to concentrate on Joan Fleming, as she clearly has a strong marketing background. The recruiting firm notes, for example, that she was one of the most outstanding marketing grads ever from Fuqua. And the job she's done with that sporting goods conglomerate has won all kinds of awards.

"Another need for DFP is to find someone who can help us with financial planning and analysis as the growth of the Company and the challenges of the various business cycles obviously make it important to have good oversight of our balance sheet and cash flow. In that regard, it seems to me that Frank Alworth could be a real plus.

"I have two concerns about these candidates. One is that they have relatively limited board experience – although Frank has served on the board of one large public company. Also, scheduling; I know they're both truly busy people. For that reason, like about 80% of first-rate prospective board candidates, they may turn down our offer of a Board seat."

Dr. Thompson was pensive for a moment. Then he said, "On the scheduling issue, we should extend the offers if we think they will be good Directors and they can always say "no" if they're too busy. Regarding the experience issue, fortunately, DFP has developed an effective Director's orientation program. Through that program, we can help our two new Directors become quickly oriented to DFP governance proceedings so they can hit the ground running and help serve our needs."

"Regarding the other two candidates," said Gen. Landry, "I like Ken – especially his strong manufacturing expertise – but I agree that he is such a close friend of Mark that he might not be as objective as we would like. In the case of Peter, it is unusual for me to prefer someone who is self-nominated, but he is a distinguished architect and I think we should keep him in our inventory of prospective directors for down the road. Let's be sure to send him an encouraging letter."

After a little discussion, the others agreed with Dr. Thompson's assessment. So, it was decided: Joan Fleming and Frank Alworth would be offered the nominations.

The final agenda item before the Nominating and Governance Committee – to be reviewed over lunch in DFP's executive dining room – concerned the adoption of some new and more extensive corporate governance guidelines. As part of that discussion, George had been asked to attend the session and cover how corporate officers should be organized when there was both a Chief Executive Officer and a Chief Operating Officer. The Committee members had wondered whether the two DFP senior officers shouldn't share more equal titles, since some of them were concerned about Mark's ability to run DFP as solidly as he had in the past, given its growth both domestically and globally.

"With early corporations here in the United States, usually there were only a few officers and their titles typically were specified in statutes," George said. "They included the President, the Corporate Secretary and the Treasurer, with the presidential and secretarial offices not to be held by the same person.

"Gradually, statutes and practices were liberalized, and titles such as Chief Executive Officer and Chief Operating Officer started to be used. For many large companies with vast operations, there is a Chief Executive Officer, who, in some cases, handles many of the outside obligations, along with strategy, financial matters, governance and leadership, and a Chief Operating Officer, a person who is more of a 'Mr. Inside' and responsible for day-to-day operations."

"What about co-CEOs? Has that been tried?" Alex asked.

"Yes, it has. A few companies have tried to use co-Chief Executive Officers, often after two large companies have merged in a so-called merger of equals. That tandem structure rarely works well in larger companies such as ours. It has worked in smaller, privately held companies when the two co-chief executive officers are related in a familial way or have worked together for many years. As I said, in those cases where two merged companies have tried to use co-Chief Executive Officers, that approach not only has failed – but it's failed miserably.

"Another issue is whether the Chairman and Chief Executive Officer should be one and the same person. Some institutional investors favor having an 'Outside Chairman' who handles many of the senior executive responsibilities, particularly with respect to the Board and shareholders, that a traditional CEO would handle. In fact, in the United Kingdom, there often is a so-called 'Non-Executive Chairman,' a true outsider, and, for larger public companies in the U.K., that is the case for more than half of them."

"If it works for them, why not...?" Dr. Thompson began.

"Not so fast! Here in this country, except in emergency situations such as bankruptcies, it is unusual to have an outside Chairman for fear that the question of who is the ultimate 'leader' will be blurred, from both a public and internal standpoint. Most senior executives who are CEOs resist adding an outside Chairman, as they believe that holding both titles and carrying out both functions are important to the effective leadership of an organization. Others – including institutional investors – maintain that having an outside Chairman will make a board better prepared to deal with an ineffective chief executive officer and more responsive to shareholder interests. While the debate goes on and on, as I noted, only a small percentage of U.S. corporations – say about 5-10 percent – have outside chairmen.

"Some companies use inexpensive but regal titles like 'Vice Chairman' to add stature. In fact, under the laws of Dakota, a Vice Chairman doesn't have to be a board member but the title gives that person some more status with customers and vendors. Here, however, I don't think that title is a fit for us."

As George continued to talk, it became clear that there would be no reshuffling of titles for now. Mark would remain CEO for the foreseeable future, with his same duties.

After the full Board approved the nomination of Joan Fleming and Frank Alworth, Mark sent them letters that included the following language:

It is my pleasure to advise you that you have been nominated for service as a member of our Board of Directors of DFP, Inc. We would like to submit your name to our shareholders for approval at our upcoming annual meeting next month. If you are willing to serve, please give me a call and we will work out the details.

Since a member of our Nominating and Corporate Governance Committee already has contacted you, I am aware that you may be concerned about the fact that you have relatively little experience in serving on corporate Boards, as opposed to non-profit Boards. Thus, we have committed to providing you with a full orientation program as a new member of our Board – a formal program that is in place for all new Directors. Once you contact me and indicate your willingness to move forward, I will put you in touch with our capable Corporate Secretary, Barbara Ramos, and she will arrange meetings for you with four or five of our senior officers and at least one of our Directors.

James R. Ukropina

Assuming you are prepared to accept our offer, I can assure you that you will have an interesting experience as a member of our Board. I look forward to hearing from you. Please call me at 555-596-4281 at your earliest convenience so that we may confirm your willingness to serve as one of our new Directors.

Very truly yours,
Mark Gregory

After receiving the letter, both Ms. Fleming and Mr. Alworth called Mark to accept the nomination.

CHAPTER 10 ·

WELCOME ABOARD
An Orientation Meeting
(Second Quarter of Year 9)

Schedule for Orientation Session for Joan Fleming

1. *Meeting with CEO – 10-10:30 a.m.*
2. *Meeting with COO – 10:30-11 a.m.*
3. *Meeting with CFO – 11-Noon*
4. *Luncheon Meeting with General Counsel – Noon-1:30 p.m.*
5. *Meeting with Controller – 1:30-2 p.m.*
6. *Meeting with George Hartfield – 2-3 p.m.*

Joan Fleming arrived at DFP's corporate headquarters in Dakota City at about 9 a.m. and asked for B.R., the Corporate Secretary. It was a reunion for them – both were Yale graduates and often saw each other at undergraduate alumni conferences.

The receptionist led Joan down the hallway and into B.R.'s office. B.R. rose to greet her.

"Joan, great to see you again! Hey – you cut your hair!"

"I'm standing here in my Armani suit and my Manolos, and you just notice my haircut?" Joan teased as they hugged. "Great to see you, too, B.R. – especially today. Sounds like a busy one."

"Not for someone who wrote her senior paper on Emily Bronte while appearing in the latest Sam Shephard play at the Drama School," B.R. teased back.

117

"That was years ago. I haven't stepped on a stage in years, and I can't say I've mentioned Bronte in any of my recent marketing campaigns!" They both laughed. "So," Joan continued, "tell me about DFP."

"Well, we know you want a good introduction to your responsibilities here. It might seem a little simplistic at times for someone like you, but I wanted to make sure we covered all the bases. Have a seat."

"Is it really that different from my nonprofit Board work?" Joan asked as she settled in and looked around B.R.'s highly-organized office.

"Well, in some ways 'no,' but in some ways 'yes.' We just think it's important that new Directors have an opportunity to meet with a number of our officers and gain a comprehensive understanding of the Company, and how senior management works with our Board. And, there's kind of a treat for you at the end of the agenda."

"Which is?"

"I've arranged a special meeting for you with George Hartfield, one of our sharpest Directors. I don't think you've met George..."

"No, I haven't – but I'm certainly aware of his reputation."

"He's a great guy – and a bit of a historian of sorts on the topic of Boards and how they've evolved. I think you'll enjoy getting his take on how our Board and other boards operate."

"B.R., I really appreciate you and the others making this time for me and sending me the orientation package. Believe it or not, I read all of the documents: The Certificate of Incorporation, the Bylaws, 10-K Report, Governance Guidelines, Annual Report to Shareholders, and all of the various analysts' reports. I'm ready to go – and I know it's going to take most of the day, so let's get started!"

"We will – but first let me run down our senior management group and what their titles are, and, more importantly, what they really do in terms of their day-to-day functions." Joan listened carefully as B.R. took her on a tour of the organization chart that she had handed her, casually describing corporate officers' formal and informal roles, with some business and personal background about each of the Directors as well. A solid group, certainly at first glance, Joan thought as she put the organization chart into a leather folder stamped "DFP."

"Joan, let me also tell you about something that should be near and dear to your heart – it certainly is to our other Directors and officers! We carry first-rate Directors' and Officers' indemnifications in the amount of $100 million. Further, under our Bylaws, Directors are indemnified in carrying out their duties to the fullest extent permitted by law."

"Thanks, B.R., it sounds like you read my mind," Joan smiled. "My pocketbook feels better after hearing that."

"Oh, one other matter. As you know, you will receive an annual retainer of $75,000 for your service," B.R. said. "That will be paid in quarterly installments – half in stock and half in cash.

"Now, let's get to your first session in DFP 101!" B.R. said as she rose. "While we walk, you can tell me about that new boyfriend of yours – I hear he's quite the tennis player!"

By the time 2 p.m. rolled around, Joan felt like she had gone far beyond DFP 101 and was enrolled in a graduate seminar on the Company. She was most impressed with Mark Gregory; he had been quite candid with her in describing the inner workings of the Company, along with the qualities of the various senior corporate officers. He even went over some of their strengths and weaknesses as they related to their future potential as Company leaders. And it was clear to her that Mark was extremely proud of DFP, as well as those who worked there, and truly believed the Company had strong growth potential.

The COO and CFO meetings were a little tougher for her, since the operating activities of a Company this size were quite unfamiliar territory – and, as for the financial details, well, that certainly would take a while for anyone to learn!

At lunch in the corporate dining room, she and Mercedes had been joined by Larry Lanski, another Director who happened to be in the area and heard Joan was there. (Well, "heard" might not be quite right: Barbara knew he had dropped by and immediately tracked him down and suggested that he get to know Joan.). Larry helped reassure her that she would fit in well with the other Board members, who would be glad to help her, if she ever felt the need. And, finally, both Larry and Mercedes gave her some insight into Mark's manner and style in running the Board meetings. Since Larry and Joan both lived in Atlanta, they also compared notes on how best to travel to and from Dakota City when the corporate aircraft wasn't available. For each Board meeting, along with a related series of Committee meetings, she knew she was taking at least 48 hours away from her business, "Fleming Images," so travel efficiency was important.

As the lunch was ending, B.R. came over to the table.

"Joan, I'm really sorry, but George's plane has been delayed. Still, he should be here in the next hour. I really think it's important for you to talk with him…"

"That's fine – I'll wait."

"You know what?" Mercedes said. "I wouldn't mind giving you some more details about the legal aspects of your Board service. Is that okay?"

"I think that's a great idea," Barbara said.

"I'm certainly ready for it," Joan agreed. "Where shall we go, counselor?"

M ercedes' office was lined with law books, and she noticed Joan looking at them as they entered.

"An affectation, of course," Mercedes said. "Almost all of our legal research these days is done online. But I still like the feel of those books. They're like comfort food to me – sometimes when I'm working on a really difficult issue, I'll get up from the computer and drag out a reference book and sit at a table, just the way I did in law school."

"Believe it or not, Mercedes, that's just how I feel about a pen and paper when I'm doing a major marketing plan," Joan nodded. "I'm very computer-literate, but sometimes the best ideas come while using old-fashioned methods!"

Joan sat down on a leather couch near the bookcases. Mercedes sat in a nearby chair.

"What I'd like to do, Joan, is give you some of my thoughts on how our Directors should operate from a legal perspective in general, and then, more specifically, tell you something about some of the challenges our Directors have faced in the past few years.

"I've practiced business law for some time and have worked with many Board members. I believe the most important role a Director can play is to help guide the Company from a policy and strategy standpoint and be supportive of the CEO and other officers. At the same time, the Director always should operate in a manner designed to enhance shareholder value. If a Director can't add value, either the CEO is not seeking his or her advice, or the Director shouldn't be serving."

"So far, except for enhancing shareholder value, it isn't really that different from how a major nonprofit board would act."

"Well, it's a lot different from a legal standpoint. You probably know that we're headquartered and incorporated in Dakota, and most of our corporate laws are similar to those adopted in Delaware?"

"Yes, Mark mentioned that as well. Why is that important?"

"More than half of the large public corporations are incorporated in Delaware, mainly for legal reasons. You see, the rules of the road for a director of a Delaware corporation aren't found only in state statutes; instead, the largest body of state corporate law governing director fiduciary duty is found in the case law from the Delaware courts. Under those cases, directors are subject to three duties – a duty of care, a duty of loyalty to all shareholders, and a duty to act in good faith. While we don't have a Delaware Roadmap to interpret our duties, Delaware law in persuasive in our courts.

"Let me say a little more about the specific nature of these duties. Assuming that the directors are acting in good faith, under the American Law Institute Principles of Corporate Governance, there is a good formulation of directors' duties suggesting he or she must act in a manner that he or she reasonably believes to be in the best interests of the corporation and with the care that an ordinarily prudent person would reasonably be expected to exercise in a similar position under similar circumstances. We are also reminded by the commentators that the duty of care includes an obligation to make, or cause to be made, an inquiry when, but only when, the circumstances would alert a reasonable director of the need for one.

"Joan, you shouldn't worry too much about what may sound like a formidable set of duties. The law, in general, permits you to delegate many of your functions to officers, employees or experts. Reliance may be warranted when you are relying on information, opinions, reports, financial statements, and you do so in good faith and reasonably believe that reliance is warranted. For example, we often call upon our independent auditors, legal counsel, engineers and others to deliver reports and recommendations to the Board for just that purpose."

"Those sound like good principles."

"They are," Mercedes continued. "Follow them, and you'll do fine. The one that usually comes into play when directors find themselves in litigation is the duty of care – although there have been a number of major cases when conflicts of interest and, therefore, the duty of loyalty, were at issue. By the way, Joan, if you ever think you may be running into a conflict with your own interests and those of DFP, don't take too long to come and see me and the CEO, so we can attempt to deal with the situation immediately."

"Of course, but why?"

"That's because if you or one of the other Directors is found to have acted on behalf of conflicting interests in carrying out your duty of loyalty to shareholders, some incredibly bad consequences may follow. First, there are exclusions in our Directors' and Officers' indemnification insurance policy and in our Bylaws for acts of self-interest, which might not be covered if the Company was damaged and you were sued. Further, under Dakota law, there's a general exculpatory provision for ordinary Board decisions – that is, a provision that ordinarily would get you off the hook if you make a good-faith business judgment – unless, that is, there's a conflict of interest or you act with gross neglect.

"In other words, if you ever get sued, in substance, the Dakota courts have concluded that you may be entitled to a defense under the Business Judgment Rule. I believe you may be familiar with the Rule but let me give you a little explanation since it may become extremely important to you one day. In effect, the rule is a judicial presumption and defense that, in making a business decision, the directors of the corporation act on an informed basis, in good faith, and in the honest belief that the action taken was in the best interest of the corporation. Accordingly, absent any abuse of discretion, a director's judgment is respected by the court because courts ordinarily do not want to interfere with business decisions."

"That sounds simple enough," said Joan.

"It's a little more complex than it sounds," said Mercedes. "Let me read you another, more legalistic definition of the Rule appearing in the American Law Institute Principles of Corporate Governance. It reads like this: A director who makes a good faith business judgment fulfills his or her duty if the director (a) is not interested in the subject of the business judgment; (b) is informed with respect to the subject of the business judgment to the extent the director reasonably believes the judgment to be appropriate under the circumstances; and (c) rationally believes the business judgment is in the best interest of the corporation. Thus, as you can see, if you make a solid business judgment and there are no conflicts, you should be in good shape – although there usually will be a focus on whether you have fulfilled your duty of care in terms of being well-informed."

Joan was curious. "Has this Board been sued before and, if so, what was the outcome?"

"Yes – two years ago," said Mercedes. "The Board was sued, but we settled the matter for a relatively nominal amount. The suit alleged that, as part of a severance package, the Board had authorized excessive compensation for a terminated officer. A few of our disgruntled shareholders filed a lawsuit alleging that the severance payment was a waste of corporate assets. When the plaintiffs' lawyer started to get further into the case, he realized that the severance payment was appropriate, since DFP and its officers – for good and sufficient reasons – hadn't done a particularly good job of warning the officer about his shortcomings prior to the time that his services were terminated. Nonetheless, we had to pay a fee to the plaintiffs' lawyer, along with a nominal settlement, to get rid of the matter on a cost-effective basis. By the way, even though we settled that case, we didn't pay much. We now have a hard-earned reputation for using settlements as a last resort. In some cases, though, a combination of monetary risk, reputational issues and senior executive time commitments dictate that a settlement is the better part of valor."

"Anything else?"

"There have been some other matters where we worried about potential litigation, particularly when there was a drop in our stock price, but the filing of a lawsuit never came to pass."

"That's good," Joan said, appreciating Mercedes' willingness to take the time to discuss these matters with her. "Mercedes, do you attend all the Board meetings? I'm a little concerned that if legal issues arise and I want to ask you a question, I might not have the benefit of your counsel and advice."

"The answer is, 'yes,'" said Mercedes. "Although, once in a while, I'm asked to leave a Board meeting when sensitive matters are being discussed that aren't specifically legal issues – you know, certain personnel or compensation issues – but those times are rare. I encourage you, at any time, to call me regarding a matter that might concern you, whether it seems like a big deal or not.

"One other matter: In certain cases, I have found the Directors may not want to raise a question with me, but instead with outside legal counsel. If so, please do so. We will certainly pay for any reasonable legal fees you incur for outside legal advice."

"We could ask her to define 'reasonable,' but you'd be here another three hours," George joked from the doorway, where he had been listening to Mercedes' last few comments. Joan laughed and stood to shake his hand.

"You must be George Hartfield."

"Guilty. And you, I presume, are Joan Fleming."

Though outwardly warm and pleasant, George felt a little uncomfortable in that he did not fully support Joan's selection to the Board. He had thought that Peter McMillan would have been a better choice. But now that Joan was aboard, George was willing to help her as a new full-fledged member of the team.

"Sorry I'm late," George continued. "But let's go and spend some time together. B.R. has reserved a conference room for us."

B.R. had briefed George about Joan's earlier meetings and conveyed the general impression that the other executives had formed: Joan would have to be brought up to speed in some of the more arcane financial and operational areas of DFP, but she clearly was a quick study and extremely bright. George thought of that assessment as they sat across the small conference table from each other.

"Joan, let me get started with some practical advice – although I don't think you will find much of it surprising. Most of us who are on this Board believe that one of our critical duties is to be supportive of our Chief Executive Officer in normal day-to-day settings and, particularly, if a crisis arises. We also have to be sure that we observe strict confidentiality with respect to all the matters we discuss in the Boardroom. As a matter of the degree of our involvement, most of us follow an approach we call 'Nose In (the corporate tent), Fingers Out.' In other words, we need to let management run the company on a day-to-day basis." (George mentioned the NIFO principle to anyone who would listen, in that he thought it was one of the most important elements of being a good corporate director.)

Joan was pleased with George's directness. Since they had gotten so quickly to the nuts and bolts of Board service, Joan asked him to describe the traits of a strong director.

"Well, let me start by telling you about some directors I've worked with at other companies, and why I admire them. I'll begin with Herb Banks, the CEO of Fargo Industries. He is always prepared; his one and only interest in serving as a director has been to increase shareholder value; he asks few questions, but when he does, they always are incisive and significant; and he has a great sense of humor and is a lot of fun to work with. Notwithstanding that, he can be persistent with a CEO from time to time when he thinks management isn't coming up with a straight answer to the question he asks. Last time I heard him, he asked the CFO if his merger deal wasn't really one that was just being made to make his corporate mountain taller and, if so, wasn't there a real risk it was about to tip over. After he said that, the merger discussion took a different tone.

"A couple of other directors I admire are Michelle Morris and Don Thomas. Michelle is a stickler for understanding how a strategic plan is supposed to work and whether it continues to be feasible as circumstances change. She's also big on budget controls. If there are large budget variances, she pokes and pokes – always in a quiet, unassuming way – to find out why and what's being done about it.

"Don, on the other hand, is more of a big picture guy and comes with a large inventory of successful – and frankly, some not so successful – business experiences. He regularly asks about what the competition – the 'enemy team,' he calls them – is doing and what the Company's new defensive alignment is. Don, as you might have guessed, is a sports fan."

George described some other directors he admired; then Joan surprised him with one question: "George, one of my friends told me that you were a practicing lawyer and once taught corporate law at law school on a part-time basis. He also said that one of your best lectures concerned the history of how Boards got started and how they've evolved over the past hundred years or so. B.R. told me we're both headed back out to the airport. Perhaps we could ride back together, and you could give me a short course on the evolution of corporate Boards?"

George remembered the similar lecture he had given to Mark at the Fargo club over lunch some years earlier. To Joan, he simply said: "I'd be glad to."

Since Joan was new to the large corporate setting, George decided to give her a more detailed version of what was now becoming his mantra. He wanted to make sure she understood the background of this complex, ever-changing world of corporate boards she had entered. As the cabdriver drove them to the airport, he laid out the history, as he saw it:

As you may know, Joan, corporations did not exist in our country until the early 1800s. In fact, prior to that time, most businesses were sole proprietorships or partnerships. In the 1800s, corporations were formed, principally representing financial institutions such as banks and insurance companies, and, later, railroads and canal companies. Most companies started with a very small board, consisting of the minimum number of directors required by law. In many cases, the board members were the principal owner, who was the president, fellow employees, relatives and a few friends.

When corporations grew and became more complex, managers realized that outside advisors could be a big help to them. As boards started to function, meetings usually were devoted principally to operating issues; once discussions had been held, the president or CEO made his decision and that decision was rarely challenged. But, as companies grew, the CEOs learned it was more difficult to sustain long-term success without an adequate strategic plan, balanced growth and some attention to better corporate governance practices. Most presidents and CEOs concluded that good corporate governance involves an effective relationship among the various participants in corporate life: The shareholders, the management, and the Board.

As state legislatures authorized broader corporate statutory laws, the general authority to manage the corporation was granted to the board of directors. Some charters, which were the governing instrument for incorporating a company, granted that authority to directors, but many also granted the alternative authority to manage a corporation on a day-to-day basis to the president, who later came to be called the chief executive officer. By the way, for Delaware corporations those charters are called 'Certificates of Incorporation' and in other states they're called 'Articles of Incorporation.' I mention that terminology only because initially you will hear some of it and find it confusing. After a few months, I assure you that a person as bright as you are will have no problem with the corporate buzzwords.

Now, back to the history. As case law developed in the corporate field, boards were given the full authority to carry out management – but implicitly it was understood they could delegate it prudently to numerous corporate officers and their agents. Finally, state law caught up with reality, and the laws in almost all states, such as Dakota, explicitly authorize the board to delegate managerial authority to the corporate officers who are elected by the Board.

Even with this delegation, state courts made it clear that neither the board nor the officers really are the ultimate source of authority, but, rather, that authority comes from the shareholders. It is they who have the right to elect directors and approve fundamental changes in the charter of a corporation, such as the authorization of stock. As corporate governance evolved, this balance between the board and shareholders has been altered. For example, by the mid-1800s, courts recognized that shareholders had the right to sue managers when they or the board wasted corporate assets or had been negligent. However, as we proceeded into the first part of the 20th Century, more governance authority shifted away from shareholders and back to members of the board.

As shareholders soon consisted of thousands or tens of thousands of parties, true management authority had to be placed in the hands of the board who, in turn, could delegate it to corporate officers. Then, late last century, the pendulum swung back and shareholders became stronger because their shareholdings were more concentrated in the hands of powerful institutional investors. For many companies today, typically, more than two-thirds of the outstanding shares are held by institutional investors, such as pension and retirement funds – and that is certainly the case for DFP.

Institutional investors began to organize themselves into groups such as trade associations and finally started to make a good deal of headway on critical corporate matters, such as influencing the dismissal of the chief executive officers of large companies. By the late 1980s, a number of large institutional investors, including public employee pension funds, collaborated to threaten boards with dramatic change, unless they took steps to either oust members of their board or some of the senior officers of the company. Also, some major proxy advisory firms developed, becoming formidable players in advising institutions on how to vote on controversial matters, such as 'poison pills.' By the early '90s, the heat was really turned up on high by a number of angry institutional investors who were disappointed by the economy and slumping stock prices.

Finally, the courts got into the act to an even greater extent, and, in the mid-1980s, the Delaware Supreme Court handed down its decision in the case of *Smith v. Van Gorkom.* There, the board of Trans Union Corp. was found to have breached its fiduciary duty of care in authorizing a sale of that publicly held Company in an uninformed manner. The court, in effect, concluded that the sale price was too cheap, even though it was more than 40 percent over the recent market price. Had the case finally been adjudicated with respect to damages, it appeared that Trans Union board members might have been liable, on a joint and several basis, for almost $25 million.

There was tremendous criticism of the decision in that case, since the merger price was a huge premium above the recent trading price for Trans Union stock. Some commentators said the Trans Union board was an able one, but others believed it was overly dominated by management. All of the so-called outside directors had strong personal relationships to the CEO, and none of the directors had a particularly large equity position in the Company.

The *Van Gorkom* decision could have resulted in large monetary liability for the directors, but it didn't. The case was settled (with most of the payments reportedly made by the company that acquired Trans Union). It caused directors to consider whether they wished to remain on boards at all. Shortly thereafter, statutes were amended to provide that directors couldn't be held monetarily liable unless they were grossly neglectful or acting in their self-interest. That so-called exculpatory provision required shareholder approval before it could be included in a company charter. Most shareholders quickly approved it, for fear that without it, directors would head for the hills. In effect, *Van Gorkom* was a shot across the bow of many boards that had been relatively complacent.

Throughout the 1990s, a number of large institutional investors started to kick up their heels. For example, they started to insist on effective corporate governance guidelines for boards of publicly held companies. Such guidelines now exist for most large companies. They provide for more independence for the board, for information to be submitted to board members on a timely basis prior to board meetings, and a continuing review of such important matters as strategy, financial condition and a management succession plan by the board or committees of the board.

In fact, Joan, DFP has adopted only a small number of corporate governance guidelines so far. At our next Board meeting, we're going to discuss a more comprehensive set of guidelines. Mark insists on adopting a Mission Statement at the same time we do governance guidelines. That way, the guidelines can help direct us toward our mission. We talked some time ago about an appropriate mission statement but Mark finally said that he thought an ideal mission statement for us would be one similar to that adopted by Hewlett-Packard. We haven't seen the amended mission statement yet but we understand it will emphasize profit, growth, employment opportunities and good citizenship. While Mark is borrowing from another company, he has done an excellent job in selecting important principles for the mission statement. They're a very good fit for us, so I expect the next meeting should be an interesting session for you.

The proposed guidelines contain material on governance practices on a number of issues. For example, recently we thought we weren't receiving adequate materials prior to Board meetings in order to be well informed about agenda items, nor did we feel the materials were arriving early enough. We also were concerned about some of the Board committees and how to select good Board members like you. The guidelines attempt to respond to these issues, among others.

Joan then asked George about a case involving director duties and the Disney board. "Didn't that case involve some serious issues for the Disney board members?" Joan asked. "Yes," said George. "There is a famous case involving the duty of care for directors, a 1998 Delaware case, in which the Disney board was challenged for approving a substantial severance payment to a senior officer. While that board authorized a payment of tens of millions of dollars to the departing officer, the courts found that the board's decision was ultimately the product of the exercise of sound business judgment.

"There are a host of cases dealing with the duty of loyalty and the need to avoid conflicts of interest in lieu of shareholder interests but, I believe, usually a good director can perceive this type of issue through the application of the old fashioned 'smell test.'"

"I've heard something about a duty of oversight. What's that all about, George?"

"Well," said George, "recently, there has been an emphasis on the legal duty for adequate board oversight over corporate operations. The *Caremark* case involved the settlement of litigation brought against the directors of a healthcare company for allegedly exercising inadequate oversight over various business segments of that company, as well as their alleged inability to assure compliance with regulatory requirements, which led to corporate fines in excess of hundreds of millions of dollars.

"In *Caremark*, the court outlined the nature of the directors' duty to monitor corporate operations. Finally, the court concluded that the directors weren't responsible for a sustained failure to exercise their oversight function.

"In general, it is necessary for directors to monitor corporate performance of the principal senior executives. There need to be programs in place that are designed to have the corporation comply with the laws and regulations.

"There should be policy statements adopted by the board or management to the effect that employee compliance is mandated as well as to maintain procedures for the officers and the board to monitor that compliance. Of all the duties, the duty of oversight is less well defined than other duties but, in the main, most commentators suggest that it does not imply an antagonistic relationship between the board and the officers. The Business Roundtable issued a good statement about this duty: it suggests that the relationship between the board and executives should be challenging yet positive, arms-length but not adversarial.

"Joan, if you have time to review a summary on one other case, partly because it was one of the first major insider trading cases and partly because it is interesting, it would be the SEC action against Texas Gulf Sulphur. In that case, insiders traded on nonpublic information about a major Texas Gulf ore strike in Canada. The court found that officers of the corporation purchased Texas Gulf securities based on that non-public information and that was unlawful. It's possible in insider-trading cases that there can be criminal prosecution, so one also needs to understand the insider-trading laws, including the so-called six months' short-swing profit rules, to avoid legal exposure or embarrassment.

"Also, if you're really into learning more about your legal responsibilities as a Director, you could read the opinions or, at least summaries of opinions, in about six or seven cases. If you could only read one case, I would read the *Van Gorkom* opinion I've mentioned. For other cases, there is a good book available called a 'Director's Handbook of Cases' that you may wish to review."

The cab pulled up to the departing passengers ramp as George was finishing his history lesson. Though fatigued by the day's long briefing sessions, Joan was glad that George had put it all into historical perspective. She was looking forward to her Board service – and looking forward to working more closely with George and the rest of the team. While George seemed to be a bit of a windy "pontificator," he also seemed to have a good sense of humor. After all, he had concluded his remarks with:

"Just remember, Joan – when in doubt, don't be late, fiduciate!"

Excerpt from the DFP Proxy Statement that was issued following the next Board meeting:

The Nominating and Corporate Governance Committee proposed a revised and updated set of comprehensive corporate guidelines that were submitted to and unanimously approved by the Board.

The guidelines were first drafted by the Committee with the assistance of independent legal counsel. Thereafter, the draft was shared with the Chief Executive Officer, who also serves as Chairman of the Board. After extensive discussions with the Chief Executive Officer, the Committee recommended the guidelines' adoption to the full Board.

The guidelines are attached to this Proxy Statement as Exhibit A. The Nominating and Corporate Governance Committee will re-evaluate the guidelines each year and make any necessary amendments.

James R. Ukropina

Exhibit A

DFP CORPORATE GOVERNANCE GUIDELINES
SIZE AND STRUCTURE OF THE BOARD

1. **Size of the Board**. The Board presently has 13 members. It is the sense of the Board that a size of 13 is appropriate under current circumstances. However, the Board would be willing to approve a somewhat larger size in order to accommodate the availability of an outstanding candidate.
2. **Mix of Inside and Outside Directors.** The Board believes there should be a majority of independent Directors on the DFP Board. (See Section 12 for definition of "Independent Director.") While the Company's Chief Executive Officer and Chief Operating Officer are the only members of Management serving as Directors presently, the Board is willing to consider other members of Management for Board membership.
   At the same time, the Board believes that Management should encourage senior officers to understand that Board membership is not a prerequisite to any higher Management position in the Company.

BOARD PROCEDURAL MATTERS

3. **Selection of Agenda Items for Board Meetings.** The Chairman of the Board, and the Lead Director (if one is used), will establish the agenda for each Board meeting. Each Board member is free to suggest the inclusion of potential items for the agenda.
4. **Board Materials Distributed In Advance of Meetings; Other Board Communications.** It is the sense of the Board that information that is important to the Board's understanding of Board business be distributed in writing to the Board at least seven days before each meeting through the transmittal of a "Board Package." Management is to make every attempt to see that this material is as brief as possible while still providing the desired information. When there are "late-breaking" developments after transmittal of the Board Package, Management may supplement the earlier transmittal by fax, e-mail or overnight courier.
   From time to time between meetings, Management should advise the Board of any significant developments through a suitable method of communication: mail, phone, facsimile message, or e-mail. The Board encourages the Chief Executive Officer to send copies of significant messages to other members of Management (showing the Board members as copied parties) such as letters of congratulation for outstanding performance, or where appropriate, letters containing constructive criticism.

5. **Presentations**. As a general rule, detailed presentations on specific subjects should be sent to the Board members in advance so that Board meeting time may be conserved, with discussion time focused on questions and issues about the presentation. On those occasions when the subject matter is too sensitive to reduce to written form, such presentation will be discussed exclusively at the meeting. Also, the Board encourages Management, on special occasions, to conduct, in effect, "virtual meetings" through the exchange of emails in an informal but secure electronic setting provided by the Information Technology department of the Company.

6. **Regular Attendance of Non-Directors at Board Meetings.** The Board is comfortable with the regular attendance at each Board Meeting of non-Board members who are senior members of management. Should the Chief Executive Officer wish to add additional personnel as attendees at Board meetings on a regular basis, it is expected that this suggestion will be made to the Board for its concurrence.

7. **Executive Sessions of Outside Directors**. The outside Directors of the Board will meet in Executive Sessions at least two times each year (in addition to the meeting held for the annual compensation review for senior executive officers). The format of these meetings will include a concluding discussion with the Chief Executive Officer on each occasion after the Board has met. Such sessions, in general, will be limited in duration and will last no more than one hour and will concentrate on significant operating, strategic and personnel issues, although any relevant corporate topic will be welcome. The name of the director who presides at those sessions shall be publicly disclosed.

COMMITTEES

8. **Number of Committees.** The current six Board Committees are (a) Audit, (b) Compensation and Management Development, (c) Executive, (d) Finance, (e) Nominating and Corporate Governance, and (f) Public Affairs. The Board believes that the name and function of the "Compensation and Management Development Committee" are important ones. They recognize the important governance functions of management development and succession planning. There will, from time to time, be occasions in which the Board may want to form a new committee or disband a current committee depending upon the circumstances. (Recently, the Board disbanded the Transactions Committee upon concluding that its duties were best handled by the full Board.)

9. **Independence, Assignment and Rotation of Committee Members**. All of the members of the following committees shall be independent directors: Audit, Compensation and Management Development and Nominating and Corporate Governance. The Nominating and

James R. Ukropina

Governance Committee is responsible, after consultation with the Chief Executive Officer and consideration of the desires of individual Board members, for the assignment of Board members to various committees. It is the sense of the Board that consideration should be given to rotating committee members and committee chairmen periodically at about a three-year interval. However, the Board does not believe that such a rotation should be mandated as there may be reasons, at a given point in time, to maintain an individual Director's committee membership or Chairmanship for a longer period. The person assigned as chairman of the audit committee shall have accounting or financial management expertise.

10. **Frequency and Length of Committee Meetings**. The specific Committee Chairman, in consultation with Committee members, will determine the frequency and length of scheduled meetings for each committee. As circumstances change, committee meetings may have to be held more or less frequently to take into account such developments as new regulatory requirements (e.g., expansion of SEC audit committee oversight rules).

11. **Charter and Committee Agenda.** Each Committee will have a charter with terms consistent with those established by the New York Stock Exchange. The Chairman of each Committee, in consultation with the appropriate members of Management and staff, will develop the Committee's agenda. At the beginning of each year each Committee will issue a schedule of agenda items to be discussed for the upcoming 12 months (to the degree these items can be foreseen). This agenda will also be shared with the Board.

BOARD MEMBERS

12. **Definition of What Constitutes Independence for an Independent Director**. The term independence shall meet the criteria for such status as required by the New York Stock Exchange from time to time. In essence, an "Independent Director" will be a person who is independent of management and free from any material relationship that, in the opinion of the Board, would interfere with the exercise of independent judgment. The Board believes there is no current relationship between any non-employee Director and DFP, Inc. that would be construed in any manner to compromise any non-employee Board member being designated independent. Each year, the Board shall make an affirmative determination of the independence or non-independence of each director.

13. **Board Membership Criteria**. The Nominating and Corporate Governance Committee is responsible for reviewing with the Board on an annual basis the appropriate skills and characteristics required of Board members in the context of the then current make-up of the Board.

138

This assessment should include issues of relevant experience, intelligence, independence, background, potential commitment to Directorship, age, compatibility with other Board members, compatibility with current board culture, prominence, skills (such as an understanding of manufacturing and marketing) – all considered in the context of an assessment of the perceived needs of the Board at that point in time.

14. **Selection of New Director Candidates**. The Board itself should be responsible, in fact as well as procedure, for selecting new Board members. The Board delegates the screening process involved to the Nominating and Corporate Governance Committee with input from the Chief Executive Officer.

15. **Extending the Invitation to a New Potential Director to Join the Board.** The invitation to join the Board should be extended by the Board itself through both the Chairman of the Nominating and Corporate Governance Committee and the Chief Executive Officer of the Company.

16. **Directors Who Change Their Job Responsibility**. It is the sense of the Board that individual Directors who change the responsibility they held when they were elected to the Board should volunteer to resign from the Board. It is not the sense of the Board that those Directors who retire or change from the position they held when they came on the Board should necessarily leave the Board. There should, however, be an opportunity for the Board, through the Nominating and Corporate Governance Committee, to review the continued appropriateness of Board membership under these circumstances.

17. **Term Limits**. The Board does not believe it should establish term limits (i.e., a maximum duration of service for a Board member). While term limits could help insure that there are fresh ideas and viewpoints available to the Board, they present the disadvantage of losing the contributions of those Directors who have been able to develop, over a period of time, increasing insight into the Company and its operations and, therefore, provide an increasing contribution to the Board as a whole. As an alternative to term limits, the Nominating and Governance Committee, in consultation with the Chief Executive Officer, will review each Director's continuation on the Board every three years. This process also will permit each Director the opportunity to conveniently confirm his/her desire to continue as a member of the Board.

18. **Retirement Age**. It is the sense of the Board that the current retirement age of 70 is appropriate.

SUCCESSION PLANNING AND MANAGEMENT DEVELOPMENT

19. **Succession Planning**. In view of the expansion of the duties of the Compensation Committee to those of a Compensation and Management Development Committee, there should be a report by the

Chief Executive Officer to all of the Board members on succession planning every 12 months. There also should be available, on a continuing basis, the Chief Executive Officer's recommendation as to his successor should he be unexpectedly disabled.

20. **Management Development**. There should be an annual report to all of the Board members by the Chief Executive Officer on the Company's program for Management Development. This report should be given to the Board at the same time as the Succession Planning report, noted above.

COMPENSATION

21. **Board Compensation Review**. It is appropriate for the staff of the Company to report once a year to the Nominating and Corporate Governance Committee about the status of Board compensation in relation to compensation paid by other U.S. companies of comparable size and character. Consideration of changes in Board compensation, if any, should come at the suggestion of the Nominating and Corporate Governance Committee but with full discussion and concurrence by the Board.

EVALUATIONS

22. **Evaluating the Board's Performance.** The Nominating and Corporate Governance Committee is to report an evaluation of the Board's performance to the Board annually. This process and the form of the report will be discussed with the full Board immediately prior to the preparation of a report. This should be done in conjunction with the Chief Executive Officer following the end of each fiscal year. This evaluation, which should be a product of input from the Chief Executive Officer and the Committee, should be about the Board's contribution as a whole and specifically reference areas in which the Board and/or the Management believes a better contribution could be made. Its purpose is to increase the effectiveness of the Board, not to target individual Board members.

23. **Evaluation of the Chief Executive Officer.** The non-employee Board members should make this evaluation annually, and it should be communicated to the Chief Executive Officer by the Lead Director, if there is one, or, if not, by the Chairman of the Compensation and Management Development Committee. The evaluation should be based on objective criteria, including operating performance of the Company's business, accomplishment of long-term strategic objectives, customer satisfaction, development of Management, ability to deal with potential mergers, acquisitions or divestitures and similar issues. The evaluation should focus on substantive matters and to a lesser degree

on governance and process issues. The evaluation will be used by the Compensation and Management Development Committee in the course of its deliberations regarding compensation of the Chief Executive Officer as well as related management development and succession issues.

24. **Selection of Chairman And CEO.** The Board should be free to make these choices in any manner that seems best for the Company at a given point in time. Therefore, the Board does not have a policy, one way or the other, on whether the roles of the Chief Executive and Chairman should be separated and, if they are to be separate, whether the Chairman should be selected from the non-employee Directors or be an employee. At the present time, combining the two positions makes sense to the Board.

OTHER MATTERS

25. **Lead Director Concept.** The Board may have one Director selected by the non-employee Directors who will assume the responsibility of chairing the regularly scheduled meetings of non-employee Directors, or other responsibilities that the non-employee Directors as a whole might designate from time to time. This functional role is now filled by a Director designated by the Board but that Director does not have a formal title, which is the express intent of the Board. This position may rotate from time to time.

26. **Board Access to Management.** Board members have complete access to all members of the Company's Management team. It is assumed that Board members will use judgment to be sure that any such contacts are not distracting to the business operation of the Company and that any such contact, if in writing, be copied to the Chief Executive Officer. In addition, Directors should not give orders to employees other than through the Chief Executive Officer. Administrative issues should be coordinated with committee chairmen or through the corporate officer or staff person who serves as a liaison between management and the committee. Furthermore, the Board encourages Management to bring managers into Board Meetings from time to time, when such managers: (a) can provide additional insight into the items being discussed because of personal involvement in these areas, and/or (b) represent managers with future potential as members of senior Management.

27. **Board Interaction With Institutional Investors, the Press, Customers, and Others.** The Board believes that the Management speaks for the Company. Individual Board members may, from time to time, meet or otherwise communicate with various constituencies that are involved with the Company. It is expected, however, that Board

members would do this with the knowledge of the Management and, in most instances, at the request of Management.

28. **Board Member Compensation.** In order to align director interests with shareholder interests, at least one half of the amount of director compensation shall be in the form of stock or stock options, with the director making the election.

29. **Amendments of Guidelines**. These Guidelines will be reviewed by the Nominating and Governance Committee every year to ensure the contents of the Guidelines are suitable for the then needs of the Company. If changes are needed, they will be recommended by the Committee for review and possible approval by the Board.

After the adoption of the governance guidelines, Mark also
asked the Board to assist him in amending the Company's
Mission Statement. He reminded the Board that it was
largely modeled after the Mission Statement of Hewlett-
Packard and was a principal force behind adding
shareholder value. The DFP Mission Statement, as
amended, follows:

DFP MISSION STATEMENT

1. Acknowledge that profit is the best measure of a company's contribution to society and the ultimate source of corporate strength;
2. Improve total shareholder return;
3. Improve the value of the products and services offered to customers;
4. Seek new opportunities for growth, but focus efforts on fields in which DFP can make a contribution;
5. Provide employment opportunities that include the chance to share in DFP's success;
6. Maintain an organizational environment that fosters individual motivation, initiative and creativity;
7. Demonstrate good citizenship by making contributions to all of the communities in which DFP has facilities and customers;
8. Emphasize growth as a requirement for DFP's survival.

CHAPTER 11

WHO AND WHY?

The Board's Committee Appointments

(Second Quarter of Year 9)

Agenda for meeting between the CEO and the Chairman of the Nominating and Governance Committee:

1. *Review existing Board committees and possible need for additional committees.*
2. *If necessary, revise and add to committee charters.*
3. *Select chairmen for committees.*
4. *Staffing of members for each committee.*
5. *Discuss how to advise Directors of changes in committee responsibilities and staffing.*

In adopting the most recent DFP corporate governance guidelines, the Board authorized an expansion of the number of Board committees. Mark asked Dr. Thompson, the Chairman of the Nominating and Corporate Governance Committee, to come by and discuss the current committees and try to determine if the Board had the right ones in place and whether any other changes were needed. Mark reminded Dr. Thompson (who, after almost seven years on the Board, insisted on others using the doctor title before his name) that there were now six standing committees – audit, compensation and management development, executive, nominating and corporate governance, finance, and public affairs. In addition, from time to time, special ad hoc committees were formed for the purpose of accomplishing such objectives as conducting investigations, examining potential conflicts of interest or improper conduct and similar issues.

First, Mark noted that some of the committee chairmen positions had not been changed in a number of years. "I think our committees are really in pretty good shape and the chairman have all been doing a good job. What do you think? Do you see a problem there?"

"I think it's good governance practice," said Dr. Thompson, "to rotate most of the committee chairmen every two or three years. Although, I know that for our University's Board of Trustees, changing of committee chairmen can be disruptive to the governance process. On the other hand, as both of us know, some committee chairmen start to build their own fiefdoms or get a little lazy, and other directors resent not having the opportunity to serve either as a committee chairman or on one of the more active committees – such as the compensation committee."

"Well," said Mark, "I suppose you're right. Let's go over some of our committees and see what makes sense for us. Let's see – let's start with the Compensation and Management Development Committee. As you said, it's been quite active, and I certainly consider it one of our most important committees. I think Larry's doing a good job. Any reason you see why he shouldn't remain in place?"

Dr. Thompson cleared his throat. "To be candid," he said, "many of the other Directors aren't happy with it. They believe there's been too close a relationship between you and Larry and that he isn't being sufficiently rigorous in reviewing incentive compensation decisions – particularly bonus decisions. Everyone thinks well of him. And they're not suspicious of your motives, but all of us feel that a fresh face would make some sense."

"Really? Well, I don't agree," Mark said. "I think you're engaged in some overkill here in terms of having the ultimate arm's-length relationships. You know, it's really hard to enlist a good Chairman for the Compensation Committee, and especially to educate him or her on the subjects they need to understand, including all of our various bonus plans, not to mention other perks and fringe benefits."

"That's the problem," Dr. Thompson replied. "Many of our Directors think you have too many plans and, when taken together, they're a little too 'rich' compared to how others are paid. It's not so much the amount of the compensation that we're concerned about – although it seems a little high. It's that we think compensation arrangements should be simplified and consolidated a bit before we continue to add a new benefit plan each year."

"Okay," said Mark. "How about Stan Towler? I think he'd do a good job."

"There's a problem there," said Henry. "Remember, Stan is a consultant to DFP. A lot of us worry about the fact that he would not be as objective and rigorous as he should be when he negotiates on behalf of the shareholders with respect to your compensation and the compensation of others. What would you think of Frank?"

Mark pondered the suggestion for only a moment. "He would be fine," said Mark. "He's a little conservative for my blood but he has experience; he's served on a number of boards and board committees, and he does a solid job. What's next?"

"Seems to most of us that we should leave the other committees pretty much the way they are in terms of staffing. On the other hand, service on the Audit Committee has become a much larger responsibility. We think those on that committee are doing a solid job – but, for what it's worth, one or two of them have asked if they could get off of it because they're worried about liability exposure."

Mark smiled and said, "Let them earn their fees. It's not that tough a job."

"Mark, maybe you haven't looked at the recent SEC rules on expanding responsibilities for audit committee members," said Dr. Thompson. "You also ought to keep in mind that a number of members of audit committees around the country have been sued in class actions. With 20/20 hindsight, they have been charged with inadequate performance of their duties of care and oversight over the financial statements of their respective companies."

The CEO thought a moment. "Why don't we add Joan to the Audit Committee? She's still fairly new and took a while to get up to speed on some of our accounting practices, but B.R. reminded me recently that when Joan got her MBA, her minor was in accounting. She runs her own Company and knows how to meet a payroll and keep her financial statements in order."

"Okay," said Dr. Thompson, "but that means she's going to have to serve on a number of committees. We already have slated her for two others. I think she can handle the workload, but we have to be careful to stagger the timing of these committee meetings so they don't overlap. She can't be two places at once.

"You know, she told me recently that she's spending far more time on Board matters than she ever expected she would, but she also said it was a lot more interesting than she had expected. I thought we had warned her that Directors of a Company this size, on average, spend at least 175 to 225 hours each year in preparation, travel and in meetings."

"You don't think she's going to burn out, do you?"

"No, I checked with her about possibly taking on additional duties, and she was fine with it."

M ark had been waiting for the right time to question one committee assignment that had been on his mind lately. Now seemed to be just that time.

"There is one other committee I'd like to discuss – the Nominating and Corporate Governance Committee," Mark said.

"Mine?" Dr. Thompson bristled. "What seems to be the problem?"

"Well – and don't take this personally – it's getting to be far too independent for me. I would like to at least continue as an ex-officio member. Since you kicked me off the Committee last year, it now only consists of outside Directors."

147

Dr. Thompson relaxed.

"Mark, you don't really know what's good for you. Many of our large institutional investors, who regard themselves as governance thought-leaders and corporate activists, are truly concerned about the membership of our Nominating Committee. As a matter of fact, they've called me at my office and urged me to be sure that you have no substantial role in that committee."

Mark frowned as Dr. Thompson continued.

"I didn't want to tell you about it because I didn't want to upset you. As you know, you discourage us from talking to some of our major DFP shareholders directly – but in this case, it turned out to be a good thing. I think we helped put out a fire by asking you to leave as an official member of the Nominating and Corporate Governance Committee."

"But, what I have to say should be considered..." Mark interjected. Dr. Thompson raised his hand for silence.

"On the other hand," Dr. Thompson said, "it *is* a good idea for you to have significant input into the selection of prospective new Directors, as well as ask questions about whether certain Directors should be retained. Accordingly, we suggest this approach: you will be an ex-officio committee member, but, if it's okay with you, at the appropriate time in a meeting you'll remove yourself from any committee meeting so that the committee members themselves can make the final decision about who's going to be on this Board. One other thing. When an invitation is extended to a potential new member, we would prefer that one of our committee members and you extend it jointly. Is that okay with you?"

Mark grudgingly agreed to the arrangement. As he did, he thought to himself that the governance process had changed a lot, even over the past few years. He was uncomfortable with his inability to involve himself as deeply as he would like in certain governance matters, such as the selection of a new Board member. Wasn't he in the best position to understand what the needs of the Company were at any given time, how the Board should meet those needs; and who should be added to or subtracted from the Board to most effectively deal with them? On the other hand, he knew the Board felt strongly that the Nominating and Corporate Governance Committee should be largely independent. And he also knew – not to his liking – that Mercedes had strong feelings on this issue. She had been particularly assertive in supporting this approach by the Board.

"One last matter, Mark," said Dr. Thompson. "I have another real concern."

"Now what?" Mark normally enjoyed his meetings with Dr. Thompson, but this one was beginning to grate on his nerves.

"Well, it's this. Our Compensation and Management Development Committee does very little concerning the latter part of its title. Not enough is being done about meaningful and effective management development and succession."

"Wait a minute!" said Mark, "I'm only 50, work out regularly, eat right, and have a clean bill of health from my doctor. You've all been quite open in telling me that you think I'm doing a great job, so why do we need to worry about development and succession? Are you trying to send me a veiled message that I'm no longer needed?"

"Hardly," said Dr. Thompson. "Instead, I'm trying to be sure that we all do one of the most – if not the most – important things that we can for a large, multinational public Company like DFP, and that is to insure continuity of solid management. Accordingly, we were going to insist that the Compensation and Management Development Committee not only continue to carry that name but also truly expand its function to manage development and its succession."

"Very well," Mark said, just as his intercom buzzed. "We'll have to work out the details later. I've scheduled some time now to meet with Geoff about our overall financial picture. He's got some interesting items that he wants to bring up at the next Board meeting."

Mark got up, shook Dr. Thompson's hand, and escorted him to the door. As the door closed behind Dr. Thompson, Mark let out a long sigh. Maybe Rich Collins had a point with his rubber "Aye" stamp after all.

James R. Ukropina

Excerpt from DFP's next proxy statement:

The Board has six standing committees: audit, compensation and management development, executive, nominating and corporate governance, finance, and public affairs. During the past year, each of the committees met at least three times and, in certain instances, held additional meetings.

The Board has formally authorized an expansion of the duties of the Compensation and Management Development Committee to include succession planning. The Board concluded that one of the Committee's most important duties is to ensure that an appropriate succession plan is in place. The plan, which was recommended by the Chief Executive Officer and the Nominating and Corporate Governance Committee to the full Board, covers not only orderly succession (with senior officers projected to work until they are of a traditional retirement age) but also includes emergency succession planning to cover the possibility that a key officer could unexpectedly be recruited to another company, become ill or lose his or her life.

A financial snapshot of the Company:

DFP INC.
COMPARATIVE QUARTERLY RESULTS
($000)
(Third Quarter of Year 12)

	Most Recent Qtr.	% Variance from Comp Qtr.	% Variance From Plan
Sales	420,000	+4	+2
Net Income	40,000	+6	+4
Earnings/Share	.60	+5	+4
Cash Flow/Share	.68	+5	+5
Stock Price versus Peer Index	+8%	-	-
Debt/Equity Ratio	60%	-	-

CHAPTER 12

A PUBLIC OFFERING

Will the Price Be Right?

(Third Quarter of Year 12)

Agenda for Board Meeting

1. *Approval of Minutes*
2. *Report on Operating Results and Related Matters for Prior Quarter – CEO*
3. *Discussion of Legislative Issues and Regulatory Matters Affecting Company – General Counsel*
4. *Review of Company's Financial Condition and Need for Capital – CFO*
5. *Proposed Public Offering – CEO and CFO*
6. *Discussion of Potential Underwriting Arrangements with Potential Lead Underwriter – CFO*
7. *Authorization of Filing of Registration Statement Covering Public Offering and Related Matters – General Counsel*
8. *Other Matters*

The early part of the meeting went swiftly; it was clear to the Directors that Agenda Item No. 4 would be the main topic of discussion for today's meeting.

"As I'm sure you noticed," Mark said, "there is a rather significant item that is coming up next. Geoff, could you review our financial condition and talk about our need for equity capital?"

As CFO Raines summarized the Company's current balance sheet for the Directors, George thought to himself about all the times he had listened as financial officers and investment bankers described the need for a public offering. The bankers in the Boardroom always insisted that the current time was absolutely opportune. Further, they often referred to an illusory conceptual marketplace "window" that seemed to open and close in an unpredictable fashion. They usually warned the Board – as they were doing on this Fall morning – that the window was now wide open for the public offering, but that it may close shortly. In fact, mused George, no client has ever seen this window – and certainly never foresaw its opening and closing. Only the bankers appear to have the sharp vision necessary to see it.

"Here's how I see the bidding," said Raines. "It appears we have the opportunity to market about $50 million of our common stock. We have a relatively immediate need for about $25 or $30 million. So what we're proposing is that 60 percent of the offering, or $30 million, be issued by the Company in a 'primary offering' and the other $20 million be sold by some of our officers or insiders, which, as you know, is commonly called a 'secondary offering.'"

"In my view, the entire offering should be a primary offering," Judy immediately said. "Why should any of the officers sell their stock just now?"

George had discussed this very issue with Mark before the meeting began. "Like all of you, I understand that the more insiders sell, the smaller the amount the Company can raise in this market," Hartfield said. "Also, I am told that if insiders sell what appears to be too much stock, these apparently excessive sales could scare off prospective buyers in the offering through a perception that our insiders no longer have confidence in the Company's future profitability."

Several Directors nodded in agreement. But George wasn't through yet.

"Nonetheless, Mark has told me – and, in a moment, Mark, you can speak for yourself – that it is important for him and for many of his officers to monetize more of their net worth. He has said that it would be difficult for him to support an offering unless the allocation is along the lines that he and others had proposed to the Board."

"Wait a second," Gen. Landry said. "It sounds to me as if the Board is being held hostage by the officers, and that is really not fair to shareholders!"

"Look," Mark said, "the other top officers and I have helped build this Company. Most of our original investors are extremely wealthy because they have experienced a lot of stock appreciation over the past few years due to our efforts – and to give the Board its due, your efforts as well. However, all of our financial advisors tell us that at this time we are far too heavily invested in this Company's stock and that we need to diversify our assets. It's not as if we won't still be significant shareholders. You all know we will continue to hold big blocks of the Company's stock after the sale, so I don't think that should really leave a concern in your mind, or in the minds of others."

Again, George thought to himself, Mark should have done some more spade work before the meeting. Had he spent a little time with some of the key Directors introducing this issue, it would have been far easier to develop a consensus on how the proceeds of the offering should be allocated between the Company and the selling shareholders.

"I have a suggestion," George said. "Why don't we rely on the Finance Committee to discuss the details of the offering and the final allocation?"

"Why should we do that?" Judy asked. "Why can't we discuss it as a full Board?"

"Well," George replied, "here's just one example. The pricing of the offering will be extremely important – right? All of the discussions about that can't involve all of the Board members because of the potential need to convene the entire Board in a real hurry at a time when not all of us will be available. As you know, the offering will have to be priced on a very short-fuse basis if one is to catch the market in that ever-disappearing 'window' of opportunity that we keep hearing about."

"I think George's idea is a good one," Mark said. "I move that we adopt it. All in favor?"

The Board passed the motion and worked out the details of the assignment, but Hugh still wasn't satisfied. "Since I'm not going to be on the committee," he said, "I feel a little left out. Mark, I want to be sure that you really think the timing is right for an offering. In my view, and in the view of some of my own advisors, we believe if the Company waits another six months, you could get a much higher per-share price for the stock. What do you think?"

"I understand your concern about timing," said Mark. "As your CEO, I don't think we should roll the dice and try to guess exactly when the peak of the market will present itself. It's possible we may not achieve the highest price in the next six months, but we're in a good position to achieve a reasonable price in the offering. After all, that's all we should ask for. Mason, could you give us your views?"

Mason Calder, an investment banker whose firm was one of the candidates to underwrite the deal, had been sitting in the meeting at the Board's request. He leaned forward from his chair against the wall where he had been waiting for a chance to speak. "At the end of the day," he said, "I can assure you that you all will be pleased with your decision to move forward…"

He droned on – not only talking about the opening and closing of windows but also the conclusion of or the end of a nondesignated "day." George wondered why bankers made such seemingly dramatic references. Such comments never seemed to advance the ball on the analysis of what ultimately turns out to be measuring complex business and financial factors in an attempt to forecast inherently unpredictable stock market conditions.

"Well, it sounds like we're going ahead," Judy said when Calder finished his presentation. "How long should it take to get ready?"

"It will take about a month to put together a registration statement," Mercedes said. "We may be able to trim a little fat off that schedule, although it will be a lot more expensive for us to do so."

"What will the offering cost?" asked Harry.

Mason playfully started to count on his fingers – to the chuckles of some Board members – before looking up. "All I can tell you is it will cost a lot of money, but I think we'll be able to raise this capital with the overall cost of the underwriters, accountants, legal and printing being around 7 percent of the total offering. Of course, that will depend on how smoothly the process goes and how difficult it may be for the underwriters to generate interest in the offering."

A few minutes later, the Board thanked Mason and the Company's outside accountants for attending the session and asked the outsiders to leave the Boardroom.

Once they were gone, Harry asked, "How are we going to select the investment banking firm that will serve as the lead underwriter in this offering?"

That's a great question, Judy thought. She told the Board that she had recently served on the Board of another public company, and two months ago had quite a negative experience with that board's investment bankers in connection with an IPO. The firm had urged the CEO and board of that company to agree to a stock issuance of one million shares at $30 per share. It, too, was a mixed primary and secondary offering, she noted. The bankers assured the Board that the market interest would probably take the stock price up to no more than $34-$36 for a nice "pickup" of near-term appreciation for the investors. Instead, the stock price went immediately to $46 but with a very small stable of long term investors. With little buying support for the higher price, the stock rapidly became a volatile security. Judy said she later learned that a number of clients of the investment bankers had made substantial gains on a short-term basis and then "flipped" the stock to others who saw the stock ride back down to $30 per share. That volatility, according to Judy, kept institutional buyers away from the stock for some time.

"In that deal," Judy concluded, "the other company used the banking firm of Betterman Brothers, one of the regional firms in this area. In my view, that firm is unscrupulous, and I would eliminate them from any consideration."

"That does sound like a bad experience," Mark said, "but Betterman Brothers is one of the leading contenders for this underwriting assignment. They have a lot of expertise in our industry, and I would prefer not to eliminate them, at least at this point."

"Look, Mark, I feel very strongly about this issue. Unless you have no other alternative, I urge you to write off Betterman Brothers as a potential candidate to lead this underwriting syndicate."

"Judy, I can see you feel very strongly and I'll keep your comments in mind. We'll run the alternatives through the Finance Committee and if you'd like to be consulted before the Finance Committee makes a final decision about the lead underwriter, we'd be happy to call you before that vote."

"You bet!" she said.

"Well, if you're looking for other candidates, I urge you to consider Thomson & Reindel, a national firm that has a lot of retail distribution," Harry said. "In my view, the Company should attract a broad public investor base and that base is accessible through a firm like theirs. Later, as DFP becomes larger, you may want to seek a broader base of institutional investors – but not at this point. If you have a lot of institutional investors in the stock, what you may see is a 'herd instinct,' with all the institutions buying the stock at once. However, once they start to dump the DFP stock, there's almost no stopping them and the DFP stock price could be cut almost in half in a matter of a few hours."

"Thanks, Harry – give the information to the Finance Committee, and they'll add them to the list," Mark said. "Harry may be right in recommending Thomson & Reindel. That firm has provided us with some excellent ideas with respect to potential acquisitions. We turned down the deals, but still, they were good ideas. That firm also was able to assist us in securing some important lines of credit when we were facing a cash flow crunch and most of its partners have excellent judgment with respect to timing and the terms of an offering.

"Also, Ron Reindel is a solid guy with good financial judgment. His track record for his clients is outstanding and he has a real green thumb when it comes to finding new sources of future profit from acquired companies. As you all well know, when dealing with large established firms, you usually will have a good team staffing your account. What's most important to us is who is leading that team and what kind of judgment and perspective the team leader will bring to issues like the best timing for a stock offering. Ron has all the qualities we need in making such calls. He and his firm are darn expensive but they really are super at what they do. Recently, I sat in a meeting where his firm convinced us we should do a debt deal rather than a stock offering so we could pay deductible interest rather than non-deductible dividends. They also talked to us about the important debt ratings for our debt which are strong. They reminded us, however, that once those ratings go south, it may take years to regain them because some of the rating agencies are slow to recognize reacquired financial stability.

"Now, Mercedes, will you address some of the legal issues we face in this situation, especially the obligations of the Directors in connection with the underwritten public offering?"

"As you know, we'll be preparing a registration statement containing the prospectus for this public offering," Mercedes explained. "Much of it will incorporate the 10-K report, which we will file with the SEC in a few weeks. I urge all of you to review the relevant documents. We are also supplying you with recent securities analysts' reports about

DFP so that you can feel that you're getting an unvarnished perspective about how DFP is regarded on the Street.

"Under the Securities Act of 1933, if there are material omissions, material misrepresentations or half-truths in the registration material, directors can be held responsible and liable. While you are going to be covered by special indemnification insurance up to $25 million for your exposure in this offering, one never knows what lawsuits will be filed, if any, and what damages will be sought. I can personally assure you that the registration statement will be carefully prepared, but you need to satisfy yourselves along those lines. Accordingly, we will be having a special Board meeting in a few weeks to do nothing other than go over the registration materials. If you cannot attend personally, I strongly urge you to do so by telephone.

"Again, process is important here – not only by doing a thorough job in reviewing these materials, but also by documenting that you did so is important to all of us."

"Mercedes is right," Hugh said. "The registration materials will be important, not only from a legal standpoint, but also from a marketing standpoint. I favor using color photographs and impressive graphics in the prospectus."

Hugh, a former partner in a large New York investment banking firm, was always a little vocal and ponderous on such issues as how the Street and ratings agencies might react to such proposals; in fact, his nickname among some of his fellow Directors was "Mr. Street," although they never used that title to his face. "At the same time, we need to understand that the registration materials are an insurance policy for all of us, so they must be accurate. Now, on to more important things.

"Geoffrey Raines has told me that he has carefully evaluated how the various investment banking firms will react to this offering and he also thinks that the rating agencies will not change DFP's ratings as a result of the offering. If they thought the offering was going to be significantly dilutive to our earnings per share over the immediate term, it would kill the stock price. I did my own checking with some of my sources at some of the Street houses and rating agencies and they corroborated what Geoff had to say."

"Don't you trust Geoff?" asked Frank.

"I trust him implicitly," Hugh said. "On the other hand, you can never be too careful about the Street reaction and the agencies. Believe me, I've learned the hard way!"

After concluding remarks by some of the other Directors about the timing of the offering, the Board approved the proposed offering in principle, with the final allocation of the primary and secondary aspects of the offering to be left to the Finance Committee. The Board meeting lasted more than four hours and both management and the Directors were pleased that it reached a successful conclusion.

Three months later, DFP issued a press release that began:

DAKOTA CITY – DFP, Inc., today reported the completion of the successful public offering of $60 million of common stock.

"The market favorably reacted to the offering and we were able to expand the offering from the originally anticipated $50 million of stock to $60 million," said DFP Chief Executive Officer Mark Gregory. "The Company raised $40 million from the offering and a number of our officers and Directors sold the balance for the purpose of diversifying their portfolios."

James R. Ukropina

A few months later, the Dakota Business Journal ran the following story:

Investor Sues DFP Over Recent Offering

DAKOTA CITY – Prominent local investor George Manda today filed a lawsuit against DFP, Inc., alleging irregularities in its recent stock offering.

The suit alleges that the prospectus contained material omissions with respect to an eroding market for certain of the Company's products. In addition to DFP, the named defendants are the Company's officers and its Directors who were on the Board at the time of the offering.

DFP's stock has dropped by about 20 percent since its recent offering, a decline that Manda claimed was a result of the alleged omission. DFP CEO Mark Gregory, who said the Company will fight the suit vigorously, disagreed.

"What Mr. Manda fails to note is that the stock prices of other corporations in our peer group have experienced similar declines," Gregory said. "This speaks about the economy – not about our recent offering."

A financial snapshot of the Company:

DFP INC.
COMPARATIVE QUARTERLY RESULTS
($000)
(Third Quarter of Year 10)

	Most Recent Qtr.	% Variance from Comp Qtr.	% Variance From Plan
Sales	350,000	-18	-25
Net Income	12,000	-21	-26
Earnings/Share	.28	-21	-26
Cash Flow/Share	.26	-24	-28
Stock Price versus Peer Index	-12%	-	-
Debt/Equity Ratio	70%	-	-

James R. Ukropina

Part II

TROUBLE

For a while, the stock returned to the level of the public offering price, but by then, the Company was in need of even more funds. Management looked internally for a source of additional funding that could be achieved on a relatively "short-fuse" basis and focused on the potential sale of its DFP Refrigeration division, because of a looming weakening economy and some cash shortages. Also, the most recent quarter was weak and well below Street expectations.

DFP Refrigeration manufactured and distributed small refrigerators and related equipment and had been profitable; however, it didn't fit into the long-term strategic plan of the Company and never would be a leader in its group. At the same time, it generated predictable earnings and had a relatively clean balance sheet with significant tangible assets that could be used as a source of leverage for a buyer who wished to finance the proposed acquisition.

One of the potential buyers was an "insider group" that had been organized by Archie Archibald, a long-time officer and employee of the Company and a good friend of a number of the Board members. Archibald was seeking low-interest financing from the Company to engage in a leveraged buyout of the division.

CHAPTER 13

THE LEVERAGED BUYOUT

A Tale of Two Proposals

(Fourth Quarter of Year 10)

Partial Agenda for Board Meeting

1. *Status Report on Proposed Sale of Refrigeration Division and Range Estimate of Sale Price – CEO*
2. *Review of Terms of Sale from Alternate Prospective Purchasers – CFO*
   a. *Archibald Group*
   b. *Argonaut Industries*
3. *Legal Duties of Directors – General Counsel*
   a. *Generally in Connection with Sale of Division*
   b. *Specific Special Duties in Connection with Sale to Related Parties*
4. *Report by Investment Banker*
5. *Possible Authorization of Sale of Division*

Archie Archibald spent several weeks getting his plan together for the leveraged buyout and brought it before the Board in a special meeting that was called on short notice. Some Board members were a little irritated at being told that they had to make a critical decision in such a hurry.

DFP announced it would auction the division to the bidder which had the best price and the most acceptable terms. Archibald and his group – which included DFP divisional officers, employees and others – had secured $10 million cash from investors and another $30 million in financing but needed

167

another $2 million to close the deal. Their financing involved using the very assets being acquired as collateral for their loan in a so-called leveraged buyout transaction. But, it turned out that Argonaut, a competitor, made its own all-cash bid – and its proposed purchase price was slightly above that submitted by the Archibald group. Another problem confronted by the Board, according to DFP's General Counsel, was that Archibald and his officers hadn't cooperated fully with Argonaut in Argonaut's due diligence investigation of the division. The Board members weren't sure whether the division's foot-dragging was intentional, or whether they were just busy with other operating matters – but either way, it was a problem. Mark had fixed the foot-dragging problem when he took Archibald out of control of the sale process and substituted the DFP CFO for Archibald, thereby eliminating what should have been an obvious conflict of interest from the start. The Board listened to Archibald's discussion of the deal terms and his explanation of other issues, and then asked him to leave the room.

"Archibald is a great guy and I think we should do what we can to accommodate a purchase by his group," Dr. Thompson said. "On the other hand, we can't play favorites."

"That's for sure," Harry said. "We need to look at this on an arm's-length basis. Is it your understanding, Mark, that our investment bankers probably could render a fairness opinion for either transaction?"

"Yes, that's the case. You may recall that Archibald also has offered us an additional post-closing earnout agreement whereby we could make another couple of million dollars over a two- or three-year period, depending on the earnings of the Refrigeration Division on a post-closing basis. The banker thinks those earnout payments would more than equalize the two competing bids.

"In my view, the fact the Archibald group has offered us an earnout arrangement and Argonaut hasn't done so is an important distinction between these two deals. Further, the Archibald group runs the operations of our refrigeration subsidiary and can clearly hit the ground running right after the closing. As a result, there's a good chance they will hit some of the earnout triggers and we'll be far better off for having taken that earnout arrangement and making a post-closing return. At the same time, there is no guarantee the earnout will be achieved, of course."

Mark went on with his analysis of the two deals. "Another aspect of this deal is that Argonaut and the Archibald group both would be acquiring the stock of the refrigeration subsidiary. Therefore, ordinarily they would be acquiring all of the assets and assuming all of the liabilities. But the fact is that Argonaut has chosen to exclude certain liabilities from its assumption obligations, including excluding potential liability for future warranty claims.

"While I don't expect many such problems in the next few years, we did have a serious warranty claim about three years ago when one of the refrigeration units caught fire and burned down a large warehouse in Southern California. In addition, the Argonaut group isn't willing to assume much of the potential environmental liability relating to our plant where the refrigeration units are produced while the Archibald group is willing to do that.

"Lastly, the Archibald group is prepared to take on any claims for unlawful termination of employees that may arise from a restructuring of the refrigeration subsidiary on a post-closing basis. Mr. Archibald has told us he plans to lay off some people in order to improve post-closing profit margins, but he and his group will take any exposure for such litigation. At the same time, the Argonaut people refuse to do so. As you can see, while the two deal prices are close, the true net economic price for the Archibald group, in my view, appears to be superior since they are paying us a higher net price by offering substantial cash with a near comprehensive assumption of liabilities, along with an earnout. Also, I'm satisfied that the Archibald group has all the financing they need. Argonaut, on the other hand, offers us no earnout and only is willing to assume some liabilities."

Mercedes knew that many of the Board members were inclined to accept Archibald's bid, and she felt it was time for a warning. "Don't forget that Board members can be sued by shareholders when shareholders perceive that the Board is playing favorites. To put it bluntly, many of you know Archibald and I can tell you are pretty good friends. If you think you can't be objective, I strongly suggest you abstain from voting. If you do vote, be sure to pay a lot of attention to our investment banker's opinion. Oh – one other thing: You also may wish to assure yourself that the process is a reasonable one that is designed to ensure the most favorable bid for the division."

Judy listened intently. She had become friendly with Archie over the years and made no secret that she was a supporter of his approach. Mark wanted her opinion for the record.

"Judy, what do you have to say about the two alternatives?"

"Insofar as I'm concerned, when we have two competing bids that are close to one another in value, we should favor our own people," Judy said adamantly. "They have worked long and hard for the Company and have been solid performers. Why shouldn't they get the nod in a close case?"

"Judy, I know how you feel, but we must have some objective indicia from the bankers that one bid is better than the other," Mercedes said. "The bankers think they can get there and are sharpening their pencils to see if the Archibald group can get a few more dollars out of their jeans."

As Mercedes spoke, B.R. noticed that Assistant General Counsel David Julian had quietly pushed open the door of the Boardroom and was motioning to her. B.R. got up, walked over to David, took the note he handed her, and delivered it to Mercedes.

"Well, it continues to get interesting," Mercedes told the Board after reading the note. "The Archibald group has increased its bid by about 5 percent – but also is seeking low-interest financing from the Company over a 12-month period."

Mercedes still warned the Board that while she probably could support the sale to the Archibald group, the Board could be sued by shareholders over its action – especially if the financing terms aren't offered to Argonaut and are particularly advantageous to the insider group.

"I need to remind you," said Mercedes, "that after the Enron matter some boards are staying away from so-called conflict transactions altogether. In my view, though, that's far too conservative a view if a deal makes sense to our shareholders. In fact, that was the law more than 100 years ago – no conflicts transactions. But then legislators built in these procedural safe harbors such as the one I outlined in my memo to you before this meeting: Full disclosure of all the facts; be sure it's fair and reasonable; and a favorable vote of a disinterested majority of the Board.

"Even so, some courts may suggest that this type of matter has to demonstrate 'entire fairness' or something along those lines – so you'll have to show fairness of result and process and you, instead of the plaintiff, may have a duty to show everything is fair. We have a good situation here, however, when there are two bidders and the bids are extremely close. Most of the deals that go down in flames from a conflict perspective are those that never come close to passing the old-fashioned 'smell' test."

Frank Alworth, a seasoned investment advisor and a corporate governance veteran, asked to be recognized.

"I want to have the floor at this point," he said, "because I think we're dealing with an extraordinarily sensitive issue. As most of you know, selling a division to a group of insiders is a lot like a transaction in which the insiders are purchasing an entire company on a leveraged or financed basis.

"Where an insider group is using leverage, supported by the fixed assets of this division, I can tell you we may run into problems and headaches that few of you can imagine," Alworth continued.

"You seem unusually concerned, Frank," Judy said. "Why is that?"

"I was on the Board of Mega Productions, a motion picture producer, and its management team proposed to take the

Company private in a leveraged buyout deal," Frank replied. "I served on the Special Committee of the Board to help referee between the interests of the shareholders and management and, damn it, I'll never do it again – because it took forever and no one was happy with our Committee."

"Do you have a suggestion on how we should handle it?" Hugh asked.

"If I had my way, what we should do here is form a Special Committee and have separate legal advisors and certainly our own investment banker," Frank said. "Fortunately, we have the latter, but there doesn't appear to be time for independent legal advice. In an ideal situation, we should have it.

"I found that in defending these transactions, a court will focus on the process used and whether you documented that process. You must be able to show you got the best price – in this case, for the division – but there's no real formula to help evaluate that, since any price is also a combination of the economic consideration and the terms and conditions of the deal.

"Of course, the advice we'd like to have here is from the managers of the division itself. They're the ones who will know how much it's worth and they're in a better position to evaluate it than anyone else," Frank continued. "Unfortunately, they are across the table from us and only our senior management can help us. Of course, our senior management is necessarily close to them – and that includes some of the Directors in this room. Another thing – as usual, we're being pressured to move quickly to do a deal. We're being told that financing only will be available for a short period of time because of the tight money market."

"Here we have the advantage of having done a respectable 'market check,' since we've had this division out on the block for an auction for about 90 days and the inside bid and the bid from Argonaut are the only ones we've received," Harry said.

"That's true," Frank responded. "I also agree that the bid packages are pretty close to one another, but I'm definitely concerned about whether Archibald and his group also are going to sign up for the same kinds of terms and conditions as Argonaut. For example, I need to know if both parties are buying the same assets? Are they assuming the same liabilities? Are they accepting the same contingent liabilities for such matters as environmental issues? Are health and benefit programs being assumed? Are we receiving similar indemnification? Are the terms generally the same?"

"Frank, whoa there! I think I can put your mind to rest," said Mercedes. "We saw these potential issues rising, so what we decided to do was prepare our own first draft of the acquisition agreement for all prospective buyers, which was pretty middle-of-the-road in order to expedite the deal. Both accepted almost all the terms of that agreement, including the same kinds of terms and conditions that you just outlined. Each party made a few minor 'tweaks' in the form of the agreement, but, in substance, both parties are bidding on almost exactly the same basis.

"Also, as we discussed, we will make the financing package available to both parties and we'll carefully record all of the process steps we've taken here to be sure that the deal is the right one for the shareholders."

"It seems to me," said Larry, "that we must offer the same financing to the Argonaut Group, but it is unlikely they'll accept it, since they're already well funded. At the same time, under these circumstances, it's my view that we must be extraordinarily careful from both a procedural and substantive standpoint to be sure that, in the last analysis, our shareholders' interests are best represented by our final decision."

"In view of Mercedes' comments, we have to go through each alternative and state on the record that we have considered all of the relevant terms and conditions of the two alternative purchases and that we acknowledge there is a potential 'conflict' involved," said Harry. "Then, any of us who is unable to be objective in the vote should abstain."

"I'm in favor of all of those steps," said Judy. "But I still believe it is in the overall corporate interest to favor the

Archibald Group so long as that group's bid is equal to or better than the Argonaut bid. In a case where the bids are substantially equal, it seems to me that the tie should go to our runner – or, in other words, to the loyal insider. After all, Argonaut also competes with us in other portions of our business."

At that point, the investment banker took the podium at the front of the Boardroom and patiently reviewed the terms and conditions of each of the competing bidders, suggested an interest rate for financing the Archibald Group, and said that the banking firm could issue a fairness opinion for either bid. He added that his firm would not opine on which was the better bid, since they were quite comparable, and since his firm's policy was to leave such choices to the client.

At that moment, all eyes turned to Mark.

"Mark, what do you think?" Alex asked. "What's your recommendation?"

One month later, the Company issued a press release that began:

DAKOTA CITY – DFP, Inc., today announced that it is selling its DFP Refrigeration Division to a group of investors headed by Archie Archibald, the current president of that division. The sale will generate about $38 million in proceeds to DFP, Inc., and an additional $4 million when the group repays a promissory note delivered to the Company by the investment group. Also, DFP may make up to $2 million if the Division meets certain earnings targets over the next two years.

As part of the transaction, DFP will be required to write off about $5 million in goodwill, which is attributable to the division that, in turn, was acquired by the Company six years ago.

DFP's stock dropped by about eight percent after the announcement of the sale of the Refrigeration Division. Securities analysts didn't expect a write-off of goodwill and, while it was a non-cash charge, the Street started to question the wisdom of the Company's aggressive acquisition program, which had resulted in seven acquisitions over the previous four years.

In addition, a local plaintiffs' law firm filed a suit on behalf of one its clients alleging that DFP's Board acted imprudently and fostered a conflict-of-interest transaction by favoring the Archibald group over Argonaut.

About six months after the suit was filed, the Company agreed to settle the case based on its General Counsel's recommendation. None of the Directors were personally liable for any of the damages since all the defendants involved in the settlement were covered either by the Directors and Officers' indemnification insurance or by the Bylaw indemnification provisions.

At the same Board meeting at which the settlement was authorized, the General Counsel had to cover another difficult matter: an allegation of sexual harassment in the Company's executive ranks.

Following a recent turndown in the national economy that had hit Dakota especially hard, DFP had a significant number of layoffs, even in its management ranks. Among those laid off was Helen Thomason, Vice President of Marketing. Helen's performance had been measurably eroding over the previous year.

But after being told that her services were being terminated, Helen went to her attorney, a well-known labor lawyer named Steven Jackson. In a letter to Mark, Jackson accused Helen's supervisor, a high-performing executive vice president, Reginald Robbins, of inappropriate remarks (comments about her clothes), unwanted touching (hugs for a job well done) and inappropriate sexual advances ("playing footsie" with her under a table at a staff meeting). In general, Helen's attorney also alleged that Reginald created a hostile working environment and, under a relatively new definition from a Dakota state court of what constituted harassment, this latter conduct could be actionable. Helen's attorney made it clear that she would file suit unless her severance demand for 18 months of compensation was approved.

An initial DFP internal investigation found no "smoking guns" supporting Helen's specific allegations, but investigators unearthed some indications that Robbins might not always have conducted himself in the most appropriate manner around female employees.

James R. Ukropina

*"Then it's moved and seconded that the compulsory
retirement age be advanced to ninety-five."*

Source: The New Yorker Collection

CHAPTER 14

THE HARASSMENT MATTER

She Says, He Says

(First Quarter of Year 11)

Agenda for Board Meeting

1. *Approval of Minutes*
2. *Operating Report – CEO*
3. *Authorization of Strategic Plan*
4. *Charitable Contributions and Political Contributions – VP of Public Affairs*
5. *Legal Status Report – General Counsel*
6. *Employee Relations Matter*

The Company had a strong employee-relations record with a limited number of claims of ethnic or sexual discrimination or harassment. But the thinly disguised "Employee Relations Matter" agenda item meant the topic would be front-and-center at that morning's Board meeting.

"Mercedes, I'd like you to begin the discussion on the Helen Thomason situation," Mark said once they reached that point in the agenda.

"Certainly, Mark. Most of you know Helen and Reginald," she began. "And I'm sure you've read the reports in your Board material about this matter. But I wanted to give you a little more context.

"As your General Counsel, I must seriously consider the allegations of any responsible employee who steps up and reports he or she has been sexually harassed. And yes, I meant to say 'he or she' – these reports come not only from our women employees but from some of our men as well. In any event, this case is somewhat serious as Helen is a fairly senior employee and, up until last year, when her sales performance started slipping, she had an excellent record.

"At the same time, I am always highly skeptical when these types of allegations arise just as someone is laid off. At this stage, after a preliminary investigation, we are in the delicate situation of not being able to either prove or disprove her allegations."

Harry furrowed his brow and figuratively put on his litigator's hat. "I must say that this fellow, Reginald Robbins, is rather flamboyant. From time to time, I've personally seen him throw his arms around both men and women to congratulate them for their performance. I understand that Helen is also alleging that he 'played footsie' with her under the table..."

"We've found no witnesses to that – or anything like it," Mercedes interrupted.

"Well, as she well knows, there aren't likely to be credible witnesses in these sorts of situations," Harry continued, "and several of us know from personal experience that Reginald's language and innuendoes can be fairly colorful. I've been up against Steve Jackson in court, and he's always prepared. I expect he can make a pretty good case about Reginald creating a hostile environment, which under present day labor law here in Dakota might result in a sustainable harassment claim."

"Maybe the answer here is to lay off Reginald at the same time we lay off Helen," Gen. Landry said enthusiastically. "What do the rest of you think?"

"Wait just a minute," said Mercedes. "Before you start talking about laying off Reginald, keep in mind that he has a tight, employee-oriented employment agreement. It is one of those agreements many of our senior officers have that, frankly, has a narrow definition of the grounds for termination for cause – with references only to gross neglect or felonious conduct. I'm fairly sure that we don't have contractual grounds to lay him off – although, if he is unethical, or even worse, a womanizer, then we need to lay him off and take the legal and financial consequences."

"Let's give him the benefit of the doubt for a moment," Towler said, obviously concerned about the direction of the conversation. "Reginald has been with us for many years and, in my view, he has been one of our best performers here at DFP. Sure, he's a little outspoken and overly gregarious, but there's a big difference between that and harassment. I think some of you are being overly protective of Helen, who, in my opinion, hasn't really performed that well for a long time!"

"I appreciate your position, Stan, but these situations are never that cut-and-dried," Mark said. "Mercedes and I have been discussing some options, and I'd like her to share them with you."

"First, we may stay the course and continue to proceed with Helen's termination," Mercedes began. "The second alternative would be to re-examine the grounds for her termination and reinstate her, although I'm fairly certain she wouldn't stand for that – and may, in fact, sue us before we exercise that option. Thirdly, separate and apart from Helen's status, we truly need to investigate more thoroughly her allegations about Reginald. If we discover that 'where there's smoke, there's fire,' we may have to discipline him, demote him or even terminate his services. As far as I'm concerned, what we have here is a business judgment for all of you to make. To help you, we have a recommendation for you from management. Mark?"

"Our recommendation," said Mark, "is to terminate Helen because her performance not only has been failing for more than a year, but, in the past six months, it has been extremely poor. Not only has she lost her effectiveness, but also her energy and her leadership in the marketing area. At the same time, she was a good performer for many years and we could take her on as a consultant to work on some special projects. Our recommendation is to do just that."

Some of the Board members seemed skeptical as Mark continued.

"Insofar as Reginald is concerned, I have to tell you that this isn't the first time I've had a complaint about his aggressive conduct from one of our female employees. We recommend that we conduct a thorough investigation of the allegations against him and also talk to some of his co-workers. We'll meet with Helen's counsel and make it clear that we're following up on her allegations and will give a report to her on the final disposition regarding Reginald. But there's an additional, fairly difficult component of our recommendation: We suggest that we put Reginald on probation while the investigation is under way."

Harry wasn't buying it. "I think both of these ideas are lousy," he said. "First, Helen has shown us that she can no longer perform, and I don't see why we should retain her as a consultant. She hasn't done good work as an employee, why should she do so as a consultant? With respect to Reginald, he seems to have been nailed by a disgruntled woman whom we laid off for good reason and now his conduct is being called into question by someone that we have already determined is unreliable. Haven't the rest of you seen situations in your own companies where people are laid off and all of a sudden they claim they have been objects of discrimination or harassment? It seems to me that what's really going on here is a lot of old-fashioned blackmail."

At this point, Joan could sit quietly no longer. "Well, after listening to all of you express your views, I must tell you that I don't think we've really looked at this situation as objectively as we should."

"What do you mean?" Mark asked, surprised at Joan's bluntness.

"Those of us who know Helen know full well she's a solid citizen and isn't apt to make a case for harassment unless she can justify it. Many of us, like Helen, have had to confront various forms of harassment in our business careers, but, for many reasons, have not publicly complained about it. In this case, my sense is that we will find ultimately that Reginald is very much to blame.

"Also, in today's society, DFP can't pursue this matter half-heartedly. DFP should retain experienced independent legal counsel who should interview not only potential principal witnesses but collateral players as well. An investigation like this should take weeks, not days. We must be sure that this is a complete investigation and attempt to obtain as many facts as possible. It also will be necessary to talk to all other women here at DFP who have working relationships with Reginald to see if they have confronted problems similar to those alleged by Helen."

Gen. Landry disagreed. "I favor a limited internal investigation because of the cost of doing more. And I so move.

"We can ask the Audit Committee to serve as a special Ad Hoc Committee to investigate the issues and have that Committee then make a report to the full Board at our next meeting, or, if necessary, at an earlier, specially called Board meeting."

Mark pondered the alternatives for a moment. "I will entertain the motion with respect to the General's recommendation," he finally said. "Also, I will promise you that once the Audit Committee completes its investigation and the rest of us have gathered as many facts as we can, I will send you a memorandum describing the outcome. Do I have a second to the General's recommendation?"

"Second," said Stan.

"Any discussion?" asked Mark.

"Yes," said Joan. "I can see that my little speech about taking a tough stand didn't make much of a dent on you. I can understand why that should be the case, at least in most instances like this, but not in this one. Also, I think you're going to approve the motion as proposed by Gen. Landry. So, I wish to tell you that I am *not* comfortable in supporting the motion and I *will* vote against it. In my view, we ought to take far more serious action at this point."

"Joan, I understand your concern," said Mercedes, "but I wish to suggest to you that a split Board vote is not good for any Board. Should we turn out to make the wrong decision and the Board is sued for it, a plaintiff's lawyer will attack the decision and, ordinarily, you and the other Directors, in turn, would assert the Business Judgment Rule as a defense. If we do, the plaintiff's rebuttal will be that there was not a unanimous vote and that a split vote should have indicated that those voting in favor of the motion should have taken more time and consideration to consider the minority view.

"Here, I think your views have been considered and I think it is somewhat unfortunate – but apparently inevitable – for you to vote 'no.' Obviously, you have to vote your conscience and proceed as you think a good fiduciary should. I simply wanted to lay out for you the potential consequences of a negative vote."

"Thank you, Mercedes," said Joan, rather stiffly. "As always, I appreciate the counsel and advice. Nonetheless, my vote is 'no' and, B.R., I want it recorded in the minutes, please."

Mark called for the vote of the others. Gen. Landry's recommendation passed 11-2, with Hugh Perry changing his vote at the last minute after weighing Joan's concerns. A brief chill went through the Boardroom.

A few weeks later, Mark sent the following memorandum to the Board members:

PRIVILEGED AND CONFIDENTIAL

To: The Board of Directors

From: Mark Gregory

I wish to advise you that we met with Helen Thomason and her attorney and have concluded that she should be retained as a consultant to the Company for the next nine months at her current base salary. She has been assigned some important special projects in areas in which she has significant expertise. We expect that she will be spending most of her time outside the corporate office conducting marketing research. In exchange for the consulting arrangement, Helen has signed a full release that releases not only the Company, but also its officers, directors and Reginald Robbins. As part of the settlement, Reginald has agreed to undergo psychological counseling.

We have also announced throughout the Company that DFP now has a "zero tolerance" policy on sexual harassment. I might add that I appreciate the Board's thoughts about this matter and your agreement that a zero tolerance policy is critical, based upon reviews of other complaints that were uncovered during the course of our internal investigations.

Now, let me turn to Reginald. I'm disappointed to report that we now have received a number of other claims concerning sexual harassment allegedly perpetrated by him, although I should add that most of the claimants are good friends of Helen. As a result of these claims, however, we have asked Reginald to limit his associations in the Company, at least for the next few months, to contacts with male employees except in emergency circumstances. During that time, we will ask our

James R. Ukropina

General Counsel, working with our outside labor law firm, to conduct a thorough investigation of the additional claims and then we'll make a recommendation to you at our next Board meeting.

In the interim, we would appreciate your keeping these matters strictly confidential. You will note that this memorandum is accompanied by a cover memorandum from our General Counsel in which she has provided us with certain legal advice and I'm supplying you with this memorandum as a foundation for that advice. Accordingly, you should regard this communication as subject to the attorney-client privilege. Should you discuss these matters with others outside the Company, you may very well destroy the privilege – not only for the Company, but also in ways that could hurt yourself and our shareholders.

A financial snapshot of the Company:

DFP, INC.
COMPARATIVE QUARTERLY RESULTS
($000)
(Second Quarter of Year 11)

	Most Recent Qtr.	% Variance from Comp Qtr.	% Variance From Plan
Sales	330,000	-12	-18
Net Income	20,000	-13	-19
Earnings/Share	.28	-14	-19
Cash Flow/Share	.29	-18	-20
Stock Price versus Peer Index	-8%	-	-
Debt/Equity Ratio	63%	-	-

CHAPTER 15

THE BOARD RETREAT

What Should the CEO Tell the Board – and When?

(Second Quarter of Year 11)

Partial Agenda for Board Retreat

1. *Crisis Management – Overview — CEO*
2. *Presentation by Strategic Consultants, LLC — State of the Industry and Strategic Issues*
3. *Discussion of Report – CEO and Comments from Directors*
4. *Report on Legal Issues and Developments – General Counsel*

Nestled among tall oaks and done in a Western lodge motif, Vista Resorts was one of Dakota's leading golf and tennis resorts. It also had outstanding conference facilities for business groups, which made it the perfect setting for DFP's annual Board retreat. While it wasn't a five-star establishment, it was just regal enough that some of the Directors were slightly uncomfortable with its upscale surroundings. On the other hand, it was well removed from the day-to-day business community, making it possible for the Board to concentrate on important operating and strategic matters – the key reasons for such special retreats.

Some of the Board members arrived a few hours earlier than the others, in order to attend an Audit Committee meeting. But by nightfall, all of the Directors had shown up for an informal dinner meeting. The pre-dinner talk centered around

DFP's operating results and the recent disappointing spiral downward – and there was no agreement on why that was happening, other than the economy in general was slowing. It soon became clear that the meeting would be stressful, especially since DFP was under increasing shareholder pressure to improve profits at every level.

Some months before the retreat, when planning the program, Mark decided that at dinner on the first night he would review the subject of crisis management. Now he also wanted to deflect the Board from current operating issues – at least for a while — and review how he and the Board might handle a crisis together.

Having been involved in a few crises himself, Mark thought it was important to educate the Board at the retreat about how a crisis might confront the Company and to share his ideas about how best to deal with it.

He explained to the Board that crises came in all shapes and sizes. He meticulously listed 18 types of crises on the white board at the front of the meeting room:

(1) Dramatic erosion in operating results or weak balance sheets.
(2) Unexpected death or serious illness of one or more senior executives.
(3) A liquidity crisis.
(4) Product defects.
(5) An act of terrorism.
(6) A natural disaster, such as a fire or earthquake.
(7) Environmental pollution.
(8) The discovery of lack of management integrity, evidenced by unethical or unlawful conduct.
(9) Sex discrimination or sexual harassment.
(10) A hostile tender offer.
(11) A proxy contest.
(12) Major class action litigation.

(13) A significant enforcement action for non-compliance with governmental regulations (e.g., a SEC or FDA action).

(14) Significant erosion in the realization of the strategic direction of the Company.

(15) Expressions of dissatisfaction by major shareholders concerning the performance of senior management.

(16) Alleged unlawful use of patents or trade secrets or unexpected lapse or expiration of enforceability of patents or trade secrets.

(17) A high-profile clash with a government or non-governmental organization ("NGO") in global business settings about workplace practices (e.g., Greenpeace).

(18) Everything else, such as confronting a political or media campaign targeted at the Company due to unfounded allegations.

Mark told the Board members that "some of these crises may not be totally familiar to you – but I'm sure that most of them are. Here's a little background about a few of them.

"When a company has a liquidity crisis, it may be doing well from a financial reporting standpoint in terms of reporting some net income, but its cash flow may be starting to dry up because of a heavy requirement for investments in items for capital spending, such as buildings and equipment, which are booked over time rather than booking the full expense in the year incurred. At such a time, numerous lenders – and vendors – may start to shut off their credit. Then, a company may be unable to meet certain financial ratio tests and various financial covenants in loan agreements are triggered. The company then is placed in default or, even worse, in bankruptcy.

"Then there is the proxy contest. There have been more and more hostile proxy contests in recent years. These usually are started by insurgents who not only want some seats on the board of directors but also want to take control of the company.

They often are ruthless and involve a lot of mudslinging. In particular, they require substantial expenditures by a corporation and, as you know, we had a proxy contest with Spayder a few years ago.

"One doesn't think of a building fire as a crisis, but out in Southern California many years ago one of the large bank holding companies experienced a major fire in its corporate headquarters and also in the division of the bank that engaged in high-level international securities trading. Fortunately that bank had a terrific crisis management plan and managed to 'offload' important data to a backup system before the fire so that there wasn't any interruption in its operations or its trading program.

"Another crisis: We often can see erosion in the realization of a strategic plan when a company starts to make a number of uncoordinated and ill-planned acquisitions. When that happens, the profit-and-loss statement starts to be adversely affected and the stock price can drop like a rock. There aren't a lot of short-term solutions to that scenario.

"Regarding crises with the NGOs, we're only starting to see a few of those – but there may be many more to come. Some of them involve apparent anarchists who don't like global business expansion. As you have read, we've had some major riots in cities throughout the world when large industrial and trade organizations meet. Some of these clashes had an impact on the facilities of large global companies."

The Directors had listened somberly as Mark continued to lead them through the list. George wrote a note to Judy as Mark talked: "I hope we're ready!"

In addition, Mark told the Board that a corporate crisis involving a specific product would be particularly sensitive for DFP, because the DFP name appeared along with the brand name on almost all of its products. For other companies, such as Procter & Gamble, in the case of some of their products, there was no obvious link between the corporate name and the name of a product brand. Also, Mark explained to the Board that he was a great believer in the proposition that a strong corporate reputation may take decades to build but it could be destroyed in a few days. Then, it would take many years to reconstruct.

The next day's first formal session began at 7:30 a.m., and the first agenda item was a presentation by highly paid and highly able consultants from Strategic Consultants, LLC. Based on their analysis of the current state of the industry, they didn't see much hope for an immediate turnaround, but they provided some step-by-step proposals for how DFP could increase its profits, cut costs and generally move forward again. In so doing, they used recently prepared – and unseen by the Board – DFP financial statements that showed a far larger gap between projected plan results for DFP and actual results than had been promised. By the time they left, the Directors were already in a bad mood – and some of them hadn't even finished their morning danish.

To complicate matters, Mercedes reported an increase in lawsuits alleging racial and age discrimination against DFP filed by some of those who had been laid off by the Company after many years of service – and the courts seemed to be looking positively at their claims. Adding to the woes, Mark disclosed that Dakota Governor Grover Hill had called him to privately express his displeasure at the Company's downsizing – and to warn him that he was going public with his unhappiness.

"Grover suggested that the Company, its management and the Board are all alarmists – and that our cutbacks are unnecessary," Mark told the group. "I thanked him for his views, but I've also assigned our Public Affairs VP – Ross Levins – to start a campaign that focuses on the facts that DFP continues to have the largest workforce in the area and that, historically, DFP has been a stable employer.

"In addition, I've authorized Ross to retain an outside lobbying firm to make direct contact with the Governor's office to see if Grover will respond to helping meet the operating problems we're facing by allocating some large state contracts to DFP. Any questions on those points?"

"Actually," George said, "I'd like to go back to the Strategic Consultants presentation. I think I speak for all of us in saying that we're quite disappointed that you didn't share with us the recent DFP financials. It looks as if there are sharp deviations from your projected financial plan budget. Remember that we very carefully started with a strategic plan and then we all helped you develop a financial plan that put flesh on the strategic plan by using range estimates of financial results, which you then used to develop that annual budget. Now, it seems much further off than it should.

"I was talking last night to some of the Board members and we think that, given these trying times, we would like to have every four weeks, if not every two weeks, e-mailed reports from you on variances from budget, the reasons for them and what you're doing about it. In short, we're not happy about what's going on. We know you're not either, but the Board has to conduct more effective and close oversight at times like these to be sure that everything that can be done is being done to turn the Company around."

As Mark noticed several Board members nodding in agreement with George's assessment, his anger started to build. "Look – I'm doing everything I can to turn this Company around! Most of our competitors are far behind us and they have made futile efforts in their turnaround programs. At least we've started to turn around a number of divisions, and I can assure you that we are working around the clock to do that and more.

"I want to think about how often we can make a cost-effective report to you on variances. Producing reports every couple of weeks or a month will take up valuable time we should be spending on the larger issues. And, I've got to tell you, it seems to me that you're overstepping your traditional role by sticking your fingers, rather than your nose, into the corporate tent."

"Mark, I think you're being far too sensitive about our request," Larry said. "We've asked for some fairly routine reports that you already prepare for your management group.

Since you have e-mail available for all of us, it won't be hard for you to just show us as copied parties."

Mark thought for a moment and concluded they were right. "Okay, I agree that you need more periodic reports. They won't be fancy but we'll send them to you every two weeks. I'll assign our CFO to make them available to you and also will set up a conference call at the end of the day each Monday afternoon so that you can ask whatever questions you want about our current results and financial condition.

"In addition, I will provide you a qualitative analysis on the nature and progress of our turnaround efforts. At the same time, I will provide you with information about what our peer companies are doing and their relative progress. Is that okay?"

"Those are certainly steps in the right direction," Larry responded, "and I know I speak for all of us when I say we appreciate your taking the time to keep us current. You know, Mark, if we're going to be decent Directors, we have to involve ourselves to a greater extent on behalf of our shareholders when matters start to get more challenging. If you were an outsider and a large shareholder, you wouldn't expect less from us. In fact, knowing you, you'd probably expect more!"

"Touché," proclaimed Mark. "I might want more and I might even want a few seats on this Board – but you probably wouldn't give them to me because, like you, I ask too many questions!"

With that, Mark adjourned the meeting and said he couldn't join the Board for lunch because he had too much to do in connection with the Company's turnaround efforts.

"Joan, I had no idea you were so good on the links!" George said as he signed for a round of drinks in the resort's 19th Hole bar later that afternoon.

"You should have read my resume a little more closely," Joan replied with a laugh. "I was in the running for Ivy League Women's Champ two years in a row."

"Good thing Mark wasn't in our group," Hugh said. "After the day he's been having, I don't think getting beaten by you would have made him very happy."

"Speaking of Mark, I was wondering – what did you two think about his handling of some of our criticism this morning?" George asked.

"I was a little shocked," Hugh said. "It was no harsher than I've seen other Boards dole out."

"I agree – it clearly was an overreaction," Joan said.

"I know he's under stress because of the financial situation, but I'm beginning to wonder if it's more than that," George said.

"Maybe you'll find out soon," Joan said. "Mark's standing over by the door trying to get your attention."

George waved at Mark, who motioned for him to come over. He did, while Joan and Hugh returned to their drinks and conversation.

CHAPTER 16

COOKING THE BOOKS
A Lead Director Is Named
(Third Quarter of Year 11)

George joined Mark in a well-appointed small library with upholstered chairs, just off the main dining room in Vista's majestic clubhouse. "Have a seat, George – and I think you'd better order a stiff drink. I have some bad news to share with you."

"Chardonnay," George told the waiter who had come up as they sat down. A few minutes later, he would wish he had ordered a double Scotch, if not some hemlock. George leaned forward as Mark began talking.

"Mark," asks George, "what's the problem now? You seem to have had your share recently – I hope this isn't a major one."

"Well, George, I'm sad to say it is." As Mark went on, George noticed how troubled he looked. "Last week, we discovered that one of our divisional presidents paid a $100,000 bribe to a government official in South Makite, a newly formed country in the Far East. The bribe was paid to obtain new business from the government there and, in fact, we landed a pretty large contract."

"That's bad – but not a disaster," George broke in.

"Wait – there's more. In addition to the bribe, we also found that our officer paid a bill for more than $30,000 for a one-week stay for the government official's family at a hotel on the Makite Peninsula. Finally, it looks like our divisional president also falsified books and records..."

"He cooked the books?"

"Right – to hide the bribery payment and other related payments, he saw to it that the expense was recorded under the 'Travel and Entertainment' account. Oh, he also dropped some of the later expenses into the account for 'General and Administrative Expenses.'

"We sent one of our internal auditors into the divisional office for a surprise audit and they discovered a paper trail that confirmed what I've just described. Also, our divisional president has admitted to what he did. He said he thought it was in the best interests of our shareholders, since the contract is a high-margin one, and that we could bear a few extra payments and still make a lot of money."

George was stunned. But Mark wasn't through yet.

"I've reviewed this matter with Mercedes and she advises me that we have at least three potential violations of the Foreign Corrupt Practices Act, not to mention the laws of Makite. First, under the FCPA, the $100,000 payment was clearly a payment in violation of the law, since it was made to a high-level government official to obtain new business and he clearly was the decision-maker for the relevant Makite agency. Secondly, our entertainment of the government official's family goes way beyond reasonable and promotional expenses and it also would be actionable under the FCPA. Finally, after getting past the anti-bribery provisions of the FCPA, we also have to worry about the so-called 'books and records' section of the FCPA. We clearly violated them when we attempted to disguise the payments under falsified accounts."

"Mark, how did you let this happen? I thought you had an effective ethics policy and that all of your officers had been extremely well trained to avoid problems just like this. Also, why wasn't it picked up earlier? Weren't these payments made some time ago?" George asked.

"George, I rely on my senior executives to assist me in enforcing these types of programs. In that regard, I have some even worse news...

"How could it be worse?" asked George.

197

"One of our principal players in helping me enforce our code of conduct has been Robert," Mark sighed.

"Granger, our COO?"

"Yes. Apparently he had a suspicion that one of our newly acquired companies, Orbitron, was using aggressive tactics in getting business in the foreign sector. He didn't follow up on his instincts, but later received the report from the auditors that there was trouble in the new Orbitron Division under the DFP umbrella. Instead of reporting it to me immediately, he decided he would take a couple of weeks to determine the facts and then forward his report to me.

"What he didn't know was that we were dealing with potential criminal conduct and various significant civil liability exposure and, perhaps, criminal sanctions for some of our officers."

"What was his explanation?" asked George.

"When I sat down with him and asked why he hadn't reported the matter, he said the facts were in a state of flux and he didn't want to prematurely alarm me. When I asked him whether he knew about the payments before they were made, he said that while he didn't endorse them, he probably had some basis to reasonably believe such payments were being made and that books and records were falsified to cover up the payments. It seems that he learned that our Orbitron division was going to obtain Makite business through a partially owned foreign subsidiary, even though the subsidiary wasn't the low bidder on the government contract."

"Mark, what are you going to do? It seems to me that you have little choice but to ask Robert for his resignation. While I think he's been a good executive for us, we've highlighted some of his weaknesses in our prior Board discussions. I'm afraid this problem may be caused by a lack of character on his part to stand up and bring this matter to our attention early enough so that we could attempt to do some additional damage control..."

"Slow down, George – I didn't have to ask him for his resignation. He came to see me early this week and tendered it. His position is that the bribe was paid on his watch and that there probably will be lawsuits and a potential criminal investigation. He's worried that his continued presence at DFP would be bad for shareholders, for our management group, and for the Board. Accordingly, he wants out.

"As you may know, Robert's wife, Meagan, and my wife are the best of friends. I rarely ask Melynda for business advice, but she has known the Grangers for a long time. When I went home to explain this to her, she urged me not to fire him.

"I pointed out that I wasn't firing him – but that I had to make a quick decision about accepting his resignation. She told me that I had to do what I needed to do but that she would be personally upset if I didn't try to rehabilitate Robert in some type of program whereby he would be sanctioned lightly but could remain with DFP. I told her that wasn't possible and that once he hadn't effectively handled his leadership position, I had to accept his resignation – and I had done so."

Without saying so, George was furious – about a number of things. First he was appalled that Mark didn't bring the matter to the Board immediately upon learning about it, although he was satisfied that Mark did not know about the misconduct until weeks after it occurred. Secondly, he believed Mark could have found a way to rehabilitate Robert and didn't actively pursue that alternative. But most of all, he was especially concerned because Mark didn't come to any key members of the Board to discuss his approach before he implemented it.   This was serious business.

"Mark, I must tell you, I am truly disappointed," George said. "Right now, I'm even thinking of resigning from the Board because I think this matter has been handled so poorly and it may have been my fault for not assisting you in putting together a better code of ethics and a comprehensive code of ethics program. We also should have a 'whistleblower arrangement' so that anyone who discovers this type of problem may easily go to a senior legal officer who decides how best to report the conduct and selects one or more Board members to be in the line of reporting. We should have done that a long time ago in the same way we've done so in a number of other companies with which I am familiar."

Mark expected George would be extremely concerned and emotional, since he also had known Granger for several years – but Mark had no idea George would be so intensely bent out of shape. On the other hand, he knew George was a good Director and wouldn't walk away from the problem, particularly if he was given an even stronger role on the Board. Mark already had spoken with the other Directors about George taking on a new role. This was the perfect time to tell George about it.

"It would trouble me greatly if you were to leave the Board," Mark said. "In fact, we have in mind a new, expanded role for you – that of Lead Director."

"I'm honored, but…"

"You should know it's a unanimous decision by the Board, if that will help you make up your mind. In the new role, you will, in effect, be a mini-Chairman and work with me on formulating the agenda for each meeting. Also, you will act as intermediary between the Board and me and work out corporate governance issues – and even operational issues like this one – as they arise. If the Board has trouble with me or they have trouble with one of our other Directors, you will be the conduit to raise those issues. We also propose to pay you an extra $50,000 in DFP stock a year for handling this new assignment." As Mark spoke, he watched George's face – and the longer he spoke, the more serious George became.

"Look, Mark, I'm not seeking an additional position on this Board. I already think we have enough committees and titles. Nonetheless, in view of the unanimous feeling of the Board, I will serve as the Lead Director – under certain conditions. We need to agree on a job description, although I think you've already covered most of that: formulate each Board agenda; act as an intermediary between the Board and the management group; and help set important policies in the area of corporate governance. If that is the proposal and you will agree that I won't have to carry a formal title, I will reluctantly go ahead with this reconfiguration – at least for a few months. We can re-evaluate it then."

Mark breathed a sigh of relief. He knew that George, while rational, could be difficult to deal with when he concluded information had been kept from him. In this particular instance, Mark had been able to head off what would have been a mini-disaster if George had left the Board at such a difficult time.

At that night's Board retreat dinner, matters began on an intense note. Nonetheless, Mark's charisma and his comedic ability relaxed the group. He said that since the Company was facing some uphill struggles, he felt it was time for his college fight song. To the delight of the group, he sang a splendid, raucous rendition – although he forgot a few words toward the end.

Mark's vocal performance was followed by a special slide show that had been assembled by the corporate communications group. It did a good job of combining some of the past 12 months' achievements at DFP with good-natured, but well-drawn, caricatures of the CEO and some of his idiosyncrasies, including a love for high-end Napa Valley wines and fast cars.

In his final toast that evening, Mark said he was pleased to report that George had accepted a new role on the Board as the Lead Director – but that he wanted to go incognito, not carry a formal title, and have no references to his title in shareholder documents. The other members of the Board applauded the announcement.

"I'd like to add – on a personal note – that I appreciate the Board's cooperation in difficult times. I'm convinced that at the next outing, matters will be more upbeat," Mark said. "Now, I've asked the waiters to bring in some cognac and cigars for those of you who might be interested."

George, who was sitting next to Joan, was wondering how she would react to this "old boys" approach. But he soon saw he had nothing to worry about when Joan rejected the cigars being proffered by the waiters and instead pulled out a small cigar case from her purse.

"H. Upmann 2000 Series Grand Robusto," Joan told George. "I wouldn't smoke anything else. Would you like one?"

CHAPTER 17

A SPECIAL COMMITTEE DEALS WITH A BRIBE AND THE CEO FACES THE BOARD
Hard Talk About Corporate Governance
(Third Quarter of Year 11)

Agenda for Committee Meeting

1. *Special Counsel introduced to Committee – Gen. Landry, Chairman*
2. *Special Counsel Reports to Committee Members concerning legal duties*
3. *Discussion of time and responsibility schedule and need for confidentiality*

In his new role as Lead Director, George wasted no time in addressing the bribery issues. After dinner, he asked Gen. Landry to chair a Special Committee to investigate the bribe and named Larry Lanski and Harry Thorpe as members of the Committee. He also asked Mercedes to arrange for an early morning meeting with special independent legal counsel to provide legal advice to the Committee.

Gen. Landry called the meeting of the Special Committee to order at 8 a.m., 90 minutes before the start of the last scheduled Board meeting of the offsite conference, and recognized Mercedes.

"I'm here for just a few minutes to introduce you to your outside legal counsel for the Special Committee, Henry Strong, of the firm of Strong, Black & Mason," she said. "Henry, who was selected by Paul Landry, is an expert in corporate governance matters and has handled alleged unlawful conduct issues for a number of companies here in town – especially when they involve senior officers. Henry, why don't you give us a little more about your background."

As Strong spoke, Larry listened carefully and concluded that this fellow knew what he was talking about and would help the Special Committee come to a rapid resolution of a difficult issue. Apparently, internal auditors already had concluded that the facts were relatively straightforward and that the bribe appeared to be an isolated payment. In other words, there were no systemic problems to address – DFP didn't have a widespread lack of integrity or a series of such payments.

"Aren't we really in a difficult situation here?" Gen. Landry asked. "If we find out that Rob Granger and his direct report made a bribery payment in the amount mentioned, isn't that a violation of the Foreign Corrupt Practices Act and a crime?"

"I think it's time for me to leave the meeting," Mercedes said as she rose from the table. "What you need is objective independent legal advice. If you need me, I will be available in the conference room next door."

'**N**ow that your General Counsel has left," said Strong, "let me just back up a bit before I answer your specific question and give you some general legal advice about this circumstance. As you know, you are directors of a corporation incorporated in Dakota and in that capacity have significant duties, including the duty to be diligent in investigating alleged unlawful conduct. You must become well informed and determine what the facts are. After you do so, then you should recommend appropriate action to the Board. Obviously you can't just sit on your hands pondering your next move.

"As has been noted, we are truly dealing with a criminal statute here and since DFP is a contractor for the United States government, there also could be ramifications for the Company's ability to do business with federal agencies in the future," Strong said.

"That could mean quite a hit for the bottom line," Lanski said. "We'd better do all we can to avoid that!"

"Right," said Strong. "Accordingly, I think we should work together to establish a fast-track time and responsibility for this Committee's activities and spell out how the Committee will organize itself. We also need to understand that once this matter is disclosed to the public, it may have a negative impact on the Company and its stock price – so you need to treat all of these matters as confidential, as I know you usually will do."

Strong worked with the Committee to lay out the schedule, which included extensive interviews with those who had been working with Granger and the divisional president who was charged with the alleged bribe.

Strong also said he had received some disquieting news. "Apparently, your General Counsel approached your divisional president, who seems to be responsible for the bribe. He said that he will not appear before this Committee at all, but, if he changes his mind, he'll only do so with his attorney at his side."

"I don't have any problem with that," Thorpe said.

"Neither do I, Harry," Strong replied. "Frankly, it is important that he have his attorney represent him. And I'll go one step further – the Company should pay for it, since we don't wish to have him pursue you and the Corporation at a later time for not providing him with adequate legal advice. In addition, in some respects, while he may be a semi-crook, our interests are parallel with his, as we need to discover what happened and whether there are any defenses to the apparent bribery payment."

"Yes, I've been thinking about that," Gen. Landry said. "Perhaps the Makite government official acted in an extortionate fashion."

"Perhaps," Strong said, "but I doubt that would be a defense in this case."

Gen. Landry turned toward the door when he heard a knock. It was time for the full Board meeting, so the Directors stood and moved down the hall, reading the agenda as they walked.

Agenda for Board Meeting

1. Call Board Meeting to order
2. Developments in Orbitron subsidiary operations
3. Resignation of Senior Officer
4. Possible Executive Session or other business

T he full Board meeting got underway on schedule at 9:30 with the members of the Special Committee coming in just before it began.

"I have some troubling news to report, which some of you already have heard about," Mark began. As he told all of the Board about the bribe and Granger's resignation, the good humor of the prior night quickly disappeared. Board members, particularly Judy, were angry with Mark.

"How could you have let controls get so far out of hand to permit a payment of this type being made?" she fumed.

Mark reached back in his reserve of energy, tough mindedness and diplomacy. (As one commentator once said, "a 'diplomat' is someone who makes you feel at home when he wishes you were"; Mark was in that mode.) Plus, he had worked out his remarks to the Board with George, who would follow Mark's comments with comments of his own.

"I'll be glad to address that later," said Mark, "But first, we have to deal with what we're facing: A corporate crisis. Fortunately, we've organized ourselves so as to use the Executive Committee as a crisis management committee and I also plan to involve that committee with the Special Committee to investigate this matter, and then deal with all of the ramifications.

"The Executive Committee will work with us to determine how best to disclose this bribery matter – first to the government and then to our shareholders and others – once we have it better defined, and also to work with us on how to establish controls that will help us avoid this type of problem in the future.

"I know that some of you think that I should have involved you earlier but, believe me, the facts for a matter of this type seem to change daily," he continued. "I thought it was important to get a relatively tight handle on what was going on here before I made a report to you and provided you with a recommendation.

"I also knew you would need outside counsel so Mercedes and Paul worked with Henry Strong to be sure he would be available this morning to meet with the Special Committee. I think all you who have met with him would agree that he is a strong legal counselor who can provide you with sound advice."

Hugh looked more and more concerned as Mark spoke. Finally, he interrupted the CEO. "Mark, in my view you aren't taking this matter seriously enough," Perry said. "We should have immediately reported this matter to the authorities and then conducted an investigation."

"Are you crazy?" asked Judy. "You don't go to a government agency until you've scoped out what the facts are, know the kind of investigation you're conducting and are able to provide a timetable to the government as to when you'll be able to give them a more comprehensive report. Once the government steps in and its own agents start conducting an examination, it can be a real witch hunt and put the Company in a much worse fix than it's already in. In my judgment, the Board should have been more active and conducted its own periodic review of the Code of Ethics and how it is operating in the foreign sector or I think we're all to blame," said Judy. (Hugh couldn't help thinking to himself: I remember Judy didn't even attend the last meeting because of a scheduling conflict with her non-profit Board meeting, which was involved in a highly visible charitable event for which she was the honoree. I don't think she's in any position to talk about what we should have done and when.)

"Mark," George said, "could you leave the room for a few minutes so we can talk among ourselves? I'd like to go into Executive Session."

While the term "Executive Session" meant different things to different people, in general, it meant to this Board that its members wanted to meet without any officer-director or current insider present. In recent years, some boards were starting to have executive session meetings at every board meeting – usually at the conclusion of the meeting. It allowed directors to talk among themselves on a candid basis about such matters as the progress of the Company, officer performance, strategic issues, agenda items that weren't being addressed to their satisfaction, or governance process issues, such as pre-board meeting packages being sent out late.

"I really don't see why it's necessary for all of you to meet without us," Mark said. "I realize you're somewhat upset about recent developments, but I think we could handle them on a more candid basis by meeting together. Nonetheless, I am going to accede to your wishes – and if you want such sessions in the future, I'm prepared to cooperate. But I hope you can hold them to a minimum." He left the meeting with a frown on his face.

After Mark left, George began: "I think we need to bring the emotions of the meeting down to a more civil level, and I also think we need to start thinking about how a good Board attacks a crisis.

"Generally, in times like these it is particularly important – if not critical – that we strongly back Mark, since he deserves this support," George said, while thinking to himself that Mark needs more work on enforcing internal controls and more discipline in how he deals with his people.

"A good Board does its best work in a time of crisis," he continued. "It's time for us to work out this situation. While it will involve some extra effort, I think we owe it to our shareholders to take hold of the problem – all along, trying to work closely with Mark."

"What about the COO position, George? What are we going to do there?" asked Joan.

"Well, that certainly is one of the mini-crises we now face," George said. "I've met with Mark and we both agree that a Special Interviewing Committee of the Board needs to be organized. Mark and I asked Larry to head the Committee and he has agreed to do so, working with me and Hugh."

"What kind of person will we be looking for to fill the position?" asked Alex.

"There's some disagreement there," George said. "While Mark fully supports the process, he and I had a pretty earthy discussion about what the criteria for the selection of the next COO ought to be. The ultimate establishment of the criteria will be a product of the initial efforts of the committee for your approval, but I think we are going to have a hang-up on one issue. I've told Mark how strongly I feel about the issue and I wanted to get input from all of you."

"Sure, George, what is it?" asked Gen. Landry.

"Mark thinks what we need from this search for the new Chief Operating Officer is an older, highly experienced candidate with vast operating experience. I told him in view of the recent downturn in the Company's profits and the rapidly changing industry, that we also must have a strong strategist, who, if necessary, could succeed Mark. Mark ultimately said he would do what the Board thought was best for the shareholders, but he clearly was troubled.

"I think we should delegate the drafting of the criteria for the Chief Operating Officer position to the CEO for final review by the Committee. Does everyone agree?" George asked. "It appears you do. Plus, I think Mark should draft the job description, but that the Committee itself must have the final word on that description and selection. Mark, himself, will be in charge of the search process, as usual."

Moving on to the next order of business, George announced that the Executive Committee would meet by telephone over the weekend to work out a specific crisis management plan concerning the bribery matter. He said he was glad the Board had authorized the Executive Committee to work in a crisis, since he expected this one would be highly fact-intensive, time-sensitive and thoroughly complex.

"I always think a Committee is the best way of handling this type of matter," he commented. "The full Board simply couldn't intensely address these kinds of circumstances on a practical and timely basis – especially since we're so geographically diverse these days."

Mark then was invited back into the room.

' **M**ark, we have decided to go with your recommendation and use the Executive Committee to work with you on the bribery matter," said George. "Regarding the criteria for the new Chief Operating Officer, you and I can discuss them after the meeting and be sure we'll both be satisfied. In view of the growth of the Company and the complexities it is facing, however, we're leaning toward a strong, mature manager – a strategist and a person who can work side-by-side with you on the ever-broadening front of day-to-day management challenges."

"George, I understand where the Board is coming from and will do my best to work with all of you," Mark said. "I want to say one thing, however, about this potential new Chief Operating Officer. While we may not totally agree on the criteria, I will accept any reasonable criteria we develop together. On the other hand, there has to be some good chemistry between the new COO and myself. If we can't work well together, there's no point in having a CEO. If you're trying to impose someone on me with whom I can't work, you'll have to choose between the two of us!"

"Mark, you know us well enough to know that we would never impose someone on you whom you thought could not be a 'partner' with you," said George. "At the same time, we need someone bright and tough-minded enough to challenge you from time to time to be sure that all of us are on the right track with our strategy, plans and decisions, which, after all, must be made in the best interest of our shareholders."

While there were a few bruised egos in the room and even some bad feelings, the Board was still intact when the meeting was adjourned.

James R. Ukropina

From the Dakota Business Journal:

Gregory, DFP Show Survivor Instinct

By Maria Bartels

Dakota Business Journal Columnist

NEWS ANALYSIS

It's been a tough few months for DFP, our largest company. First, there was that nasty bribe business that made Dakota City residents far more aware of the Makites than they ever before had reason to be. That, of course, forced the resignation of DFP's COO, Robert Granger. Then, there was the worry – both inside and outside the company – that it might have been just the tip of the proverbial iceberg.

But, as the sound bytes roared and the headlines screamed, DFP CEO Mark Gregory made a calculated decision to stand firm: The bribe, he told anyone and everyone who would listen, was an isolated incident. Our local TV station played the clip over and over again of him saying "This problem isn't systemic – I'll stake my reputation on that!" According to sources in the securities industry, he met repeatedly with shareholders and securities analysts to reinforce his position and said both internal and external investigations would prove it.

Lucky for him, he appears to have been right.

Apparently the irregularities were caused by one bad apple who had become a DFP Division President a few years ago but, in Gregory's words, "clearly didn't have the judgment and perspective to serve in that position." That executive also turned out to be a former CPA who knew his way around financial reporting requirements and was able to "paper over" the bribe for at least a few months. He finally admitted his guilt and confirmed that he had acted alone.

Meanwhile, according to a reliable source, the Audit Committee of DFP's Board of Directors reviewed and strengthened internal managerial controls as well as accounting and financial reporting practices, especially in the foreign sector, in hopes of avoiding future problems. At the same time, a comprehensive crisis management plan was adopted for future crises.

So, now, DFP is again able to focus its attention on its operations.

And, most important, Mark Gregory advised this reporter that it appears that the search for a new COO is nearing an end. After Granger's resignation, there was a lot of internal corporate discussion about the kind of COO the company needed, and, through another source at a headhunting firm, it now looks like the leading candidate – Andrew Sommers, a high corporate achiever at several companies, whose credentials nearly match Gregory's – has the strategy/operations mix they've been looking for. A company spokesman said that a DFP press release will be issued as soon as a new COO is elected.

It's unclear yet whether Sommers will come on board – sources say he's holding out for a significant compensation package – but if he does, he can expect a continuing roller-coaster of a ride at the state's largest-and-still-growing conglomerate.

#   #   #

CHAPTER 18

THE AUDIT COMMITTEE AND FINANCIAL REPORTING

To Reserve, or Not to Reserve?

(Second Quarter of Year 12)

Agenda for Committee Meeting

1. *Introductory Comments by Officers, including CFO, Chief Accounting Officer, General Counsel, Internal Auditor, Independent Auditors concerning closing of year-end financial statements and special issues, if any, arising in connection with year-end closing of books*
2. *Review of draft audited financial statements*
3. *Discussion with auditors about independence of firm and comments about financial statements*
4. *Discussion with CFO and other Officers about financial statements*
5. *Discussion of major year-end proposed adjustments or changes to certain items in financial statements*
6. *Executive session with Independent Auditors*
7. *Executive session with Internal Auditor*
8. *Executive session with CFO*
9. *Executive Session among Audit Committee members only*
10. *Final Meeting with CFO*
11. *Committee to authorize recommendation of financial statements for inclusion in DFP's 10-K*

F rank Alworth, Chairman of the Audit Committee and a well-known investment advisor in his day job, reconvened the meeting after a recess. The Committee already had spent more than four hours going over year-end financial statements and disclosure documents. Although he was skilled at reviewing financial statements and related material, the audit committee process was a rigorous one for him – not to mention the others.

The Audit Committee agenda definitely was a full one. First, the CFO had discussed year-end results, carefully going over the profit-and-loss statement, the balance sheet, the cash flow statement, and the footnotes to the proposed financial statements, as well as the Management Discussion and Analysis Section of the 10-K Report ("MD&A"). They also discussed a relatively new requirement under which the CEO and CFO had to certify to the accuracy of the financial statements.

The members of the Audit Committee had extensive questions about how certain accounting adjustments in the financial statements were made at year-end, especially concerning the recognition of revenues and booking some additional reserves – both traditional sources of trouble. They also had discussed with the independent auditing firm that firm's independence from DFP, in accordance with the SEC rules. Since the audit firm had been doing some tax-related work, one Director expressed a concern about all future non-audit services being approved by the Chairman of the Audit Committee prior to being undertaken by the audit firm. All agreed that this approach would be the best practice and the Committee immediately had voted in favor of requiring such approval.

The Audit Committee elected to defer some important issues until the end of the meeting. The Committee reviewed with the General Counsel her year-end report concerning pending litigation and regulatory proceedings. The internal Auditor reviewed with the Audit Committee his findings concerning internal control weaknesses and certain other issues discovered during the last three months of the year's internal audit activities. The General Counsel also reported on arrangements with third parties, such as commission agents and joint ventures in the foreign sector, in order to assure that no additional problems had arisen during the course of the year under the Foreign Corrupt Practices Act.

Then, it was CFO Raines' turn again. "At our last Audit Committee meeting, we discussed some highly important issues and I wanted to give you a follow-up report," Raines said. "As you'll recall, we had a very lengthy discussion and then made some managerial changes here at DFP due to some problems with our financial reporting and audits.

"We did a lousy job in a couple of respects and didn't have the kind of backup through our independent auditing firm that we would have expected. As a result, DFP had to restate its financial statements for a consecutive three-year period ending two years ago. While the changes were large enough to require restatements, they didn't involve amounts that were all that material. Nonetheless, as a result of those restatements, a number of our lenders have demanded we employ tighter financial systems and controls. As a result, we have hired a new Internal Auditor with experience both at one of the large independent auditing firms – not ours – and with another substantial company. He assures us that those kinds of matters will never occur on his watch."

"I'm not sure anyone can make that kind of promise and keep it, but I'm glad to hear he's going to try," Frank said.

"Yes, it's good for all of us, Frank. Meanwhile, as a result of our restatements, we also are now under an informal review – but not an investigation – by the Securities and Exchange Commission for inadequate financial reporting and insufficient related-party disclosure. In particular, we've been criticized for poor financial reporting of some of our derivative transactions, as our reporting was not totally consistent with the relatively new financial reporting and accounting principles. This is the case, even though our auditors had reviewed all of our journal entries, as well as the final presentation in our financial statements and footnotes.

"Some of the most significant criticism came from parties who charge that we have spent too much time with some relatively small and exotic off-balance sheet transactions which, they claim, we didn't disclose well enough. They also complain that we have a few equity incentive plans with affiliated partnerships and joint ventures that are too rich and that were poorly disclosed. Although we believe that all those plans were fully justified and approved by shareholders – and ultimately will increase shareholder value – we made a mistake by not placing a 'cap' or 'ceiling' on how much a lower-level executive could make through one of these affiliated partnerships."

"Are we talking about a lot of money, Geoff?" asked Frank.

"I should say so," said Geoff. "Last year one of the senior officers in one of our subs made even more than Mark did. Ultimately, we disclosed that fact in our executive compensation table in our annual meeting proxy statement. Actually, our counsel had said it was a close call for disclosure because that officer might not be regarded as a senior executive officer of the parent corporation, thereby excusing disclosure – but we thought that was too 'cute' a defense for non-disclosure.

"As you also know, at this time our stock price is headed south rather sharply and this fellow's bonus has gone into the stratosphere. Accordingly, all hell may break loose at the Annual Meeting. Naturally, we're going to have another Audit Committee meeting next month to go over all of these issues."

"Next month is not going to be soon enough," said Larry. "I'm asking that you prepare a status report with all of your recommendations and current action steps about these issues and have that to us in the next 10 days. Even though these Audit Committee meetings seem interminable, we should meet again in about two weeks to be sure that everybody is on the right track and the appropriate curative steps are being taken."

(At this point, Larry slipped a note to Joan: "We've already gone five hours and we've hardly started to discuss the really important issues. I'm afraid this meeting may never end!")

Then came one of the more difficult issues. In that earlier discussion with management and the auditors, the committee had learned there was a disagreement between the independent auditors and DFP's financial staff about the dollar amount of a financial reserve that should be taken to recognize a potential contingent liability for various litigation that had been filed against the Company, its officers and Directors with respect to the bribery matter. As usual, the independent auditing firm called for a relatively large reserve and management was resisting establishing a reserve at all. But, if a reserve had to be established, management took the position that it should be only 50 percent of the amount suggested by the independent auditors.

"Well, let me see, my colleagues," Alworth said. "We have the responsibility not only to review financial statements but also to consider any disagreements between management and our independent auditors with respect to significant issues just like this reserve issue. With the blessings of Mercedes, I went out and hired my own lawyer, who's an expert not only on corporate law but also is a strong CPA. He told me the following: If you're a director, always insist on conservative financial reporting. If independent auditors suggest a larger reserve and management opposes it, if we are truly in doubt, it is important that we recognize expenses early and defer income until later unless it is clearly earned. Of course, we still should listen to management carefully.

"I asked my lawyer to look at the public records about this bribe and he says a larger accounting reserve is absolutely called for. He believes that not only will the responsible officer be fined but also that the Company will have to pay significant fines, both here and in Makite. That's because not only did DFP's agent pay a bribe in violation of the Foreign Corrupt Practices Act, but also because that very same officer tried to engage in a cover-up by cooking the books. He expects the Justice Department will want to make an example of DFP and I agree with him. Accordingly, I propose that we support the auditors and have them book larger reserves. What do you think?"

The other members of the Audit Committee listened to management's position on why the reserve should be a relatively small one.

"It seems to us," said Geoff, "that in doling out penalties and fines the government and courts will take into account that DFP is a first-time offender when it comes to a violation of the Foreign Corrupt Practices Act. Clearly, we had one renegade employee who took action – paying bribes – without any authorization. Our biggest problem was that our COO didn't address the matter adequately, but he paid dearly by having to resign from his office.

"We also think that under the Federal Sentencing Guidelines criteria, DFP had an 'effective' compliance program in place – an important fact. As most of you know, to be 'effective' a program doesn't have to be perfect. Also, when senior management learned of the violation, we immediately retained outside legal counsel and shortly thereafter made a report about the facts to both the U.S. Justice Department and to the Securities and Exchange Commission."

"That may be the case," said Frank, "but DFP's management didn't take as prompt an action as some thought it should. Also, the bribe was certainly a large amount."

"All true," said Geoff, "although the bribe was made through a subsidiary in which we only have a minority equity position. Ordinarily, we might be off the hook for such a payment – except, in these circumstances, admittedly our agent was following the guidance or non-guidance of an officer or a principal here in Dakota City. So we don't have a defense whereby our government might not have jurisdiction over a payment made through a minority foreign subsidiary. At the same time, however, the fact that the payment was made on a more indirect basis might, our counsel says, lower the amount of a fine and, therefore, a necessary accounting reserve; we continue to think a reserve of $400,000 is in order. We also believe this matter should be settled and behind us in the next few months. Finally, whatever reserve we set up, it may be discoverable in litigation or in regulatory proceedings by plaintiffs' lawyers or the government. Therefore, the establishment of a large reserve may be inviting a self-fulfilling prophecy of a large liability."

After that speech had been made, representatives of management were asked to leave the room.

The Audit Committee then met privately with the senior partner of the independent auditing firm. After that, he was asked to leave and the three members of the Committee met privately.

Alworth led off with comments about the process and the substance of the issues at hand. "Not only did this meeting take a long time but, insofar as I'm concerned, we didn't get these materials soon enough to leave any reasonable time to review them," he said. "I don't know about you, but I find it difficult to give careful attention to more than 200 pages of documents to be discussed at this Audit Committee meeting on Friday morning when I only received them in my office on Thursday afternoon.

"I realize these are fast-moving times, but when you have to look at the report from the audit firm to management, materials from management sent to our committee, the financial statements, the footnotes, the management discussion and analysis and related materials, it is incredibly difficult to do a job that I'm comfortable with in such a short period of time," he added.

"What do you suggest, Frank?" asked Larry.

"First, I'll be talking to Mark about delaying the publication of the financial statements next year to provide us with adequate time for our Audit Committee to make a careful review of the draft statements and related material. But now, it looks like we are down to one issue – and that is, what should be the amount of the accounting reserves?"

After lengthy deliberation, the CFO was asked to join the meeting and to discuss an approach through which a larger accounting reserve would be taken, increasing the litigation reserve from $800,000 to $1.6 million. The CFO ultimately acquiesced in that position and, as it turned out, it was a sound one.

As a final item, the Committee asked that the DFP compliance program be reviewed by outside legal counsel once again. Since DFP was now a large contractor to the U.S. Government, it was subject to the federal government's whistleblower program. Under that program, adopted around the time of the Civil War, whistleblowers could be awarded significant fees for blowing the whistle on corrupt conduct. The compliance program needed to deal with that eventuality and put out small fires before they became big ones, said Larry to the CFO. Nonetheless, the CFO understood that compliance review had to be a top priority. In fact, he was becoming impatient with the Board. He was wondering if the Board members were more concerned about shareholders or their own backsides.

James R. Ukropina

The following is an excerpt from the next DFP Proxy Statement:

The Board of Directors authorized a Special Committee to investigate an alleged bribe paid by one of the officers of the Company to a government official in Makile. The Company engaged outside counsel as well as independent auditors to work directly with the Special Committee to review the matter. After a comprehensive investigation, the Committee concluded that while it could not establish that an unlawful bribe had been paid, it was sufficiently concerned that it recommended to the Board that the relevant officer be terminated.

The terminated officer, Jonathan Henry, was not among the senior corporate officers of DFP but was affiliated with Orbitron, a corporation acquired by DFP. Special Counsel to the Special Committee prepared a report for the Committee that ultimately was delivered to the Board. The Board concluded it was apparent that the alleged bribe was not made as one payment but in a series of payments which, in and of themselves, may have included a few so-called grease payments under the Foreign Corrupt Practices Act and, therefore, those payments would have been lawful.

Nonetheless, the payments were made without the authorization of the Chief Executive Officer of the Company and its General Counsel, which had been required as part of the Company's policy for any questionable payments in the foreign sector. Accordingly, Mr. Henry was terminated without a severance payment. Mr. Henry has sued DFP for unlawful termination and also alleged that others in the Company violated the Foreign Corrupt Practices Act over a number of years. The Special Committee, which already had met for more than 50 hours in examining this matter, has resumed its meetings and is now investigating those allegations.

From the Dakota Business Journal:

New Head Named for Dakota Foundation

DAKOTA CITY – Roy Robinson, who has headed the Fargo Foundation for the past five years, has been named the new Executive Director of the Dakota Foundation.

"I look forward to joining the Dakota Foundation and following up on the magnificent work done by Walker Chalmers," Robinson said. "His record of grants to encourage medical research and development in technology is stunning."

Many of those technological developments funded by Chalmers and the Dakota Foundation caused the incubation of new startup companies in Dakota in which the Foundation maintains major – and quite successful – investments. Based on his ability to recognize such potential, Chalmers was recruited as Executive Director of a large New York City foundation and the search for his successor has taken nearly nine months.

The tax-exempt Dakota Foundation, a 501(c)(3) charitable organization, was originally funded by DFP, Inc., after its Board authorized seed capital in the form of a cash gift and a large block of DFP stock. While the Foundation doesn't operate under the name of DFP, it is well known that DFP originally caused its formation and, through it, has been a strong supporter of social projects as well as medical and technological innovation.

CHAPTER 19

THE DAKOTA FOUNDATION BOARD
Is It a Sin to Raise Money?
(Second Quarter of Year 12)

Partial Agenda for Foundation Board Meeting:

Agenda Item No. 4: Discussion of nature and timing of Annual Fund Raiser

Not only was the Dakota Foundation one of DFP's pride-and-joys, but also it was a large shareholder of DFP. The number of shares with which DFP had funded the Foundation now represented about three percent of the Company's outstanding stock. Otherwise, DFP's formal involvement was relatively minimal; three of its Board members – Stan Towler, Judy Moran and Harry Thorpe – also served on the nonprofit Board but they accounted for a minority of the board members. DFP also had started to curtail direct charitable contributions except to colleges and universities that were "feeder" schools for new DFP employees and to local charities in cities where DFP had important facilities. Some of DFP's shareholders applauded this more restrictive corporate giving program because they thought charitable gifts could be better made by them directly rather than through the Company.

Since DFP had discontinued its dividend payments in order to provide more capital for reinvestment, the Foundation had to do more and more of its own fund-raising for its annual working capital through community events – and it wasn't particularly happy about it. But the Foundation staff was fairly happy with Geoffrey Raines, the DFP Chief Financial Officer who also served as a financial advisor for the Foundation. He had invested Foundation funds in some local start-up companies, and while one of them "went south," three others had huge profits and the Foundation's assets rose to more than $60 million.

Rounding out the Foundation Board were seven local community leaders. While the Foundation seemed to be prospering financially, its Board wasn't – at least when it came to leadership. For months, there was a sharp division on the Board as to who should be the Chairman, and finally, Harry Thorpe was elected. He promptly started an executive search process for a new Foundation executive director. The search resulted in Roy Robinson being recruited away from the Fargo Foundation to serve as the Executive Director for the Dakota Foundation and to run the group's day-to-day affairs.

Right now, Harry was regretting that appointment.

"I tell you," Roy was saying to the Board, "this is a great way to raise money! Casino nights and casino weekends are all the rage – I was reading an article in *Fundraising Quarterly* just the other day about it..."

"Roy, I'm not so sure," Harry said. He looked around the room for support. The Board had a relatively typical membership lineup for many local foundations:

- Two women who had been community leaders and former friends, but who now didn't get along with each other.
- A distinguished academic who, while brilliant, had a difficult time making a short statement about any Board agenda item.
- A local businessman, who, while highly successful, couldn't understand why the Foundation didn't make large distributions to charities while it also grew its capital.

- A wealthy owner of a local car dealership who himself made large gifts to the Foundation each year but who rarely attended any Board meetings.
- And, finally, the arrogant grandson of one of the community's local leaders, who was blessed with more money than civility. Some of the other Board members wanted to replace the grandson with a new Director, but his family was such a large contributor to the Foundation that the other Directors were reluctant to do so.

"I'm telling you, Harry, it's a great idea! This year's fundraising event should be 'Monte Carlo Saturday' followed by a silent auction."

"Just a minute, Roy," said one of the community leaders, Lorraine Sanders. "As you probably know, I'm a strong Baptist and think that kind of gambling event borders on being a sin. Why can't we have line dancing or a polka night or something exciting like that to generate a large turnout?"

Her antagonist was ready for battle. "You may remember, Lorraine," said Helene Truman, "that we tried something like that about 10 years ago, and the turnout was almost non-existent. The fact is, we have to offer something that is really exciting to our usual supporters as well as to the young people in this town, or this event will be a giant catastrophe."

"I would be happy to conduct a research study on what other nonprofit corporations do concerning their annual charitable events and then supply you with an extensive report at our next Board meeting," said the academician, Randall Leonard. "I could list all of the possibilities and accompany each with a set of pros and cons for various competing events, supply you with potential budgets and then give you an estimated return on our costs and expenses. Then we could meet a few more times, get down to a short list of alternative events and finally decide on which one we would like to support."

"Thank you, Dr. Leonard," said the local businessman, Casey McCord, "but as you know, this event has to be announced in the next few weeks, and by the time you finish that process we will be well into next year. Accordingly, I'm going to support Monte Carlo Saturday and ask for a vote on this matter. Plus, I'm still waiting for that report you promised me six months ago on how we can increase our charitable contributions..."

"Now, Casey, let's slow down," said Harry, going into "Chairman" mode. "We don't have to vote on this matter right away – but you're right, we don't have much time to study the matter, either."

Tom Ford, the wealthy car dealer, tried to cut to the chase. "As far as I'm concerned, this discussion is a giant waste of time. We all know that Monte Carlo Saturday will be extraordinarily successful for us and," taking a quick glance at Lorraine, "that is hardly a sin.

"Let me make this offer: I'm prepared to underwrite all – and I mean all – the expenses for a Monte Carlo night or a Monte Carlo weekend, because if we take any more time discussing this issue I'm going to lose a lot of business opportunities down at my dealership. Therefore, it's less expensive for me to be the underwriter than to wade through a lengthy Board meeting. I think highly of all of you, but if railroads were run this way, they would be bankrupt before you know it." (That last comment prompted Judy to write a quick note to Stan: "I thought most of them already were!")

"We really appreciate your willingness to underwrite our event, Tom," said Lorraine, "but perhaps we can take just a few more minutes to discuss other alternatives – one of which might be to show some classic films from the archives of one of the leading production companies."

"Old movies? I don't think so. Frankly, I don't need more time to discuss this matter," Tom insisted. "If you want me to be the underwriter on the terms that I've outlined, I will be. If not, I have to leave for another business meeting."

227

Harry realized he had to move the meeting along. "In view of these circumstances, I would like to call for the vote. All those in favor of Monte Carlo Saturday, please say, 'Aye.' Do any of you not favor the event?"

Lorraine sat there with her arms crossed and a sour look on her face. Everyone else had their hands raised or were nodding in approval.

"Okay, duly noted," Harry said. "Monte Carlo Saturday is approved with only one Director abstaining." He looked over and saw Helene beaming in approval, silently giving a "thumbs-up" to Tom.

The fundraiser was a huge success. Tom donated the hottest sports car from his showroom floor as the grand prize for a raffle, and it received a lot of attention from the local citizens. Even Mark purchased a pocketful of lottery tickets for the car (he could imagine all the legal implications Mercedes might have brought up if he'd actually won!), but it wasn't his lucky night – or then, maybe it was. Also, a large, unexpected contribution was made to the Foundation by local heir Ellsworth LaPeer, thereby insuring his grandson yet another term of survival on the Board.

It was the beginning of several successes for Roy as the Foundation's new Director. Over the next several months, he was able to win grants from numerous funding sources, which meant the Foundation relied less on DFP for financial support. In fact, the Board's majority agreed that it no longer would actively solicit funds from DFP; to honor its long association with the Foundation, however, DFP agreed to make additional contributions to the Foundation over the next few years before discontinuing its support.

And, notwithstanding the seemingly petty discussion about the fundraising event, the Board was deadly serious and highly professional with respect to authorizing grants for important social and scientific projects. It was unified in attempting to assure itself that all of the grants were cost-effective, and for the advancement of scientific projects and improvement of the community. For example, the Foundation Board had received a recent report concerning important biological research done with respect to a strain of corn that could be grown in difficult environments with a relatively high yield. Also, one of its grants caused a report to be issued by a Dakota State professor with respect to potential liver damage from the dangers of a highly popular fast food.

On critical issues of nonprofit board governance, the Foundation board also got high marks. It regularly reviewed the Foundation's principal purpose, its current strategy to achieve that purpose, and the cash flow being generated to fund operations. Board members also reviewed compensation decisions carefully. They wanted to attract and retain the right staff people. Also, counsel advised them that an authorization of excess compensation could result in fines on directors under applicable federal law.   In short, the Foundation was an important "value-added" factor to the state's progress in science, technology, medicine and other fields.

CHAPTER 20

FACING MULTIPLE CORPORATE CRISES
When It Rains, It Pours
(Fourth Quarter of Year 12)

Agenda for Executive Committee Meeting

1. *Environmental issues.*
2. *Possible product recall program.*
3. *Other business.*

During the last Board retreat, Mark had presented a list of 18 specific crises that DFP could face. Now, one of them – No. 7, environmental pollution – was no longer hypothetical. The heat was on.

As the Executive Committee came into the meeting room, Mark was pleased the Board had delegated to this group the initial handling of any corporate crisis. That step had been taken because a crisis is always time-sensitive, fact-intensive and extraordinarily demanding in terms of the amount of focus and time that would have to be involved in order to come up with a suitable strategy. On the committee were George Hartfield, Paul Landry, Larry Lanski and Mark.

In order to help the Executive Committee understand the dynamics and history of the crisis, Mark briefly reviewed DFP's acquisition a few years earlier of Burton Products, whose plant had been the focus of an environmental pollution story in the Sunday edition of the Dakota Eagle.

Burton's top product, manufactured at that plant, was a dietary supplement called "Tough Athlete." Now known as

"DFP's Tough Athlete," it had become very popular with teenage athletes. The manufacturing facility was on the banks of the Placid River, upstream from a popular and pristine recreational area in the northern part of the state. A number of factories of other large companies also were situated along its shores.

DFP's management had been extremely impressed with the quality and environmental safety of the manufacturing facility at the time Burton Products was acquired. Since then, however, there had been some warning signals that pollutants were being deposited into the river, but it was unclear whether the DFP factory was responsible for them as opposed to another factory upstream. However, according to the article in the Sunday paper, an expert in water quality for "Keep Dakota Clean" – a local affiliate of "Greenpeace" – identified special lubricants coming from the DFP factory as a significant source of the recently discovered pollution. In the article, one of DFP's large investors, a so-called "green mutual fund," had demanded immediate closure of the DFP factory until the problem could be resolved.

After listening to Mark's explanation of the situation, the Executive Committee weighed the alternative strategies for dealing with the issue, ranging from calling for both internal and external investigations to shutting down the facility immediately. It became clear after two hours, though, that more information was needed from the company's onsite inspectors, who were going through the plant with a fine-tooth comb, so the committee members agreed it would be best to reconvene the meeting at 10 a.m. Tuesday. In the meantime, it approved the issuance of a corporate response expressing deep concern over the problem and assuring that DFP was working swiftly to determine how best to deal with it.

Mark was exceedingly concerned about the potential factory closure, since the products manufactured at the former Burton facility were some of DFP's most successful – not to mention that they all had an extremely high profit margin. He got little sleep on Monday night as he pondered the crisis options. Then, early Tuesday morning, he got what he later referred to as the "wakeup call from Hell."

He immediately recognized Mercedes' calm, business-like voice on the other end of the line and knew she wasn't likely to be calling him at 6 a.m. with good news.

"Mark, I'm sorry to wake you so early," she said.

"That's okay, Mercedes. What now?"

"It's bad – I just received notice that two teen-agers in Illinois who used 'Tough Athlete' have died."

"My God! What...?"

"Two other teenagers are in a hospital in that same area – but it appears they may recover, due to early action by attending paramedics."

"Get me up to speed quickly. What happened?"

"Apparently someone put poison in the bottles – we're still trying to sort it out."

"What's been done so far?"

"Just some initial fact-finding – and it's the first glimmer of relatively good news, if there can be such a thing in this situation. Our head of quality control got there quickly and visited the local nutrition store where the kids purchased the products. He believes someone injected a poisonous substance into, at most, only a few bottles containing the supplement. Those who died or became ill all had purchased the bottles at the same store – and we haven't heard any other reports of deaths or injuries."

"Get me as much additional information as you can before the 10 a.m. Executive Committee meeting. And I want you there, too, of course!" Mark said as he bolted out of bed.

As he was getting dressed, he pulled out the list of crises, a copy of which he kept in his wallet. Sure enough, he was right. DFP was now facing two of the worst in a long list – No. 4 and No. 7, a product defect and an environmental pollution problem – and both of them at the same time! Damn, thought Mark, his father taught him that problems and crises come in bunches – just like bananas – and the old guy was right.

'So," Mark told the Executive Committee when it reconvened that morning at 10, "it appears that some real sicko injected poison into the bottles with a microscopic hypodermic needle punched through the sealant – it doesn't look like we were responsible. Still, we have almost 60,000 bottles of the supplement on shelves throughout the country, retailing at $30 per bottle. And, more than $12 per bottle was expected to be clear profit. What should we do?"

"Mark, I don't think we have any choice but to issue a press release, largely following the draft you gave us," George said. "We should express our sincere and profound regret and sadness about the deaths and the illness of our customers. We should announce the initiation of an immediate investigation into both the pollution allegations and the nature and scope of the product poisoning. After all, you were the one who said that without prompt action the hard-earned reputation of DFP could be shattered in a matter of a few days. Also, we have to remember that a DFP product – doctored or not – has killed two young persons and may kill others. And, we have a plant on the river that is now looking like it's polluting our state, and some of our investors are threatening to dump their stock."

Gen. Landry added, "It seems to me that the next issues will be whether the plant should be shut down during the investigation and whether we should adopt a total recall program for 'Tough Athlete.' Let me warn you that I've been through similar issues before and there is a real tendency for a CEO to unduly 'walk on eggs' because overly conservative legal counsel doesn't want the CEO to admit any responsibility for the problem."

"That's true," George said. "At the same time, there is a lot of potential liability here."

"I know it's hot news in the legal community, too," Harry said. "My partner told me that a buddy of his at one of the large plaintiffs' law firms here is threatening a DFP shareholder class action suit against you and the Board on the basis that you haven't been doing an adequate job of compliance with health and safety regulations. Oh, and he added that the entire Board should be held liable to shareholders under the *Caremark* case."

"I guess that's to be expected," Mark said. "But we can't worry about that now. First, let me address the pollution question. I visited our plant this morning and it seems there's only one potential source of pollution – and it could be addressed and repaired in a matter of a few weeks. My instincts are to shut down the factory and correct the problem, even though I realize that will cost us hundreds of thousands of dollars in lost revenue.

"Regarding the product recall, here are my instincts: Given the Company's long record of first-rate quality control, we shouldn't be held responsible for one or two poisoned bottles. Nonetheless, it is pretty clear that we might have done a better job of placing a better sealant on the Tough Athlete bottle so when it was opened it would be apparent that someone already had tampered with it."

"As Directors, shouldn't we go a little more slowly in deciding what we should do?" Larry asked. "I worry that if we ultimately conclude that a third party really was involved and move too hastily, the recall would have been unnecessary."

"Maybe so," George said, "but in dealing with crises there are two types of parties – the quick and the dead – and only one is successful." Uncharacteristically for him, George punctuated his remarks by pounding his fist on the table. He continued: "The speed of our response is critical!"

Mark continued to listen carefully and pondered the alternatives. This was a particularly complex period for the Company, since its profits had been slipping, and the stock price, again, was declining. Nonetheless, he knew that he had to remove short-term profit considerations from these discussions and attempt to do the right thing in the right way. Then, for the Board's sake, he should be sure to document their diligence through the Board's minutes.

"I've asked a few other experts to join us this afternoon to help us make sure we cover all the bases," Mark said. "Let's see what they have to say." He buzzed for Barbara, who led them into the room.

The team included a prominent medical expert; an in-house lawyer who specialized in product liability; an environmental lawyer from an outside law firm who also was a distinguished chemical engineer and had handled similar matters for large companies; DFP's Vice President of Corporate Communications; and a Senior Vice President from the Company's external financial public relations firm. Mercedes and Geoffrey already were in the Boardroom, and for various reasons, the General Counsel reminded the group that the upcoming discussion was privileged under the attorney-client doctrine.

After the committee had heard the experts, the meeting was interrupted by a call for Mark from the offices of DFP's financial public relations firm in New York City. Mark listened for a minute and then put Tony Darling, that firm's representative, on the speakerphone in the Boardroom.

"Mark, I thought you and your Board members should know that your stock price is going south quickly on heavy volume," Darling said. "An unscrupulous short seller has floated a rumor that the pollution problem is far greater than reported. He says clean-up costs will be in the range of tens of millions of dollars and will be followed by a serious class action suit for inattention to health and safety regulations by the officers and the Board.

"It is important that the Company take a firm stance on this matter shortly, and, if at all possible, attempt to announce a range estimate of the financial cost for fixing these problems," Darling concluded. With some gallows humor, he added that DFP shouldn't announce that any costs the Company might incur could be tax-deductible; one large corporation had done so in the past, only to see special legislation introduced by a congressman to block the deduction.

No one saw the humor in the story, as a chill came over the room. George, knowing that no CEO could be ready to make a definitive recommendation in the circumstances, wanted to give

Mark some time. "In my view, the best thing for us to do would be to permit Mark to meet further with his experts and come up with a program and press release that he can recommend to the full Board in a telephonic Board meeting tonight..."

"How about early tomorrow morning, George?" Mark asked. "We could finalize the press release then, and ask for a short suspension in the trading of our stock until the press release is issued."

"First thing in the morning would be fine, Mark."

Also, George suggested that Board members lean heavily on management in crafting the solutions to the pollution and product recall problems, as well as in how those solutions should be presented to the press. "Nothing is worse than having a whole Board or a group of its members prepare a press release," George said. "That's a big invitation for another paralysis by committee."

The phone rang again and Mark picked it up. He listened for about a minute before hanging up.

"One of the hospitalized teenagers has died," Mark said. "And, talk about politicians kicking us when we're down – apparently our friend the Governor just held a press conference calling us 'kid-killers.'" His somber look wasn't lost on the Committee members.

"Let's adjourn now, so Mark and his group can get to work," George said. He rose, and as he walked past Mark to leave the room, he sympathetically patted him on the shoulder.

The next day, the DFP Corporate Communications Department issued the following press release:

DAKOTA CITY – DFP Chief Executive Officer Mark Gregory today announced that DFP has temporarily shut down its production facility on the Placid River until it can resolve the issues of whether its manufacturing process produced adulterations in a leading dietary supplement called "DFP's Tough Athlete" and whether the facility was causing environmental pollution.

"There is clear and convincing evidence," said Mr. Gregory, "that DFP's Tough Athlete product is safe and that three teenagers who died in Illinois after taking the dietary supplement each had consumed Tough Athlete pills from a single bottle of the product that clearly had been tampered with by a third party.

"DFP expresses its profound regret and sadness concerning the deaths and illnesses occasioned by the consumption of one of our most popular products," Mr. Gregory said. "While an early investigation suggests that the product was, in fact, tampered with by a third party and that no further problems should result from the product, until we engage in comprehensive analysis, the product will not be marketed. The Company also has decided that it will do an even better job of making its products tamper-proof, so that a consumer will know if a bottle or container of the product has been altered prior to opening it.

"DFP is fully insured for matters of this type and the cost of the recall will be largely covered by DFP's product liability insurance policy," Mr. Gregory continued. "We also have established financial reserves for health hazards relating to DFP's product manufacturing facilities. The amount of our current reserve will cover anticipated modifications in our production facility on Placid River."

Mr. Gregory also said DFP plans to augment its budget for its health and safety program for both its customers and employees. In addition, the Company has formed a new Board

James R. Ukropina

committee to provide oversight with respect to that program and has retained legal counsel to insure that the program is in compliance with all applicable laws and regulations.

Once the Street learned of the Company's position on the shutdown of the Placid River facility and its ample insurance coverage, the DFP stock price increased by 5 percent. Securities analysts not only were impressed with the definitive action taken by management and the Board but also were heartened by learning of the insurance coverage and financial reserves that had been in place.

Even Gov. Grover Hill, who had been critical of the Company when he first uttered that DFP's management consisted of a bunch of "kid killers," reversed his position. "I have just been informed that a sick individual has been arrested in Illinois and he admitted to tampering with DFP's Tough Athlete product," Gov. Hill said at a press conference. "At the same time, the product recall still is a good idea for all of our constituents since it is not clear how many stores he visited in Illinois or, perhaps, in our own state. Apparently, the individual's employment was terminated at DFP a number of years ago and he decided to carry out a vendetta against one of this state's most respected corporations.

"Earlier," Gov. Hill continued, "I prematurely had urged our State Attorney General to file an environmental pollution action against DFP. In view of the responsible manner in which that Company has pursued an environmental cleanup program and product recall, I have withdrawn that recommendation but, of course, I've left the final decision to the Office of the Attorney General."

The statements by Gov. Hill weren't an accident. DFP Director Stan Towler, a former state controller, had reminded Gov. Hill that the media might look askance at his relationship with the Company if they knew he had taken a number of "short campaign trips" on company chartered planes that some might question and had never reimbursed the company as he had promised to do.

DFP decided to initiate a product recall program, and it was successful but the plant repair program was far costlier than anticipated. There was a negative impact on DFP's bottom line, even after insurance and reserves for such contingencies.

After the crises had been addressed and resolved, Mark sent this memorandum to the Board:

To: The Board of Directors

From: Mark Gregory

Re: Lessons Learned

I thank you all for your advice and support in connection with the product recall matter and the crisis involving our production facility on the Placid River. Often, I am asked what lessons management has learned when encountering such challenges. In this case, one I learned was to listen to the Board's advice when you suggested we should shut down the production facility, move to a nearby idle production plant and not lose all that much of our production volume. As you know, we did so and, due to our efforts and some good luck, as well as renaming our Tough Athlete product, we were able to gain some new sales volume shortly thereafter. (Thanks for the help on the product name change. We now have two new names: "Bobby Brawn" and "Brenda Brawn.") We now use slightly different food supplement formulas for each with a rugged sealant in each bottle.

We work hard to avoid crises but, through these matters, I've also learned that you need to manage the kind of crisis you've always tried to avoid because total avoidance simply is not possible with an active, large Company. For example, if you have enough employees for a long time, one of them even may assault another. In business circles, that phenomenon has its own unfortunate name – "Going Postal," to signify all the assaults by certain postal employees on their fellow employees.

Your willingness to permit us to develop comprehensive recall and shutdown programs with a related disclosure message to all of our constituents also was useful. It was difficult to move on a thoughtful basis, but it was helpful that you had the confidence in me and the rest of our senior management team so that you left the ultimate recommendation in our hands. I also was pleased that the Executive Committee was available to meet on such short notice and will take advantage of that process in the future in similar circumstances.

One hard-learned lesson by way of the environmental pollution problem is that we should pay more attention to early warning signs of operating problems, especially those having environmental pollution potential. As you know, we had some reports of relatively minor pollution but ignored them because they seemed insignificant in the total context of our operations.

I have now learned that a small probability risk in connection with large issues involves matters that we all must address immediately, given the potential damage to our balance sheet and to our public image. In that connection, I have asked our General Counsel to appoint one of our senior attorneys to provide you with a comprehensive recommendation on environmental compliance programs as well as a general regulatory compliance program.

That counsel will meet with the Audit Committee at least twice a year so that you will have the factual basis for the type of oversight that would appear to be appropriate. In addition, our Director of Corporate Affairs will attempt to have DFP engage in a more pro-active, well-funded community program to re-establish our reputation for quality control and environmental compliance.

Finally, in terms of ethical conduct, some recent problems have caused me to believe that we should place more emphasis on our corporate ethics program. We have installed a new program that includes, in effect, an ethics officer. We have asked one of our highly respected senior legal officers to take calls from any of our employees or officers who are concerned about any violation of ethical or legal requirements. The entire Board will receive a report from that officer once a year about our ethics program and our experiences with our employees under that program.

James R. Ukropina

Again, I thank you for your support. We certainly will be better equipped to deal with the next crisis, which, unfortunately, may be inevitable, notwithstanding our comprehensive efforts to implement the right types of compliance programs and early warning devices.

*"In a moment we'll have a few words by the chairman of the
board. But, first, Mahler's Eighth Symphony."*

Source: The New Yorker Collection

CHAPTER 21

THE ANNUAL MEETING OF SHAREHOLDERS
The Soul of Corporate Democracy
– or Something Else?
(Second Quarter of Year 13)

Agenda for Annual Meeting:[*]
1. *Chairman calls meeting to order*
2. *Corporate Secretary establishes quorum*
3. *Election of Directors*
4. *Ratification of approval of independent auditing firm*
5. *Report by CEO on recent operating results*
6. *Question-and-answer period*
7. *Other Business*
8. *Adjournment*

As Mark sat on a stage watching the auditorium fill, he remembered that some commentators called the annual meeting of shareholders the soul of corporate democracy. Frankly, he thought, it was an expensive pain in the neck – or worse. And he knew that this annual DFP meeting would be one of the Company's worst ever.

---

[*] The events and remarks occurring in this chapter represent broad creative license in approaching the topic of annual meetings in a satirical manner. To the extent satire is used in this book, this chapter is an extreme example of an average annual meeting, although there are some that border on chaos.

The business media had targeted DFP as a bad corporate citizen for engaging in widespread layoffs and for allowing bribes – Mark was still reeling over a periodical cover that portrayed him in a prison uniform, and he recognized some of the country's best-known shareholder activists coming into the meeting room. These activists, who only seemed to own a handful of shares for the sole purpose of attending meetings, were joined by older DFP shareholders who depended upon their shares as their retirement nest eggs.

On top of that, the Company's stock had recently declined – along with a decline in the stock prices of other companies in DFP's peer group. Further, DFP was renegotiating its labor contract with the union leadership and a good deal of acrimony had developed in those negotiations.

Some employee shareholders, who were also union members, sat in the audience and held ugly placards, with dollar signs all over them, critical of high compensation for the executives. Others held signs supporting higher wages for themselves as union members.

To make matters even worse, a number of disgruntled shareholders appeared at the meeting, ready to support a proposal whereby a shareholder rights plan (known in the business world as a "poison pill") could not be adopted without shareholder approval. The Board had made it clear that it was considering adopting such a plan in order to permit it adequate time to deal with hostile takeover bids. A number of the shareholder activists regarded such a plan as placing too much authority in the hands of the Board and creating a potential "Maginot Line" around the management group and the incumbent Board members to the detriment of shareholders, who might benefit from a hostile, but high-premium tender offer bid.

And, sitting in the front row was Leon Stevens, a well-known shareholder activist. Mark knew Stevens had promised to appear and demand that the Company's charter documents be amended to repeal staggered terms for the Board of Directors. Under the staggered term provision only one-third of the DFP

Board seats were vacated every 12 months, which meant it took at least 24 months before the majority of the Board could be replaced.

Previously, Mark would have been able to call upon Robert Granger – the former, but now-resigned CFO – to help him with many aspects of the meeting. Now that Granger had left following the bribery scandal, Mark didn't really have a veteran DFP corporate officer at his side. In fact, Andrew Sommers, the new Chief Operating Officer, only had joined the Company shortly before the annual meeting. Sommers was due to give a few brief remarks about recent operating results, but couldn't help with some of the more difficult parts of the meeting, including responding to tough – and often unusual and thoughtless – questions posed by irate shareholders. On the other hand, Sommers was a knowledgeable expert about DFP's industries and should be – and was – well prepared to respond to thoughtful, sophisticated questions from the audience about industry trends, and difficult issues facing the major corporate players in those industries.

Unfortunately, Sommers had already become a lightning rod for some of shareholders' criticism, since he was receiving a compensation package in excess of $1 million annually, assuming that he was able to achieve his various target bonuses over the next 12 months.

Prior to the meeting, DFP's corporate communications staff had worked mightily to come up with a strategy to improve shareholders' sentiment at the meeting. It had prepared a colorful and exciting videotape for the shareholders that would "open the show" – a slick presentation demonstrating some of the turnaround activity DFP had undertaken, as well as some of the Company's community activities and contributions throughout the prior 12 months. The lights dimmed, and the video began.

The end of the video was met not with applause but with a hostile yell from the audience.

"How much did that cost you?" shouted a disgruntled

shareholder at the back of the room. "Shouldn't it have been delayed until next year – assuming you're still around?"

Mark took a deep breath and began.

"I wish to call the meeting to order and ask our Corporate Secretary, Barbara Ramos, to take care of the formalities – Barbara."

"I hereby certify that holders of more than the majority of our shares are present at this meeting, either in person or by proxy," the Corporate Secretary said. "Accordingly, there is a quorum present. I have been asked to advise you, the shareholders who are present today, that while we very much appreciate your attendance, we will have to follow our agenda closely as we have a number of action items and reports. Those of you who have comments or questions about any agenda item must wait until that item is up for discussion and then you can pose your questions and make your comments. At the end of our agenda, under 'Other Business,' there will be plenty of time for general discussion."

Mark groaned inwardly as Stevens stood up. "Mr. Chairman, I demand to be recognized. I flew here from Chicago this morning and only have a short time to make my presentation."

"Mr. Stevens, you are out of order," Mark said.

"By the time you get the Dakota City police here to put me back in order, I will have made my presentation and left, so I suggest you listen to me now or bog down this meeting forever."

"Mr. Stevens, you are out of order!" Mark tried again. But Stevens wasn't stopping.

"First of all, with respect to Ms. Ramos' certifying a quorum, I warn you that you should never trust what a woman says! I really doubt there is a quorum here and you haven't satisfied me there is one. Further, a few months ago your General Counsel said that my shareholder proposal to condition any shareholder rights plan on a shareholder vote was too late for inclusion in your proxy statement. While that may be literally true under the SEC shareholder proposal proxy rules, I believe you did other shareholders and me a grave injustice by not including it. Accordingly, I'm going to move that the Bylaws be amended to do away with staggered terms for you and your fat cronies on the Board. As far as I'm concerned you are all a bunch of jerks, and that's appropriate when you have a bunch of staggering Directors!"

Applause erupted from scattered locations throughout the auditorium.

"Mr. Stevens, I'll give you one more minute to conclude your intemperate remarks," Mark said. "Even though we don't have police here, we have security staff and they will be pleased to lead you out of this room if you do not control yourself."

"Well, Mr. Chairman, if that's the way you feel about it, I'll terminate my remarks – but I guarantee I'll be back next year and out for your head. I might add that if you'd purchased my publication on what it takes to have good corporate governance and had paid any attention to it, you'd never be in this fix."

"As I recall, Mr. Stevens, one issue of your publication that you sell to Boards like ours costs about $1,000 a year and contains only about 50 pages. I don't believe that type of $20-per-page periodical is cost-effective for our shareholders."

Mr. Stevens left the meeting room shaking his fist in the air. "You haven't heard the last of me – and I won't stand for this treatment," he said as the security staff headed in his direction.

The DFP corporate communications staff and the internal law department staff had insisted that the meeting be recorded. Outside legal counsel, however, warned management that such a recording might be regarded as "unlawful" under Dakota law, but Mark thought that it was worth taking a chance, especially having announced that the meeting would be recorded and that anyone who objected could leave. By now, Mark had lost his cordial bedside manner and it was clear that he was ready to take on the most aggressive shareholder with a sharp elbow. As it turned out, selective editing of the transcript permitted management to emphasize some of the "high points" of the meeting – although there were relatively few, other than the motion to adjourn.

One of the most vocal questioners among the shareholders was a representative of a labor union, who accused Hugh Perry of taking large management fees to manage DFP pension funds. Accordingly, he maintained that Perry was no longer an independent Director. Others shouted in agreement and raised other issues – including the cost of the recent Board retreat and Mark's salary. At times, the rumbling of the crowd got so loud that even voices on loudspeakers couldn't be heard, but Mark persevered. Finally, he had the formal business of the meeting behind him and began an extensive question-and-answer period.

A s he did, a poorly dressed man in the back row banged some cymbals, stood on his chair and, to the shock of everyone, started to disrobe, showing his ample stomach protruding over his belt line.

"Uh, what are you doing there, sir?" Mark said as he looked around quickly for the security team.

"I had to do something special to get your attention," the man said, stopping his strip tease. "I've been sitting here in the back of the room for over two hours trying to get your attention. Last year I came to this meeting and no one would recognize me. I also was afraid I'd get stuck behind some windbag who wouldn't sit down. Now I'm going to ask my question: When are you going to increase the dividend or split the stock?"

"Well, I can tell you are really anxious for us to do so," Mark said, "but I'm sorry you haven't listened to our report. We dropped our dividend last year because operating earnings were not strong enough to justify the kind of cash flow that would fund our historical dividend rate. That was an incredibly difficult decision for this Board since many of us are also large shareholders and we know that retirees like you rely on that dividend. Regarding a stock split, all that gives you is more pieces of the same pie but your percentage ownership doesn't change. A split might have the collateral advantage of bringing our stock price into a more suitable trading range but that isn't a problem for us now. I hope that answers your concerns, but if you want to give us your address and phone number, we will be happy to correspond with you when our earnings improve and our dividend can be re-established. As a better alternative, we might start a stock repurchase program which, at the right price, could be good for everybody."

"Okay, you asked for it," the frustrated man said, as he turned his back toward the CEO, bent down, took down his trousers and revealed his loud underwear in protest. Before he could go any further, two security officers grabbed him from behind, lifted him up under both arms and then removed him, feet first, from the meeting. Outside the auditorium, they turned him over to local police officers, who charged him with indecent exposure and disturbing the peace.

Back in the auditorium, meanwhile, a petite and attractive older woman stood up and said, "Mr. Chairman, I would like to be recognized."

"Yes, Mrs. Jones, it's nice to see you again. What can I do for you?"

"I want to thank you for the way you handled that rude, overweight gentlemen here in the back of the room," she said. "At one shareholders meeting I was at earlier this year here in Dakota City, he threw a bottle against the wall in order to get the attention of another chairman and the chairman almost fell off the podium. You certainly demonstrated a lot of style and grace and I want to compliment you for being a cool customer."

At that point, a number of shareholders, who were growing tired of the meeting, applauded. One of them moved that the meeting be adjourned. Before asking for a vote, Mark looked to the two proxy agents of DFP who actually held proxies on a majority of the shares at the meeting covering almost any new business that would come before it. After getting a nod from them, Mark asked for a vote. The proxy agents carried the day with their voting authority to close down the meeting until next year.

Part III

REBOUND

James R. Ukropina

CHAPTER 22

THE FINANCE COMMITTEE DELIBERATES
When Too Much Cash Isn't a Good Thing
(Fourth Quarter of Year 14)

Partial Agenda for Committee Meeting

1. *Review of financial condition and existence of large cash reserves*
2. *Review of possible alternative uses for cash*
3. *Review of ratings of DFP debt issues by rating agencies*
4. *Review of recent stock price activity and possible response to hostile bid*

Traditionally, the Finance Committee had been responsible for reviewing the Company's financial condition, its credit rating, and its relationship with major shareholders and lenders. In addition, from time to time, the Finance Committee reviewed the ever-changing investor profile of DFP. But this meeting was largely devoted to a "high-grade problem," the existence of new, huge cash reserves for DFP.

Finance Committee Chairman Larry Lanski, himself a former CEO of a large New York Stock Exchange company, opened the meeting with the report that the Company had accumulated more than $500 million in "excess" cash during the past 18 months due to several factors, including: A more profitable than expected sale of a large division, significant unexpected profits from a new product line, a substantial court judgment in favor of DFP from a lawsuit it had filed against a competitor, and a faster collection of customer receivables.

"We are now like a 'mini-bank' because we are so cash-rich," Larry said. "Unless we redeploy our capital effectively, you can count on some corporate raider regarding us an extremely attractive acquisition target with a hostile bid for our stock, which doesn't yet reflect our improved cash flow position."

"My recommendation is that we attempt to come up with a plan that will help us rapidly deploy our cash," said Hugh Perry, the representative of the large Dakota public employee pension fund which, in turn, was a large DFP shareholder. "If we don't declare a special dividend, buy in our stock or make a shrewd acquisition, we are a prime – and I mean 'primo' – candidate for a takeover bid."

"It's my view," said Harry Thorpe, the trial lawyer, "that we should make a friendly acquisition and make one in a hurry. We have to be able to negotiate a good price but, most importantly, we need to put some of our shares in friendly hands before one of the raiders attempts to scoop up a majority of our shares and take over the Company. At the same time, whatever we do has to be in the best interests of shareholders."

"I agree," said Larry. "In addition, we should make sure that we have all the appropriate anti-takeover defenses and shark repellents in place that we can adopt to fend off a potential hostile bid. I'm going to suggest that the Executive Committee look into that."

"My suggestion," said Harry, "is that we give these recommendations more thought and have one of our virtual meetings over the next few days, over the secure Internet communication system set up for us by Mark. We can exchange views on Friday afternoon between 3 and 6 p.m., and then we'll leave it to you, Larry, to consolidate our views and summarize them for a written consent we all can sign. How does that sound to the two of you?"

Larry and Hugh nodded in agreement. Having listened to hours of reports from the DFP staff they didn't see the need for another face-to-face meeting. The meeting was recessed, and it would be reconvened in the form of the virtual meeting later in the week.

To: hthorpe@dfpdirectors.com; hperry@dfpdirectors.com
From: llanski@dfpdirectors.com

Gentlemen: I've had a chance to reflect further on the issues raised at our meeting earlier this week concerning the deployment of our cash reserves. In addition, I have conferred extensively with DFP's CFO and also its General Counsel. Importantly, we also have sought the advice of outside legal counsel specializing in takeover matters, given that how we propose to deploy these unexpected large cash reserves is a very substantial fiduciary issue. Counsel advises us that any sensible deployment is defensible but that we need to be certain that the funds are deployed in a way that will benefit shareholders and that we document our rationale for our recommendation. (By the way, Mercedes, our General Counsel, asked me to remind you that anything we say in these e-mail messages could be picked up in discovery in a later legal proceeding. I'm not sure what the big deal is but I promised I would mention her concern.)

In that regard, we considered one alternative: a special cash dividend. While the dividend would be an extraordinary one and well received by some of our shareholders, we expect many of them would not respond favorably, because dividends are frequently taxed at ordinary rates. Of course, most of our institutional investors would not pay a tax on the dividend but, on balance, this does not seem like a good idea.

Our best idea is for DFP to acquire another high-quality company for a combination of stock and cash. That would permit us to conserve some of our cash and also issue more equity to other parties who are sympathetic to the company's long-term strategic objectives. I hesitate to use the term "friendly hands" when describing these parties, because it has a bad connotation as someone who would be a rubber stamp for our board and management. Instead, I see prospective merger partners as parties who would share our long-term strategy for growth of the company on a grassroots basis, along with some carefully selected acquisitions. What do the two of you think? Larry

James R. Ukropina

To: llanski@dfpdirectors.com; hperry@dfpdirectors.com
From: hthorpe@dfpdirectors.com

Have considered Larry's proposal that DFP look closely at high-quality acquisitions with potential stockholders who are sympathetic to our long-term strategy. I strongly concur with this approach. If that tack is undertaken I suggest DFP immediately retain a first-rate investment banking firm to embark on a search for prospective acquisition candidates. Most importantly, DFP should not waste any time. I hear rumors from my friends down at the courthouse that DFP is now regarded as an extremely attractive acquisition candidate. (Also, I strongly concur with Mercedes. Let's be careful in what we say and how we say it in these messages. I'm not concerned about the substance of what we say but how someone can distort one of our observations by taking it out of context.) Harry.

To: llanski@dfpdirectors.com, hthorpe@dfpdirectors.com
From: hperry@dfpdirectors.com

Have studied your two transmittals and am in general concurrence. While I think that speed is important in connection with the potential acquisition, at the same time we must proceed carefully enough to ensure that any acquisition deal can be justified on a financial and operating basis. You may recall that DFP looked at some potential acquisition candidates not too long ago and found the cupboard pretty bare. I also have heard that Arthur MacHenry, the CEO of FoodStuffs, Ltd., is starting to look around for potential acquisitions. As you may recall, they are the largest player in our industry and have some major resources they could bring to bear in competition with us for an acquisition candidate. I also was told that our old friend Roger Spayder is starting to poke around again and seems to be interested in DFP – but only at the right price. I assume that last point is motivation enough for us to move forward. Hugh.

To: hthorpe@dfpdirectors.com; hperry@dfpdirectors.com
From: llanski@dfpdirectors.com

Gentlemen, yesterday I met with Mark Gregory and Andy Sommers, and both urged us to finalize our recommendation. Accordingly, I've asked Mercedes to draft a form of unanimous written consent, which I will sign and then send to the two of you, so that we may unanimously approve a series of resolutions whereby we propose the search for a merger or acquisition involving a price of up to $400 million. DFP would use cash and stock, but not so much stock as to prevent the stock portion from being tax-deferred when received by the sellers.

We also are recommending a special dividend, although a small one, to bring attention to the fact that we have large cash reserves. Hopefully, this publicity will cause our shareholders to bid up the price of the stock, which, after all, is the best defense for a hostile takeover bid. The higher the stock price, the tougher it will be for a raider to offer a premium well above the pre-announcement bid price.

At our next Board meeting, I will prepare to cover our recommendation with the full board and the rationale for our recommendation. I would welcome your comments to our Board members after I have made my initial report. Best regards. Larry.

One week following the Finance Committee meeting, the Executive Committee met. While it had not yet declared a corporate crisis, it concluded that certain steps should be taken to respond to the possibility of a hostile bid.

First, the Executive Committee authorized a contribution of $5 million to a number of local charitable organizations in the Company's service areas. Those organizations were to be the beneficiaries of an acceleration of some long-term pledges for major gifts from DFP. (The Executive Committee members were concerned that those pledges would not be honored by a "raider.") Next, the Executive Committee, after receiving informal approval from all Board members, authorized "golden parachute" contracts for all of the senior executives. These provided for compensation from 24 months to 36 months of an executive's annual pay in the event of a hostile takeover bid. The parachute arrangement had two triggers: the first trigger was the change of control event, and the second trigger was an event such as a demotion or a change of job location. Finally, they placed projected benefits of a deferred compensation plan in an unfunded so-called "Rabbi Trust" arrangement in order to make it more difficult to strip out and liquidate the assets in the plan for the use of the raider and not for plan participants (the "Rabbi Trust" arrangement actually was originated by a Rabbi to protect the benefits in a plan developed for himself.)

The Executive Committee also considered a shareholder rights' plan. The plan had·some real teeth, inasmuch as it called for the potential issuance of large blocks of equity securities at bargain basement prices to all incumbent shareholders at the time of a hostile bid, except to the bidder. There was a heated debate about the plan among the Committee members. Those pushing for it called it "the best defensive weapon in a corporate arsenal. Why, more than 50 percent of large companies have them. What's the big deal? Even if we have a poison pill, we can always waive it. It just gives us more time to consider a complex bid."

To the naysayers, it wasn't so simple: "Our shareholders will think we act like porcupines and are anti-fiduciary because we want to deter premium offers."

Mark wanted the plan, but feared that some major institutional investors might try to unseat some Board members if it was adopted. Mark agonized about the issue – but for too long.

At a later date, the Monday morning quarterbacks would argue that the failure to adopt the pill bordered upon "stupidity."

Mark turned his full attention to further growing the Company. He decided – after difficult deliberations – that the food and food appliance industries in which DFP was involved were becoming so competitive and capital-intensive that DFP could be attractive to a larger company on a benign basis. Sadly, he had decided DFP couldn't continue to go it alone and find large chunks of capital by itself. He had heard a maxim voiced in a number of forums recently: "Eat or be eaten!" Accordingly, Mark had received the green light from a number of Directors to start to explore some friendly business combinations with some of the big players in both the food appliance and food industries.

All of the Directors with whom he had spoken – he had skipped a few because he worried about their ability to keep a confidence – had given him a go-ahead to explore potential business combinations. A number asked him for periodic status reports, but Mark said they would be difficult to assemble and communicate and he didn't want to approach the Board until he virtually had a deal in hand. In that regard, he knew he was running the risk of being second-guessed – but it was a risk he thought worth taking from a shareholders' perspective. As it would turn out, once again Mark had misread the sentiments of the Board.

The company Mark had selected as an appropriate merger partner was Hurly Burly Industries ("HBI"). Hurly Burly had been a successful competitor in the food business for some time, and, notwithstanding some price wars between the two companies, the two CEOs were good friends. They signed a confidentiality agreement and started to negotiate.

Frank Foster, the CEO of HBI, was about ready to retire, so he agreed that Mark should be the CEO of the newly combined company and that the two Boards should be combined on an even-steven basis. Foster, in substance, planned to acquire DFP – but on a totally friendly stock-for-stock basis – and, thereafter, the two companies would merge. HBI's management agreed, subject to Board and shareholder approval, to pay a 30 percent premium over the recently quoted market price of DFP, for a total acquisition price of $3.25 billion. Mark was ecstatic that the merger was coming together so quickly on such a friendly basis and called for a special Board meeting to be conducted by telephone in view of the extreme time pressures and for fear of a news leak to the Street.

James R. Ukropina

Each quarter, the Board received a report with the operating data concerning one of DFP's manufacturing plants. An excerpt from a summary of the most recent report is shown below: (average production unit uses 7.3 pounds of raw material)

PLANT OPERATING METRICS AND FINANCIAL PERFORMANCE

Plant Earnings (in $000)		% Margin
Net Sales	$50,000	
Cost of Goods Sold	$41,000	
Gross Margin	$ 9,000	24.0%
Sales & Administration	$ 3,300	5.4%
Other Fixed	$ 1,400	5.1%
Depreciation	$ 2,100	
EBIT	$ 4,300	8.6%
Tax	$ 1,376	2.8%
Net Income	$ 2,924	5.8%
Plant Cashflow (in $000)		
Net Income	$ 2,924	5.8%
Depreciation	$ 2,100	
EBITDA	$ 5,024	10.0%
Capex	$ 3,000	
Change in Working Capital	$ 350	
Free Cashflow	$ 1,674	3.3%
Productivity		
Cost per Ton	$ 2,733	
Cost per Unit	$ 1.86	
Quality and Customer Performance		
Defects per 000 units	2.1	
On time delivery	98.20%	
Claims paid / sales	0.25%	
Capital Efficiency		
Raw Material Inventory	$ 600	
WIP Inventory	$ 1,000	
Finished Goods	$ 800	
Total Inventory	$ 2,400	
Accounts Receivables	$ 6,400	
Working Capital	$ 4,000	
Plant Capital	$22,050	
Capital Employed	$26,050	
Return on Capital Employed: Net Income -	$ 2,924	
Capital Employed -	$26,050	
ROI – 11.2%		

A financial snapshot of the Company:

DFP INC.
COMPARATIVE QUARTERLY RESULTS
($000)

(First Quarter of Year 15)

	Most Recent Qtr.	% Variance from Comp Qtr.	% Variance From Plan
Sales	800,000	+10	+12
Net Income	90,000	+11	+13
Earnings/Share	1.25	+11	+12
Cash Flow/Share	1.50	+14	+15
Stock Price versus Peer Index	+7%	-	-
Debt/Equity Ratio	1.2:4	-	-

CHAPTER 23

BUSINESS COMBINATION STRATEGY
Let's Make a Deal
(Third Quarter of Year 15)

Agenda for Special Telephone Board Meeting
1. *Call Meeting to Order – CEO*
2. *Establish quorum, take roll call and assure that everyone can hear one another in accordance with Bylaw provision for a telephonic meeting*
3. *Discussion of "Project H"*

"I call this special telephonic Board meeting to order," Mark said into the speakerphone. "I think all of you will be pleasantly surprised by my news. I want to tell you about a possible, exciting business combination – what I and others on our team are calling 'Project H.'"

Mark proudly mapped out the proposed business combination with HBI – including the favorable terms he had negotiated, the fact that he would be the CEO of the newly combined Company, and the point that the two Boards would be combined to form a new Board to govern the combined business enterprises. He phrased his presentation carefully and had practiced it in advance; he knew there would be questions about such matters as pricing and such significant legal issues as fiduciary duties, but, in the last analysis, he didn't foresee any major stumbling blocks. After all, he thought, everyone should be able to see this was a great deal. Unfortunately for him, Mark had miscalculated the Board's

262

reaction because, for the sake of expediency, he had chosen only to talk to a few Directors prior to the meeting and they turned out to be the Board members who were "low-hanging fruit."

"That's wonderful!" Judy said. "Those HBI guys are great – and it sounds like they're excited about this merger."

George, meanwhile, was personally proud of Mark's initiative and negotiating skills, but he couldn't help expressing a concern.

"Look, Mark – if Frank Foster is prepared to pay a 30 percent premium – or $750 million over our current market cap – others might pay more, and that would be better for our shareholders," George said.

"Perhaps," Mark responded, "but I truly doubt it. I think we should push this deal through while the iron is hot!"

Gen. Landry was more vehement than George had been. "Mark, what were you thinking? This is a multi-billion dollar deal. We can't simply take the first suitor who comes our way. When I was on a board last year in a similar position, our legal counsel told us we had a duty to auction off the company for the highest price. As I recall, he referenced something called the *Revlon* doctrine. There – as well as here – we needed an investment banking opinion, advice from outside legal counsel and a plan of attack to be sure that we do the kind of diligence that should be done."

At this point, Mark thought he needed to let Mercedes express herself about the need for some time-consuming and careful diligence before proceeding. "Mercedes and I have conferred about this matter and agreed, to some extent, to disagree – because I think speed is essential. But let's hear from her directly."

"Well, let's narrow in on the legal issues," Mercedes said. "Most of you have participated in my orientation program, where I covered one important legal case that I want to again summarize. Way back in 1985, the Delaware Supreme Court handed down a decision in the case of *Smith v. Van Gorkom*. In that case, the Board of Trans Union Corp. was found to have breached its fiduciary duty of care in authorizing the sale of a publicly held company in an uninformed manner and for too cheap a merger price – even though that price was 40 percent over the pre-announcement trading price. No fairness opinion was obtained from a banking firm. While the court made it clear that one isn't always needed, it hinted that it's pretty important to have independent advice on pricing a big deal. Like this Board, the Trans Union Board consisted of extremely capable Directors, but the court found the Board had become dominated by management."

If this had been a videoconference, everyone could have seen Mark grimacing as Mercedes spoke. She had warned Mark she had an ethical obligation to give this sort of feedback to the Board, but, still, he wished she wouldn't be so brutal about it. She continued:

"All of the so-called outside directors on the Trans Union Board seemed to have strong personal relationships with the CEO, and none of them had large equity ownerships. The court found that the board had not acted in an informed manner, and the decision in *Van Gorkom* could have resulted in a large monetary liability for the directors – say, about $25 million. It didn't, because the case was finally settled with most of the payments attributable to the directors being made by the acquiring company. Nonetheless, that case has caused lawyers like me to caution directors to consider how you should approach a matter of this type. Also, I can assure you that, if you take the first deal out of the box, some institutional investors may suggest that you have not approached this matter on a prudent basis. Criticism will follow and even, perhaps, lawsuits.

"Also," added Mercedes, "last week I attended a high-level seminar in Chicago on mergers and acquisitions. I learned that only about 20 percent of business combinations really turn out to be defensible from a shareholder return standpoint and many of them are ill-considered and unsuccessful. Also, at that seminar we covered the *Revlon* doctrine, which I also discussed with outside counsel who you will hear from later.

He thinks the auction idea might not apply in a stock-for-stock deal or a strategic merger, but we'll have those issues confirmed for you."

"It seems to me there are a lot of loose ends here – legal and otherwise. It's those issues that worry me," Gen. Landry said.

"Well, General, the good news is that a lot of difficulty that could be encountered in a business combination can be avoided through careful due diligence," Mercedes said. "In that regard, you would need to pore over HBI financial statements and financial schedules, examine environmental contingent liabilities, review management information systems to be sure that they are compatible with one another, and worry about contingent liabilities, contract files, litigation files, patent matters and the like. We need to review our product compatibility, our joint markets, and, of course, potential antitrust issues. We would expect the same from the people at HBI."

"Mark, I hate to be a wet blanket," said George, "but we need to assemble a team of good people, both internal and external, who are well trained in accounting, law, contract analysis and, importantly, the skills and character of the management group of HBI. I also recommend we hire a private investigation firm to be sure that HBI has the kind of integrity in its senior management team that appears to be the case. And, not to open up old wounds, let's not forget how we blew it with Obitron."

"George, that's a great reminder," Gen. Landry interjected.

George didn't respond before continuing. "HBI, like ourselves, also is involved in the foreign sector. We would want to check out its code of conduct and its history, if any, of questionable payments. And that's just one area. We also would want to be sure that it has strong relationships with its key managers, suppliers, distributors and principal customers."

"All those are good points, George," said Mercedes. "In addition, once we complete the diligence, we could finalize pricing. Some companies try to work out pricing themselves but, as General Counsel, I think it is imperative in a deal of this size that you retain a good investment-banking firm. First, such a firm is far more experienced than any of us in how pricing should be handled and what appropriate multiples should be used on earnings and cash flow. A good banker also will have a pretty strong impression of how the Street will react to an announcement of a DFP business combination with HBI.

"Finally, I remind you that, as Directors of a Dakota corporation, you are entitled to rely on experts, such as bankers, and, in good faith, you can justifiably rely on their advice after due inquiry. With respect to due inquiry, you should ask bankers to deliver an opinion to the Board that any deal that DFP would make is fair from a financial perspective to all of our shareholders. You also need to query any bankers about how they arrive at such an opinion, what assumptions they used and what the key elements are of their rationale."

"I've done a lot of M&A deals," Larry said. "In my view, making acquisitions is not only a science but also somewhat of an art – probably a healthy combination of the two. For example, we need to study our respective product lines and operating systems to see if they're compatible, study our customer demographics to see that the customer base is compatible and, importantly, satisfy ourselves that the two management groups could effectively combine with one another. How will the people interface? Who will get paid what? Who will remain at the corporate staff level?

"Some of the most successful acquisitions are those characterized by intense, broad-based preliminary diligence by both parties, post-signing and pre-closing diligence and intense but fair negotiations on pricing. With a deal like this, we will need a pricing formula to be sure that if the facts change, such as the development of unexpected contingent liabilities, then we can make appropriate adjustments in the pricing formula. We also need to be able to pay key managers in both companies, on a post-closing basis, generous compensation to ensure that they'll stay with the combined company and not get enticed away by larger, competing enterprises.

"And, of course, there will be the usual 'social issues' – What will the new company be named? Will DFP retain its name as a division of the new company? Where will the corporate headquarters be located? Issues like that."

"Oh, remember," said Mercedes, "you now have the ultimate inside information. Not only will disclosure or tips to outsiders cause grounds for legal liability for you, they could kill the deal. Loose lips sink ships!"

As Mark listened, he realized that this wasn't going to be as easy as it had seemed at the start of the phone call.

Following the Board meeting, Mark asked Harlan MacArthur, a major New York-based player in the merger-and-acquisition field, to head an investment banking team to assist DFP in combining with HBI.

Mark called another special telephone meeting of the Board that afternoon to let the Directors know the status of the investment banking firm's engagement and to move forward with potential proceedings in the business combination with HBI.

After the call, one of the Directors, former State Controller Stan Towler, leaked to one of his golfing buddies that something "big" was in the works for DFP and HBI. Unbeknownst to him, his golfing buddy, Fritz Unger, was indebted to Roger Spayder for a longstanding unpaid $25,000 personal loan. Unger knew that Roger Spayder had a deep interest in DFP and also was aware of the long-time war between Spayder and Gregory.

'Roger," Unger said in a telephone call that night to Spayder, "I'd like to get together for cocktails tomorrow night. I have some information that I know will be of interest to you – and I can assure you that it will be worth a lot to you. In fact, I expect you'll find it so valuable you'll cancel my note."

"Maybe so, Fritz," said Spayder skeptically, "but I can't see you until 7 tomorrow night and I don't have time for socializing.

Come to my office then and one of our security guards will let you in."

Early the next evening, Unger went to Spayder Enterprises headquarters and was escorted to Spayder's office. Spayder didn't even rise from his chair, nor did he shake hands. "Well, what do you have for me?" he blurted out.

"As you know, Roger, I owe you about $25,000. I want an understanding that if you capitalize on this information, you'll cancel my loan. Is that a deal?" asked Unger.

"It is," said Spayder, "so long as the information is that valuable."

"I'm sure you'll find it worth far more than $25,000," emphasized Unger. "Here's the scoop. I learned from a DFP Director that your buddy Mark Gregory is talking with that fellow Foster over at HBI. I did some more sleuthing with a disgruntled executive secretary at DFP and learned that they're just about ready to strike a deal to merge the two companies. I understand the effective price is around $45 per share. I'm no financial genius like you, but it seems to me that DFP would be worth far more than $45 a share to you for many reasons, some of them corporate, some personal. Is that the case?"

"Bingo!" said Spayder. "Your loan is cancelled."

Unger started to leave, but Spayder wasn't finished. "Oh, by the way, Fritz, let me do you a favor. Now that I've cancelled your note, remember you'll have constructive income to report to the IRS –be sure and report it. I certainly plan to try to take a business deduction for loan forgiveness."

"With friends like you, I'm not sure I need any enemies," Unger said as he turned to leave. "But I'm glad to have the loan off my books anyway."

Spayder planned to make a cash bid at a 40 percent premium instead of HBI's 30 percent premium. While the bid was being financed in part, Spayder confirmed that the loan facility was in place, thereby eliminating any argument that his bid would be soft. Since the difference in pricing represented hundreds of millions of dollars that could be recovered by shareholders, Spayder knew his bid was bound to be almost irresistible to everyone on the Board – that was, everyone except Mark.

To make matters worse, Spayder called Mark before making the bid and told him that he had heard DFP might be "for sale." When Gregory angrily denied that, Spayder assured him that he had no intention of making a hostile bid for DFP. Given their earlier experience with Spayder, Gregory and most of the senior officers at DFP didn't take a lot of comfort from Spayder's words, since he frequently had broken his promises or not kept his commitments in a business deal – and it was a good thing they didn't this time. Further, even in exchange for internal DFP financial data, including projections, Spayder had refused to sign a standstill agreement that would "freeze" his takeover conduct while negotiations were underway. Mark's conclusion? The handwriting was on the wall – Spayder was about to initiate his raid for DFP.

James R. Ukropina

A SUMMARY DESCRIPTION OF DFP IN ITS 15TH YEAR
(AS AVAILABLE OVER THE INTERNET)
DFP, INC. (NYSE: DFPI)

Business Summary

DFP, Inc., together with its consolidated subsidiaries, is a global manufacturer and marketer of kitchen equipment for the home, restaurant and institutional use. It also manufactures and markets branded convenience food products as well as products for the home. The Company operates in three business segments: Kitchen Equipment, Home Equipment and Food Products. The Kitchen Equipment division includes the world famous Grillit barbeque. Its Food Products division manufactures and distributes gourmet food, coffee and dietary supplements, especially for youthful consumers. Home products include cookware essentials, tableware and home furnishings.

Financial Summary

DFP was founded 15 years ago in Dakota City, Dakota. Its net income increased 22% in the first quarter of the current year. Revenues reflect an increase in international equipment and earnings increased by 25%.

Officers

Mark Gregory, 53
Chairman and CEO
Andy Sommers, 51
Pres. and COO
Geoffrey Raines, 61
CFO and Sr. VP

Directors

Frank Alworth
Financial Consultant and
Investment Advisor
to the Dakota Foundation
Joan Fleming
CEO of Fleming Images

Judy Moran,
Former COO of
Grillco, Inc.

270

Mercedes Magruder,
43
Sr. VP and Gen.
Counsel

Mark Gregory
CEO and Chairman of Board of DFP

George Hartfield
CEO of Ernest Exploration Co.

Paul Landry
Retired Air Force General and former CEO of Hurst Mfr. Co.

Larry Lanski,
Former CEO of Zephyr Communications, Inc.

Hugh Perry
Investment Advisor for Dakota State Teachers Retirement System

Andy Sommers
DFP Chief Operating Officer

Dr. Henry Thompson
President of Dakota State University

Harry Thorpe
Trial Lawyer and Partner of Thorpe and Burns, LLC

Alex Todihara
Entrepreneur

Stanley Towler
Former State Controller and Consultant

Recent Research Reports

Sat	May	11	Investment Review
Fri	May	10	Manchester's Company Profile: DFP
Fri	May	10	Market Edge Industry Group Analysis

Upcoming Events

May 15		Earnings Announcement

Location

345 Dakota Place
Dakota City, Dakota 98765

Phone: (555) 182-7964
Fax: (555) 182-7965

James R. Ukropina

Employees (last reported count)**:** 3,500

Financial Links
·Institutional Ownership
·Upgrade/Downgrade History
·Historical Price Data
·Free Annual Report
·SEC Filings from Edgar Online

Competitors:
·Sector: Consumer Non-Cyclical
·Industry: Food Processing and Kitchen Equipment

Company Websites
·Home Page
·Investor Relations
·Divisions

Ownership
· **Insider and 5%+ Owners:** 45%
· Over the last 6 months:
   ·2 insider buys; 40,000 shares
   ·4 insider sells; 35,000 shares
· **Institutional:** 31% (57% of float) (141 institutions)
· **Net Inst. Buying:** 1.25M shares (+0.97%)
   (prior quarter to latest quarter)

Statistics at a Glance — NYSE: DFPI

Price and Volume		Per-Share Data		Management Effectiveness	
52-Week Low	$25.52	Book Value (mrq*)	$9.00		
Recent Price	$27.00	Earnings (ttm)	$5.0	Return on Equity	12%
52-Week High	$31.44	Earnings (mrq)	.36	**Financial Strength**	
Beta	0.36	Sales (ttm)	$3.2		
Daily Volume (3-month avg)	612.3K	Cash (mrq*)	1.4	Current Ratio (mrq*)	2.9:1
		Valuation Ratios		Debt/Equity	1.2:4
Daily Volume (10-day avg)	538.0K	Price/Book	3.0	Total Cash (mrq)	$685MM
Stock Performance		Price/Earnings (ttm)	5.5		
52-Week Change	-12.1%	**Income Statements**		Daily Volume	110.2K
52-Week Change relative to S&P500	+3.7%	Sales (ttm)	$3.2B		
		EBITDA (ttm*)	$.387B		
Share-Related Items		Income available to common (ttm)	$352MM		
Market Capitalization	$2.1B	**Fiscal Year**			
Shares Outstanding	81.4MM	Fiscal Year Ends	12/31		
Float	48.3MM	Most recent quarter (fully updated)	3/31		
Dividends & Splits					
Annual Dividend (indicated)	None				
Dividend Yield	N/A				

See Profile Help for a description of each item above; **K** = thousands; **MM** = millions; **B** = billions; **mrq** = most-recent quarter; **ttm** = trailing twelve months; (as of 31-Jan-2002, except **mrq*/ttm*** items as of 27-Jan-2002)

DFP Quarterly Balance Sheet

	Period Ending			
	March 31	**Dec 31**	**Sept 30**	**June 30**
Cash and Cash Equivalents	$1,200,000	$4,117,000	$3,928,000	$3,518,000
Net Receivables	$133,627,000	$114,928,000	$3,928,000	$3,518,000
Inventory	$124,986,000	$86,612,000	$78,926,000	$71,764,000
Total Current Assets	$324,920,000	$222,147,000	$247,000,000	$205,000,000
Property Plant and Equipment	$265,218,000	$247,300,000	$242,800,000	$225,000,000
Intangible Assets	$47,892,726	$48,962,000	$48,968,000	$48,988,000

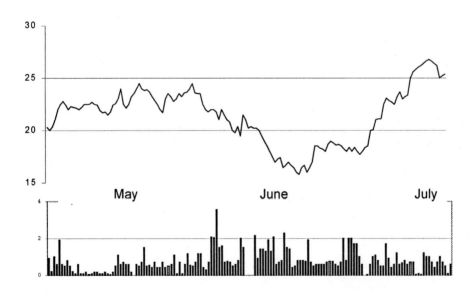

CHAPTER 24

THE SPAYDER BID
Doing the Right Thing
(*Third Quarter of Year 15*)

Partial Agenda for Board Meeting

1. *Discussion of terms of tender offer*
2. *Comments on legal duties of Directors – General Counsel*
3. *Additional Comments by independent legal counsel on fiduciary duties, SEC issues, antitrust issues, possible need to form a special committee, possible requirements for response by board – e.g., in favor of bid; reject bid; issuance of "stop-look-and-listen" letter (i.e., we'll be back to you soon); other alternatives*
4. *Comments by CEO*
5. *Executive Session*

Mark looked grim as he entered the Boardroom and started handing out a stack of papers. "I think, as a refresher, you should all read this before we get started," he said. It was a press release from Spayder Enterprises. George took his copy and read:

SPAYDER ENTERPRISES ANNOUNCES CASH TENDER OFFER FOR DFP, INC. FOR $3.5 BILLION

Spayder Enterprises (NYSE) announced today that it intends to commence a tender offer for all of the issued and outstanding shares of DFP, Inc. for $50 per share in cash. In total, the bid amounts to $3.5 billion.

It also announced that if the offer is consummated and it acquires more than 90 percent of the shares of DFP, after completion of the offer it intends to acquire the remainder of the shares that are not tendered in the offer on a compulsory basis in accordance with state merger laws. Shareholders of record of DFP who tender their shares directly will not be obligated to pay brokerage fees or commissions, or, except as set forth in the Letter of Transmittal, transfer taxes on the sale of their shares.

To date, DFP's Directors have not decided whether to recommend acceptance of the offer and they have advised Spayder Enterprises they are now seeking an opinion from an independent investment advisor as to whether the offer is fair.

Obviously, George had been in on several discussions about the potential Spayder bid, but seeing it in black-and-white really brought it home. Trying to keep his perspective, he remembered that while the premium bid price of about 40 percent over the recent market price seemed substantial, only a year ago the stock had traded at above the proposed bid price – and many securities analysts expected it to return to that level within the next 24 months. Thus, the Board faced a difficult decision. The pricing might be right but the bidder seemed to lack fundamental integrity.

He listened carefully as Mark introduced the investment bankers and legal advisors. Not only was there a mergers and acquisition lawyer, but also legal experts on tax issues, antitrust matters and federal securities laws. Each concluded that, while there may be a few "hiccups," a Spayder bid for DFP would be well-received in the stock market and it was highly likely that his hostile bid would be accepted by a majority of DFP's shareholders and approved by the regulators.

Mark remained adamant that the deal shouldn't go through. "I have the utmost respect for our experts, but I urge you as a

Board to vote against this bid," Mark said. "We did not build this Company to turn it over to a man like Roger Spayder..."

As she listened to Mark's emotional appeal, Judy couldn't help but think about his past reluctance to adopt a shareholder rights plan that would have protected against such a bid.

"If you'd adopted a poison pill some time ago," Judy said at one point, "you wouldn't be in this position. We could have had flip-in and flip-over provisions – all the bells and whistles. Now, if we did it, it could be regarded as overly defensive and not in the interest of our shareholders, at least from a fiduciary perspective."

Needless to say, Mark wasn't in a good mood – and Judy's "'reminder" didn't go down well. "Thanks, Judy," he said with an edge in his voice, "for telling me what I should have done. But that is water over the dam, and I want to be listened to on this matter.

"Here are just a few of my reasons for opposition," Mark continued. "First, Spayder's $50 price is inadequate. As you know, our stock traded around $60 per share less than a year ago. Also, a cash tender offer is taxable to our shareholders, while a stock swap deal with HBI would be tax-free or tax deferred – and, a merger of HBI-DFP, in the long term, would be a much better deal for all of our shareholders. Doesn't anyone care about the long term in our society?"

As Mark spoke, his thoughts crystallized even further. "Like you, as a member of this Board I am a fiduciary, but, to an even greater extent than you, I also have additional duties as the Chief Executive Officer: duties to our employees, to our customers, to our vendors and to the various communities that we serve. Let's look at the deal from their standpoint.

"As we all know, Spayder rarely, if ever, keeps his word. He already has told me there won't be any layoffs after his tender offer, but we all know that significant layoffs have occurred after every deal he's done.

"Also, in his last deal he did, as soon as it closed, the customers of the acquired company faced some devastating price increases for key products because he artfully dodged the antitrust laws and was able to gouge them. In another recent deal, he shut down a plant that was extremely cost-effective and moved its operations to a large and outdated facility that he personally owns."

"Even if all this is true, Mark, what about our duty to our shareholders?" Hugh asked.

"I've talked to some of our investment bankers and all of them think we can do better than this price over the long term," Mark said. "Candidly, none of them can opine that Spayder's tender offer is financially inadequate – but I certainly think it is ethically inadequate.

"I've also received calls from some of our key suppliers, and they've indicated that if the Company is taken over by Spayder they don't want to do business with him because of his terrible reputation and his unwillingness to pay his bills on a timely basis. Finally, I know personally that he has been kicked out of two country clubs for lack of social decorum and he is married to his fourth wife. To me, personal behavior still counts for something!

"There, I think a lot is on the table – let's discuss it further."

In the ensuing discussions, it became increasingly clear that the Board was substantially persuaded that, notwithstanding Spayder's inferior character, his cash bid of $50 per share was more than fair given the current economy and the Company's prospects over the next year or two. It also represented a $1 billion cash premium over the pre-bid stock price and most directors didn't have the stomach to turn their backs on that amount.

Judy, as usual, was no shrinking violet. "Mark, here is how most of us think about it. Spayder is an extremely bright, but incredibly aggressive and difficult person. At the same time, he is offering our shareholders cash – so they can cash out of their stock, and don't have to be part of this organization down the road. While he's a rapacious cost-cutter and certainly in the 'slow pay' category as a customer, to the best of our knowledge he has never violated any laws – and it's unlikely he will ever do so, because he is so well advised by some very good, large law firms.

"And while I'm not condoning his personal behavior – he may have lost a number of country club memberships and a few spouses – that doesn't make him a bad businessman. In fact, he's been able to expand the operations of most of the companies he's acquired. It's true that he leaves a lot of bodies along the road, but what we have to ask ourselves is whether this price is a fair one under the current difficult economic circumstances, whether he can deliver the cash at the closing of the tender offer and whether it is in the best interests of our shareholders for us to be supportive. At this time, I think most of us are in favor of moving forward."

"Before we go much further," said George, "I want to be sure that we have all been heard. We've had some long discussions about the Spayder bid, but we need to be certain this is a good time to sell the Company. It seems to me that our internal profit projections do not justify the alternative of continuing to remain as an independent Company, since we would never achieve the type of returns that could replace the proposed acquisition price.

"Since we have a lot of cash and we could add some more debt, we could make a self-tender for the shares, but that would mortgage the Company's future. We also have rejected the use of a poison pill but, upon reflection, I wish we'd put one in place since that would give us a little more time to think about this deal.

"I think we also must conclude that there will be significant layoffs here at our local office, particularly with the corporate staff. Also, some of our key production and marketing people will be terminated. Accordingly, if there is going to be a bid and we're going to support it, we need to have an understanding with Spayder about some continuity arrangements and some stability for key people. I know him well enough that I think I can negotiate those matters effectively."

Joan Fleming then weighed in. "George, I'm sure you can negotiate anything that makes sense. On the other hand, I worry about Spayder's reputation for not keeping his commitments. Isn't it possible we can get a higher price from another bidder?"

Larry said that, with Mark's authorization, recently he had called a CEO of a large food conglomerate who might have been interested in the Company and would serve as a "White Knight." "Unfortunately," he said, "the CEO said that while he would like to make the acquisition, his company recently made another large acquisition and was still digesting it. So, he had no current appetite for another one."

"Most of you still don't seem to understand the situation," Mark said. "We have a large amount of cash in our own cash drawer that we haven't had a chance to deploy, because we're being conservative for the long-term benefit of our shareholders. What Spayder will do is use most of that cash to help fund the purchase price and, in effect, buy the cow with the cow's milk. As a result, his net price only will be about 80 percent of what he's paying.

"In other words, he is paying a very low multiple of our earnings. If you want to put DFP up for auction, I'm sure we could do much better than he is suggesting! In fact, there is a pretty good chance we could find a 'White Knight' rather quickly."

"Mark, if anyone wants to step in and submit an 'overbid' in excess of Spayder's tender offer they can do so," George interjected. "If they do, we can address that at that time. Remember, Spayder isn't asking for our support, but he has suggested that, under these circumstances, we should endorse his bid. We can decide that at a later time. After all, we are probably in a better position to evaluate a bid than any of our other shareholders, who don't understand the Company's near-term and long-term prospects."

"Mark, I think you need a friend in court," said Hugh. "I agree with you that this deal will cause a lot of layoffs here at DFP, which is particularly worrisome to me because DFP has a number of union employees who are loosely affiliated with employees of the state government agencies our firm represents as an investment advisor. And, I've heard from some of our local union leaders that they're incredibly concerned about the current economic prospects and unemployment situation here in the state. They've asked me to take a very hard look at whether the Spayder bid makes sense from an employment standpoint.

"But while I'm really concerned about that issue, as a fiduciary first and a money manager second, this bid still looks extremely attractive. Also, you should know that Spayder called one of the senior officers of the Dakota Employee Pension Fund and asked him to lean on me to vote in favor of this deal. The officer told me that I should use my best judgment, but that I should be careful not to lose a bird in the hand."

"Hugh, I appreciate your concerns for our employees," Mark said. "You appear to be the only Director who cares about anything other than money." In response, a low collective groan came from all of the Board members.

George felt it was time for a break. "Mark, do you mind if we take a little recess?" he asked. "I'd like to talk to you privately for a moment." After the recess was called, George went with Mark into an adjoining office.

'M ark, let me start by saying I admire your desire to do the right thing here. We all want to do the right thing. But I think your personal bias against Spayder is grossly distorting your thinking. Also, we all think that this cash price is generous and that a paper or stock deal through Foster's company isn't even a close second.

"There is another matter I want to advise you about. Spayder called me this morning and told me he knows you've been talking with Foster. He says that if you and we oppose this deal, he's going to encourage some of his good friends who are large DFP shareholders to file lawsuits against all of us. They will first allege to the Dakota City newspapers – and then in court – that you and we are in breach of our fiduciary duty by opposing the bid. He also will go public with the idea that the reason you are opposing this deal is that Foster has promised that you will be the Chief Executive Officer of the new Company and your selfish position is what is actually barring the DFP shareholders from a big payday."

"You know what, George? Spayder is a real lowlife and a scumbag – and that's just the kind of allegation I'd expect from him. As you well know, I'm already a Chief Executive Officer, and being the CEO of a larger Company is not going to be a treat. I would look forward to that role only because the Foster deal is a better combination for our shareholders.

"While I'm inclined to react aggressively toward Spayder and bring a defamation suit against him, I remember our last encounter with Spayder many years ago, when the Board thought I overreacted. So this time I won't, although it's tempting."

"Mark, I have to give it to you straight," George insisted. "This deal is too good for the shareholders, and we can't pass it up."

"Are you telling me you're going to abandon me? You know what kind of guy Spayder is!"

"Well, 'abandon' is a pretty strong term, Mark. I have nothing but the greatest admiration for you – but we all have a duty to the shareholders. And my duty, as I see it, is to vote in favor of the Spayder bid."

"George, how can you do that! We've built this Company together – and Spayder will destroy it."

"Mark, I'm not the only person who sees it this way," George said. "Spayder's gotten even more support than you know."

"Which means?

"Well, I was talking with Roy Robinson over at the Dakota Foundation. He told me that not only does the Foundation support the tender offer – but also that they will be very vocal in publicly supporting it."

For once, Mark was speechless. The very Foundation that DFP had created and funded was now turning on its benefactors. He couldn't believe it. In a couple of moments, he regained his composure.

"George, could you go back in and ask the Board to wait about 45 minutes before reconvening? I have a few calls I'd like to make and I want to get my thoughts together."

"Sure, Mark. We'll be waiting for you."

M ark returned to his office, picked up the phone and hit one of the speed-dial buttons.

"Hardy, do you have a second?"

"Sure, Mark, I always have time for you." Mark had attended business school with Hardy Powers, who was now a senior partner for one of New York City's largest investment banking firms, and Mark often had turned to him in times of crisis – both personally and professionally.

"Hardy, I have an extremely important question to ask and I need your unvarnished objective advice. Tell me the truth: Do you think Spayder's tender offer will be successful?"

"Mark, I know this will come as incredibly bad news, but there's no question the offer will be successful," Hardy said. He could hear Mark sigh, but he knew that deep down Mark already knew this. "Our firm already has started to arbitrage the deal and, as an arb with a big position, we are certain that at Spayder's premium bid price, more than 80 percent of the DFP shares will be tendered. In fact, it's likely to be more than 90 percent. These days, cash tender offers are relatively scarce because of the tight economy. We expect that most of the big banking houses will tender their shares, along with all the other institutional investors."

"Are you sure, Hardy? Really sure?" asked Mark.

"Mark, I know how important this is to you, so I want to be as objective as I can. If I thought you had a real chance to fight off this offer, I would tell you – heck, I'd even join you! You know how I like a good fight."

"That's good to hear, Hardy," Mark said, glad to have a friend willing to try to lighten the mood at times like this.

"But that's not a viable option, frankly. One other thing: I've heard you've been talking with HBI about an exchange offer or merger in which it would swap shares of HBI stock for DFP shares. Unfortunately, even though an exchange offer and a cash tender offer can now be put on the same fast track, from a process and regulatory standpoint, there's no way that a paper offer will compete with a cash tender offer."

That's top-secret info, Mark thought when he heard Hardy mention the HBI stock exchange option. Hardy was more connected than he realized.

"Also, everybody knows Spayder is a tough hombre and he's willing to go to the mat to make his tender offer successful," Hardy continued. "Foster also is a fairly tough businessman, but he's too much of a 'nice guy' to take on Spayder – hell, nobody wants to take on Spayder.

"I'm sad to report, Mark, but that's my best judgment about what's going to happen here."

"Well, Hardy, that's not what I wanted to hear, but I appreciate your being honest with me. Hey, let's look on the bright side – if it happens, I'll have more time to play golf with you!"

After hanging up, Mark took his personal balance sheet from a desk drawer and calculated what he and his family would make from the multibillion dollar Spayder tender offer. Not only would he see his shares increase in value, but also, under the terms of the DFP Option Plan, all of his vested and unvested stock options would be accelerated. The total amount was staggering.

But still, Mark thought, while the immediate financial implications of this offer were terrific, the ethical implications weren't. Mentally, he kicked himself for not having the foresight to expect that Spayder might make an offer. As someone once told him, you have to see the "invisible" in order to accomplish the "impossible."

Knowing the Board was waiting, Mark pulled out a yellow legal pad and started to write a formal statement to deliver to the Directors. He had a lot to cover in a short period of time, but he wanted to be sure he got it right.

While Mark was writing out his remarks, George went back to the Boardroom and said Mark would be along in 45 minutes or so. Several of the Directors took out their cell phones and headed out to the hall, while others checked their e-mails on their laptop computers and Blackberries.

George went over to a side table and poured himself a cup of coffee. Joan walked over to join him.

"How's he doing?" Joan asked. "This has got to be an emotional roller-coaster for him."

"Mark's a strong guy – we've seen enough examples of what he's gone through over the years to show us that he's going to be just fine, whatever happens."

At about 11 a.m., they heard the door to the Boardroom open and turned to see Mark walking through the door, carrying his yellow legal pad.

CHAPTER 25

VOTING ON THE SPAYDER BID
Conscience vs. Reality
(Fourth Quarter of Year 15)

'Thank you for waiting. I'm ready to start now," Mark said as he sat down. "I call the meeting back to order. Could each of you succinctly state your position on the Spayder bid?"

Mark listened as each Director had his or her say. There were no surprises; everyone supported the business combination. Even Hugh, though still expressing concerns about layoffs after the merger, said that, after agonizing deliberations, he had no alternative but to vote in favor of the business combination, because it would be better for the shareholders.

"Very well," Mark said after the Directors finished. "I'll call for the vote, after which, I'd like to make a few personal remarks. All those in favor, please say 'aye.'"

The "ayes" resounded throughout the room. There were no "nays." Mark didn't vote immediately, and the Directors shifted awkwardly while waiting for Mark to cast his vote. It seemed like an eternity as Mark rose to walk to the podium, but it was probably no longer than a minute. For the first time in a long time, Directors could hear the quiet ticking of the big clock on the Boardroom wall.

Mark shuffled through his notes before slowly reading the following remarks[*]:

I concur and vote for the resolution to combine DFP and Spayder Enterprises because, as Directors, we must recognize the primacy of the shareholders' interest under current conditions. On behalf of management, I thank each of you for sticking with me in some earlier difficult decisions. My vote as a Board member stands to make this vote unanimous.

However, my conscience votes 'NO.' No, on behalf of you who are frustrated by an environment that puts a higher price on immediate values than upon promising prospects.

As Chief Executive Officer, I represent employees and customers with a different perspective than Board members can have under these conditions. On behalf of them, my conscience votes 'NO.' No, for DFP employees who have freely chosen DFP and entrusted DFP with their financial and psychic well-being. No, for the employees, who during many years, have created the premium over the costs that shareholders invested – a premium that now will go to shareholders. No, for all of the employees who responded with me to vote against Mr. Spayder in his proxy contest long ago when he tried to take control of DFP.

As we all know, DFP is a Company limited only by the capacity of its people and markets. It's a Company with a bold plan of growth for its products and services, with wave after wave of innovation, and it's a Company driven by a market in customer orientation and supported by our traditional operating strengths. But tomorrow, after the tender offer, we are apt to find this

---

[*]These remarks are largely based upon remarks made by a distinguished executive and my lifelong friend, John Lillie, when he addressed the Board of Lucky Stores when it faced the second of two hostile bids.

Company limited by financial capacity and dominated by financial engineers.

Finally, I vote 'NO' for our customers, who will pay more for less. My conscience votes 'NO' for them and for you, many of whom I know share many of my feelings.

In order to combine ourselves with Spayder Enterprises, I can assure you that we, the management, will undertake our tasks diligently – driven by our professional pride and integrity – but encumbered by our dignity.

There was silence in the room as all of the Directors let Mark's remarks soak in. All of them knew he was right – but that his version of corporate and personal ethics had been supplanted by a judicial system that virtually demanded that directors accept a high-premium offer regardless of difficult circumstances.

While certain cases, including the old *Time-Warner* case, had justified turning down premium bids in favor of lower bids with potential strategic advantages, most courts were not sympathetic to the *Time-Warner* doctrine, at least the courts in Dakota. George thought to himself: while about half the states had adopted statutes permitting director consideration of the interests of other stakeholders, such as employees, customers, suppliers, communities and creditors, in the last analysis courts wanted those interests subordinated to maximizing shareholder profit. One expert said, "You manage day-to-day issues for the stakeholders but, in the long term, corporate governance is for the shareholders."

At that point, George stood up, walked to the front of the room and put his arm around Mark's shoulder. "Mark, you know we had to vote the way we did – you know that. Often shareholder interests and stakeholder interests are compatible. In a hostile premium bid, however, the shareholders must prevail." In his mind, Mark wasn't so sure, but he shook his friend's hand and the meeting was adjourned without further word.

A few weeks later, Roger Spayder's company issued a press release that began:

SPAYDER ENTERPRISES COMPLETES
TENDER OFFER FOR DFP

DAKOTA CITY – Spayder Enterprises today announced the successful completion of its $3.5 billion tender offer for all of the issued and outstanding shares of DFP, Inc. It said the remaining conditions for the consummation of the tender offer had been completed and the tender offer, as extended, had expired.

Spayder Enterprises commenced the tender offer more than 30 days ago to purchase all of the issued and outstanding shares of DFP's common stock. The tender offer was the first step in a merger transaction that will result in DFP being merged with and into Spayder. As a result, DFP will become a wholly owned subsidiary of Spayder Enterprises.

At the expiration of the tender offer, shares totaling more than 96 percent of the issued and outstanding shares of DFP had been tendered. Spayder Enterprises needed at least 80 percent tendered to move forward with its plans to acquire DFP. As a result of the tender offer, the New York Stock Exchange will suspend trading in DFP's common stock effective today.

"Mark, you won't believe who's on the phone," his executive assistant told him. "It's Roger Spayder."

Mark listened in disbelief after picking up the phone. "Mark," Spayder said, "I want you to stay on and run the Company, at least for a transition period. I'll make it worth your while. We're not buddies, but I think it's a good move for both of us – assuming, of course, you can still stomach me."

Actually, Mark understood Spayder's reasoning. The transition period would be difficult and someone with Mark's experience at a high level should be able to keep the Company running on an even keel and on a good profit path – plus it would ensure that many top employees, who were Mark's friends, would not be forced out too quickly. Mark still hated Spayder, but he could last for a while.

Mark responded, "Well, Roger, you've got a lot of chutzpah, I'll give you that. I can think of a thousand reasons not to accept your proposal, but, if we could get an ironclad employment and management agreement, I might do it. After we agree on reasonable operating and capital budgets, I'll want full operating authority and, if you interfere, I'll want a pot of money. Is that clear, Rog, baby?"

"O.K., Mark, you win. Have your lawyer call mine and we'll work out the terms."

Mark knew his days would be numbered in the job, but it would give him some time to help DFP adjust to its new owners. Plus, he was heartened to be asked to continue as a player with the Company he had helped build – even if time was running out for the Company as he knew it.

After consulting with his wife, who admired Mark's desire to soften the blow to DFP – not to mention retaining a good employment lawyer – he called Spayder a couple of days later and accepted the position.

CHAPTER 26

GEORGE'S LAST BOARD MEETING
What It's All About
(*First Quarter of Year 16*)

Agenda for Board Meeting

1. *Approval of Minutes*
2. *Review of Corporate Integration Program for the combination of operating segments of Spayder Enterprises and DFP – COO*
3. *Review and authorization of integration of incentive plans, pension plans and retirement plans of combining companies – COO*
4. *Appointment of new officers – HR Director*
5. *Discussion of potential contraction of workforce and layoff program with possible modest severance program – HR Director*
6. *Staffing of Board of Directors – George Hartfield, Acting Chairman*
7. *Scheduling of Future Board Meeting – Acting Chairman*
8. *A Resolution Honoring George Hartfield – Corporate Secretary.*

As George watched the Board members walk in, he realized he would miss them all on many levels. Though individually they had their foibles – as he acknowledged he did – the Board members as a team had grown tremendously as they had helped steer the Company over the years. Even now, with most of them leaving in the wake of the

Spayder purchase, they had indicated that they felt a shared camaraderie not unlike that of a high-caliber college athletic team that had gone through a championship season.

So much had happened in the decade-plus of George's Board services, he thought – and especially in the four months since the Spayder bid had been accepted. Though Spayder initially had asked Mark to stay and actually had treated him well at first, the old bitterness had resurfaced quickly within both men – and Mark recently had been asked to resign. He had received a generous severance package, in exchange for a one-year non-compete covenant under which Mark promised not to compete with Spayder or DFP. In the package, Mark had asked for one additional matter to be included: He wanted to be allowed to attend this final Board meeting, at which George would be honored for his years of service. Spayder agreed.

Ironically, George would be presiding over his own final DFP Board meeting. Spayder had asked George to serve as an outside Board Chairman until Spayder himself could take over that post, since Spayder was on a trip to Glasgow, Scotland.

"I'd like to call the meeting to order," George said. It still seemed strange to him that Mark wasn't leading the session, but it allowed him to take a few minutes before calling the first agenda item to reflect on his experience as a DFP Director and his pending resignation as a Director on the new Board.

"I believe that all of you should be proud of your service as DFP Directors," George began. "I'm sure you all would admit that much of it has been hard work and we were subject to a lot of criticism – a good deal of it unwarranted, I might add – but we had a positive experience overall. Working with someone like Mark Gregory is a treat, although from time-to-time," he said as he looked directly at Mark, "like any good CEO, you presented us with some real conundrums."

"I second that, George!" Judy teased. Mark gave her a mock look of innocence, and turned back to George as he continued.

"We all have been well compensated for our service, but no one should ever join a board for the compensation. As we all know too well, most directors incur far more risk and time expenditure than is justified by the compensation. Many don't see it that way, but if you put in between 175 and 225 hours a year, as do most of us on this Board, we would earn much more if we billed our time at our regular effective hourly rates.

"At the same time, I must tell you that the collegiality of this Board and the camaraderie we have developed are very special. Without question, this has been an energizing experience – although I'd only want to go around this track once in a lifetime. The ups and downs we had with DFP operations, financial results and ultimately with the business combination with Spayder Enterprises were more than any director should have to experience in one Boardroom career. I've enjoyed it and hope all of you have too.

"Now, for the first agenda item..."

After the first seven agenda items had been taken care of, George intoned, to the amusement of the other Directors: "I can't believe I'm doing this, but Mark said I had to, so here's the next agenda item: A Resolution Honoring George Hartfield. I recognize Barbara Ramos. Would you read the resolution, please?"

Barbara read the following:

WHEREAS, George R. Hartfield consistently has held positions of leadership for the DFP Board of Directors as Chairman of the Compensation Committee, Chairman of the Nominating Committee and as its Lead Director;

WHEREAS, George Hartfield has performed admirably on behalf of the shareholders of DFP and has brought extraordinary leadership to the Board and to its committees with his intellect, judgment and perspective;

NOW, THEREFORE, BE IT RESOLVED, that as George Hartfield retires from this Board, his colleagues salute him as an outstanding leader and Director for DFP, thank him for his consistent willingness to contribute to the most important Board responsibilities, and assure him of the continuing friendship of his colleagues, with their admiration and best wishes.

When she finished, Mark stood up. "I think this is one resolution on which we can all agree. Is that correct?" The Board members quietly applauded and nodded their heads in sincere appreciation. Mark turned to George.

"George, in addition to the resolution we've just unanimously passed, I'd like to add my personal appreciation for everything – and I mean everything – you've done for this Company, and for me personally, over the years. Do you have anything you'd like to say?"

"Thanks, Mark, and a sincere thank you to the rest of you as well," George said as he turned to the assembled Directors. "I know we all agree that voting for the Spayder deal was one of the hardest things we've ever had to do, and I had thought about addressing that. Instead, I decided to share with you a letter that Mark gave to me earlier this week. It's from a longtime employee-shareholder, and I think it says more about our duties and responsibilities than anything I could write."

George pulled the letter from inside his coat pocket and adjusted his glasses before beginning:

Dear Members of the DFP Board of Directors:

My family and I have been employees of DFP for the past 15 years. We have acquired a large number of shares of stock through the Company's Employee Stock Purchase Plan and also have been fortunate enough to receive stock option grants. We want to thank all of you for being excellent stewards of the Company and acting in the interests of both shareholders and employees.

Many of us realize what a difficult decision you had in deciding whether to recommend the offer of Spayder Enterprises for all of the DFP stock. As employees, we had real concerns, since we knew Mr. Spayder continually has demonstrated that he is a hard-hearted cost-cutter and already has announced – after promising not to do so – that he will lay off about 10 percent of the DFP employees.

Notwithstanding Mr. Spayder's broken commitments, most of us are very pleased that the DFP Board decided to go ahead and endorse the bid. We know the economy is becoming more difficult every month and if you had not recommended the tender offer, we fully expect that the DFP stock might have dropped by more than 20 percent in the current stock market.

Many of us, like those in my family, have become millionaires as a result of owning DFP stock, so we think you did the right thing when you recommended the tender offer to all of us. My husband and I also plan to take early retirement from DFP and live on our savings from your generous retirement program. Others are planning to leave DFP to join other companies — before Mr. Spayder fires them. Even so, we all had a wonderful experience with DFP and most of us are ready to turn a new page in our lives. We thank all of you again for making a difficult decision – but one that made sense to almost all of us in our capacity as long-time shareholders of DFP.

Sincerely,
Emma Jones

George stopped and put the letter down. "It's those kinds of letters that make you feel good about being a director." The Directors nodded in assent.

"But," George added with a grin, "I can't let you go away *too* happy. I also must tell you that our General Counsel advised me that a lawsuit has been filed against all of us by some of our more aggressive shareholders, charging us with recommending the sale of DFP stock to Spayder Enterprises at too low a price.

I understand as well that a related plaintiff may be suing Spayder for paying too much."

"It just never ends, does it, George?" Gen. Landry said.

"Well, General, I'm not too worried about these suits. I expect ultimately that they will be settled for a nuisance value. I just wanted to mention them to show you that, as the world turns, there are some unusual people out there – but at least, as the letter from Emma Jones showed, there are a few who are grateful for what we have done."

With that, George turned to Mark. After they shook hands, George made his last comments as a DFP Director:

"It's been a great ride, folks. We made a lot of decisions together – a few poor ones, but mostly solid ones. I think we left our shareholders in much better shape than we found them. I guess that's what it's all about.

"Meeting adjourned."

EPILOGUE

Not Quite Completing the Circle

Eighteen months after the last DFP Board meeting, the newly combined companies (DFP and Spayder Enterprises) were operating in an acceptable manner – but clearly not retaining their competitive edge in the marketplace. Spayder, who had the reputation of losing interest quickly in new operations and moving on to seek out new deals elsewhere, was still eyeing a company in Scotland that he thought would be a good fit with one of his other properties.

While Spayder was in Europe, the management of the largest global food conglomerate, FoodStuffs, Ltd., decided to pounce. Arthur MacHenry, its CEO, had been watching Spayder's operation from afar, and thought it was underperforming. Though Spayder Enterprises was making a tidy profit, FoodStuffs' business development team had drawn up confidential plans to restructure it in a manner that was projected to be much more cost effective, while at the same time continuing FoodStuffs' reputation as a high-expectation, but employee-friendly, company.

So, FoodStuffs acquired Spayder Enterprises – with very little complaint from Spayder, whose newest personal acquisition in Scotland was about to come to fruition. Plus, he would make a handsome sum on the sale of Spayder Enterprises to FoodStuffs. He did ask, however, to remain as President, at least until his next deal was signed. He didn't yet know of FoodStuffs' idea as to who should come back as CEO to replace the retiring CEO of FoodStuffs: Mark Gregory.

Though Mark had become a leading consultant, a business school adjunct professor and an outstanding commentator on a financial television network, he privately had yearned to return to the leadership of a large corporation. He accepted the job.

When Spayder heard of the appointment, he resigned before Mark could fire him.

As Mark began making his plans for the Company, he realized the circle was complete – except for one thing. He had his assistant set up a dinner with George Hartfield.

Mark and George were having a great dinner at the Fargo Club, animatedly discussing the strange turn of events over the previous 18 months. A vintage merlot from the Napa Valley of California was being served when Mark finally asked the question:

"George, why don't you come out of retirement and rejoin our Board?"

George didn't see that one coming. He took a sip of his wine and put down his glass.

"I'm flattered, Mark – but no. I think you're ready to forge your own relationships with a new Board. You hardly need my help. But remember – a Lead Director may continue to make sense for you in the future, even though all of your earlier experience as a Board Chairman should mean that you might not need to call on him or her as much as you called on me. Of course, if you ever need my input, I'm as close as the nearest phone.

"But for now, I'm staying retired – or at least semi-retired."

"Okay, George – sadly, we'll go without you. And, oh, by the way, this time our Board table will be a round one."

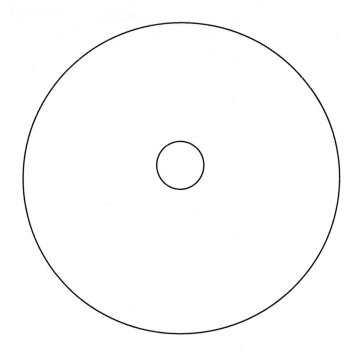

**New Board Table
(Year 17)**

Part IV

CLOSING COMMENTARY

James R. Ukropina

FUNDAMENTAL MATTERS CONCERNING BOARD SERVICE

In preparing this book, I was asked by friends and colleagues to include a section on certain fundamental matters concerning Board service:

1. What factors should I take into account when joining a board?
2. What traits characterize a good and a bad director (what I refer to below as the "varsity director" and the "junior varsity director")?
3. How can I, as a director, help management "see around the corner" for signs of impending trouble?
4. What will the board governance process look like in coming years of the 21st Century?

I've attempted to answer those questions in the pages that follow. Included in the answers is an excellent checklist of corporate "warning signs" prepared by one of the top commentators on good corporate governance, former Lockheed Martin CEO Norman Augustine.

1. **What Factors Should I Take Into Account When Deciding Whether To Join A Board?**
   A. Is the Company that has invited me to serve on the Board (the "Company") one that has interesting operations and is apt to be in a growth cycle for some time to come?
   B. Who is the CEO and, if a different party, who is the Chairman? How well do I know him or her? Does the CEO have the kind of integrity, experience and ethical outlook that will help to minimize the chances that the Company (and the Board) "will get in trouble"?

C. Do I have the time to devote to Board activities? (Many Boards of large companies require from 175 to 225 hours per year for travel, preparation, meeting attendance and similar activities.)

D. Does my schedule conflict with the Board meeting schedule, including scheduled Board Committee meetings? (Note, many Board Committee meetings now are held on days other than on the Board meeting date.)

E. Does the Company maintain adequate directors' and officers' indemnification insurance? Are there expansive indemnification provisions in the Company's Bylaws?

F. Which firm serves as the Company's independent audit firm? How long has it served in that position?

G. What law firms does the Company use? Are they experienced in corporate law, federal securities law and governance matters?

H. Who are the other directors, and what roles do they play in the governance process? Is there a lead director? If so, who is that party? Can I talk to a few directors to get a "feel" for how the governance process works?

I. Are the packages of Board meeting materials sent out to directors well before the Board meeting? If so, what is the typical lead time?

J. Does the Board have many "virtual meetings" by which the Chairman of the Board sends out multiple e-mails between Board meetings to secure the sentiments of Board members on relevant issues? If so, is this done effectively? Is this a particularly time-consuming process?

K. What major lawsuits are pending against the Company or the Board, if any? Are there any threatened or anticipated lawsuits or regulatory proceedings that may soon be filed?

L. Do the outside directors routinely meet alone?

M. Is there a management succession plan in place?

N. Does anyone in top management have the reputation for being self-serving?

2. **What Traits Characterize a Good and a Bad Director (the "Varsity Director" and the "Junior Varsity Director")?**

No one really knows exactly what goes into the recipe for a good director, including the author. Nonetheless, here's some food for thought consisting of a list of good and bad traits (with help from Norm Augustine on some of the more critical traits).

A. **Varsity Director**
   i. Independent-minded, but with a collegial personality embracing a team approach.
   ii. Highly ethical with a strong moral compass.
   iii. A quick study who asks incisive questions and will not take an evasive answer for a response.
   iv. The ability to see around corners (see checklist below).
   v. Thorough preparation for Board meetings with a review of all meeting materials and an appetite for collateral materials about the Company, such as securities analysts' reports. A strong desire to understand how the business really "works" and a decent grasp of the applicable business model.
   vi. A desire to ask for an opinion or a report from an expert when one is needed, especially if management has not established that its views are independent (e.g., a fairness opinion from a banking firm for a large or unusual acquisition transaction).
   vii. An understanding of the difficulties of advancing good leadership and a willingness to support the CEO in a crisis.
   viii. Reasonable patience.
   ix. Willing and able to speak succinctly in making comments so as not to unduly impose on the limited time available for all directors.

x. Attention to important detail, including any significant variance from strategy or variances from budget.

xi. Creativity that will help management look at alternative solutions when difficult operating issues arise.

xii. A willingness to focus on policy matters, strategic issues and critical compensation issues without undue involvement in day-to-day operations.

xiii. An understanding of the legal aspects of performing the fiduciary duties of a director and, if little understanding, a willingness to review such publications as the "Corporate Director's Guidebook" published by the Business Section of the American Bar Association. (For the Third Edition of the Guidebook, see the August 2001 issue of the *Business Lawyer* at pages 1575-1632). Also, for updates on good corporate practices see ongoing publications or surveys published by organizations like Korn/Ferry International and the National Association of Corporate Directors.

xiv. A fundamental understanding of financial issues and accounting principles in order to qualify as "financially literate" for service on the audit committee and to keep pace with financial discussions during board and board committee meetings.

xv. A willingness to bring personal "political clout" to bear when it can help the Company.

xvi. Has no material conflicts of interest with interests of the corporation.

B. **Junior Varsity Director**
In many respects, the Junior Varsity Director has "inverse" or inconsistent traits with those listed above for the Varsity Director. As noted below, there are some additional special liabilities a Junior Varsity Director may bring into the Boardroom.

   i. Not thoroughly prepared for Board meetings and the questions posed by the director reflect lack of preparation.

  ii. Lack of focus on boardroom activities during Board meetings with multiple interruptions to take telephone calls and check voicemail messages.

 iii. An unreasonable desire to speak more often than is necessary with little consideration or attentiveness to management and other directors in the boardroom.

 iv. Tendency to get lost in the "details" and inability to see the big picture.

  v. Little familiarity with the day-to-day operations of the Company and limited understanding of the relevant industries in which the Company operates.

 vi. Focuses on a single issue with potential for being a narrow zealot.

 vii. Has a superficial understanding of issues and is prone to making non-substantive and non-constructive comments (e.g., quick to criticize new plans but never offers a constructive alternative).

viii. Poor relationships with the general counsel and the corporate secretary because does not respond on a timely basis to requests for documents that must be reviewed and executed by directors (e.g., the Annual Meeting Proxy Statement; the 10-K Report; 10-Q Report; written consent forms; and similar documents).

 ix. Flagrant disregard for the corporate chain of command. Communications with junior officers and staff undermine senior management.

  x. Gross disregard for confidentiality.

3. **How Can I Help Management to "See Around the Corner" for Signs Of Impending Trouble?**

Where there is a good governance process, the members of senior management, particularly the CEO, should do all they can to prevent the Board from being "surprised." In certain cases, however, the business cycle becomes so frantic that the CEO is not able to see trouble looming on the horizon. In my experience, and in the experience of others, there are certain corporate developments that should serve as potential warning signs of impending trouble.

I have found no better list of such items than one prepared by my friend and colleague, Norman Augustine, the former CEO of Lockheed Martin and a veteran board member. His extremely helpful list is set forth below:

Managing Business Risk:

Fifty Warning Signs of Impending Trouble

1. ☐ Management with questionable ethical standards
2. ☐ Start-up business
3. ☐ New products or processes
4. ☐ Recent mergers or acquisitions
5. ☐ Operations in politically/economically unstable countries
6. ☐ Business in fields of rapid technological advancement
7. ☐ History of management turnover
8. ☐ Recent reorganization
9. ☐ High financial leverage; demanding covenants
10. ☐ High multiple
11. ☐ Declining margins
12. ☐ Speculative investments in facilities/inventories to support future growth
13. ☐ Significant off-balance-sheet debt or transactions
14. ☐ Declining market demand; small or declining market share
15. ☐ Aggressive financial positions (leveraged derivatives, futures, etc.)
16. ☐ Inadequate reserves or history of misapplying reserves
17. ☐ Hazardous manufacturing processes or products

18. ☐ Inadequate insurance
19. ☐ Highly-regulated business
20. ☐ Insiders selling significant amounts of stock
21. ☐ Dependence on few suppliers, customers or products
22. ☐ Lack of formal delegations of authority
23. ☐ Weak, changing or unverified control systems, including IT
24. ☐ Diversification into new markets or geographical locations
25. ☐ Arrogant, autocratic, risk-taking management
26. ☐ Business characterized by episodic major events
27. ☐ Activities (including past acquisitions) affecting the natural environment
28. ☐ Significant pending litigation
29. ☐ Lack of successors for key employees
30. ☐ Poor or deteriorating credit rating
31. ☐ Volatile stock price
32. ☐ Large fixed-price contracts
33. ☐ Militant labor force
34. ☐ Susceptibility to natural disasters
35. ☐ Weak or untested management; management with spotty track record
36. ☐ Outside directors do not meet alone on regular basis
37. ☐ Vulnerability to fraud
38. ☐ Inadequate cash resources; consuming cash
39. ☐ Impacted by events outside control of management
40. ☐ High public visibility
41. ☐ Lack of checks and balances
42. ☐ Significant near-term debt payments
43. ☐ Several inside directors; CEO selects directors; large board
44. ☐ Recent rapid growth
45. ☐ Assets vulnerable to devaluation; frequent write-offs

46. ☐ Disputes with outside auditors or recent change of auditors
47. ☐ Restated or obscure financial reports; dependence on pro forma accounting
48. ☐ Excessively paid executives; unreasonable financial goals
49. ☐ Related party transactions or family ownership
50. ☐ CEO just left to pursue personal interests

Score:
5 or less: It's time to wake up!; 6-10: You're headed for trouble; 11-15: You're in trouble; 16-19: You're in deep trouble; and 20 or more: Prepare three envelopes.*

*A reference to the joke about the just-fired CEO handing three numbered envelopes to his successor, with instructions to open the envelopes in sequence whenever he/she faced a crisis. As the new CEO encountered a succession of serious problems, it was discovered that the three envelopes contained the messages, "blame your predecessor," "blame bad luck," and "prepare three envelopes"!

4. **What Will Board Governance Look Like In The Coming Years Of The 21st Century?**
Again, I call on my friend Norm Augustine for his views of the Board of the 21st Century along with a few of my own thoughts.
   A. Both of us believe that boards will become increasingly independent of management but, to be effective, Board members will need to have a constructive relationship with management.
   B. Effective boards in the 21st Century will understand the difference between concentrating on appropriate governance issues (like policy questions, strategic issues and significant compensation and personnel issues) and involving themselves unnecessarily in day-to-day management.

C. Increasingly, boards will have either a "lead director" or a "coordinating director."

D. Directors will have to become increasingly competent in connection with technological developments in the relevant industries.

E. In recent years, boards have decreased from about sixteen members to about eleven. Norm and I both think boards will stay about this size for some time. As board service becomes even more intense and board committees become more active, boards may have to expand somewhat in order to accommodate multiple and expanding committee responsibilities.

F. Boards will accommodate increased international participation and representation from new board members, and teleconferencing and phone meetings will become more frequent.

G. Director compensation will continue to increase but there will be expanded use of grant of stock options or issuance of stock to directors in lieu of cash.

H. There will be more "virtual meetings" in which directors will converse with one another, and with management, over the internet. For example, the "reply to all" button on the personal computer (a dangerous button in my experience) will be used more frequently as board member sentiments are distributed to all board members and key members of management in response to a management inquiry for board input.

I. More women and minorities will be available for board service as certain ceilings on advancement are further removed.

J. There will be heavier reliance on committees of the board to address special issues.

K. There may be an increasing but possibly detrimental use of individual report cards evaluating individual performance by each director.

L. There could be even more reluctance by board candidates to join boards due to legal liability exposure, intense pressure on boards by institutional investors, increasing time commitments for board service and potential issuance of report cards referenced in item K above.

M. There will be an increasing number of private meetings among outside directors (i.e., without management present).

N. There will be an increase in the ratio of outside directors to inside directors.

O. Board activities will become much less formal – focusing more on two-way meaningful discussions about strategic progress rather than formal presentations about the prior quarter's financials.

GLOSSARY OF TERMS

Listed below are more than 200 terms either used in this Book or in boardroom discussions that may be helpful to the reader as well as to those who are going to a corporate boardroom for the first time or will revisit one after a long absence. For the user of this Glossary (and for the lawyers and accountants who are "purists"), keep in mind that these explanations are definitions, and definitions are, as stated, not precise. Instead, they are working definitions designed to give the user a fundamental – but, in many cases not a complete – understanding of a term or a subject. Of course, if one really wants to understand a concept like "GAAP" (Generally Accepted Accounting Principles) there are thousands of pages of such principles available for you. Then you can read voluminous interpretations thereof and you will have just started to skim the surface of what GAAP is all about.

Many of the explanations for the terms have been taken, in whole or in part, from the "Securities Law Glossary" authored by the American Bar Association and published by the Securities Law Committee of the ABA Young Lawyers Division. Most are general in nature and are not intended to be detailed or comprehensive technical descriptions of a particular concept. Further, definitions may change over a period of time as legal and business dynamics evolve.

Some of the other definitions have been taken from the Seventh Edition of Black's Law Dictionary, published by the West Group. The definitions taken from Black's include articles of incorporation, board of directors, buyout, cash flow, closing, certificate of incorporation, committee, common law, consent, director (and certain categories of directors), earnout agreement, proxy, proxy contest, proxy solicitation, proxy statement, write-down or write-off and ultra vires. Other definitions are those of the author, including CEO, COO, conflict of interest, and Lead Director. Following is a list of the terms explained here:

Ad Hoc Committee	Consolidation
Agenda	Contingent Liability
Amortization	Control Person
Annual Meeting of Shareholders	Conversion Price
Annual Report	Conversion Ratio or Conversion Rate
Arbitrage	Convertible Bond
Articles of Incorporation	Convertible Issue
Audit	COO
Auditor	"Cooked Books" or "Cooking the
Balance Sheet	Books"
Basis Point	Corporate Governance
Bear Hug Letter	Corporate Governance Guidelines
Bear Market	Corporate Opportunity Doctrine
Bid	Corporate Secretary
Black-Scholes Formula	Covenant
Board of Directors	Credit Event
Book Value	Cumulative Voting
Bull Market	Current Maturity
Business Judgment Rule	Current Ratio
Buyout	Current Yield
Bylaws	Debentures
Call	Derivative Instrument
Callable Bond	Dilution
Capital	Director
Capital Gain	Directors' and Officers' Liability
Capitalization	Insurance
Capitalize	Disintermediation
Capital Loss	Dividend
Cash Flow	Dutch Auction
CEO	Earnings
Certificate of Incorporation	Earnings Per Share (EPS)
Certification	Earnings Report
CFO	Earnout Agreement
Chairman	EBIT
Closing	EBITDA
Collateralized Bond Obligation	EDGAR
Commercial Paper	Entrepreneur
Committee	Equity
Common Law	Euro Bonds
Confidentiality Agreement	Eurodollars
Conflict of Interest	Exempt Securities
Consent	Exercise Price
	Fairness Opinion

	FASB
FCPA	Material Adverse Change or MAC
Federal Funds	M&A
Federal Funds Rate	MD&A
Fixed-rate Loan	Merger
Flip-In Plan	Mezzanine Investment
Flip-Over Plans	Money Market
Float	NASDAQ
Freeze Out	Note
GAAP	Off-Balance Sheet Financing
GAAS	Officer
General Counsel	Opportunity Cost
Golden Parachute Agreement	Option
Goodwill	OSHA
Hedge	Poison Pill
Indemnification	Preferred Stock
Indenture	Prime Rate
Initial Public Offering (IPO)	Principal
Inside Directors	Private Placement
Insider	Profit Margin
Insider Trading	Pro forma
Institutional Investor	Prospectus
In-the-money Option	Proxy
Investment Advisor	Proxy Agent
Investment Banker	Proxy Card
Investor	Proxy Fight
Issued Shares	Proxy Solicitation
Lead Director	Proxy Statement
LBO	Public Offering
Leverage	Put
Leveraged Lease	Quick-Asset Ratio
LIBOR	Quorum
Line of Credit	Rating
Liquidity	Related Party Transaction
Liquidity Risk	Resolution
Listed Stock	Restricted Securities
Lock-up Option	Return on Equity
Manipulation	Return on Investment
Margin	Revolver
Marginal Tax Rate	Revolving Line of Credit
Market Capitalization	Risk
Market Value	Roll over
Marketability	Rule 10(b)-5
Schedule 13-D	Subordinated Debenture
SEC	Swap

SEC Form 3 and SEC Form 4	Target Corporation
Secondary Offering or Distribution	10-K Report
	10-Q Report
Severance Payment	Tender Offer
Shareholder	Time Value
Shares Authorized	Treasury Bill
Shares Outstanding	Ultra Vires
Shark Repellants	Underwriters
Shelf Registration	Underwriting Syndicate
Short Sale	Venture Capital
Short-Swing Profits	Venture Capital Investments
Social Issues	Voting Right
Spread	Warrant
Squeezeouts	White Knight
Staggered Terms for Board of Directors	Working Capital or Net Working Capital
Standstill Agreement	Working Control
Stockholder of Record	Write-down
Stockholders' Equity	Write-off
Stock Option	Yield to Maturity
Stock Split	
Street	

EXPLANATION OF TERMS

AD HOC COMMITTEE – A temporary or special committee (e.g., a committee to investigate charges of unlawful conduct); not a standing or traditional committee.

AGENDA – List of topics to be covered at a meeting. Often the order in which Agenda items are set is important as that order may serve to prioritize or de-emphasize a significant issue.

AMORTIZATION – The gradual repayment of the principal amount of a debt through equal periodic payments which are sufficient to meet current principal and interest and charges and liquidate the principal debt at maturity.

ANNUAL MEETING OF SHAREHOLDERS – Under state statutory requirements, corporations must hold one meeting per year at which shareholders are represented in person or by proxy (typically the latter). At this meeting, at a minimum, directors are elected for at least a one year term and a report is made concerning financial matters. Special items also may be on the agenda for the meeting, including ratification of auditors, amendments to charter documents, mergers or acquisitions, proposals made by shareholders and similar matters. Voting for some meetings is now conducted over the Internet and, in some cases, the meeting proceedings are webcast. Most annual meetings are constructive events but a few have turned into "circuses" dominated by single-purpose shareholders. Now, some observers question whether annual meetings are cost effective when taking into consideration the interest of all shareholders.

ANNUAL REPORT – This document includes the formal financial statement issued yearly by a corporation to its shareholders. The annual report usually contains a discussion by management of a Corporation's operations and shows, among other items, liabilities and profits during the past year of operation. It often includes a letter from the Chairman and Chief Executive Officer to all shareholders along with photos and graphics depicting various aspects of the Corporation's operations during the prior fiscal years along with commentary and projections about the Corporation's future prospects.

ARBITRAGE – Strictly defined, buying something where it is cheap and selling it where it is dear; e.g., a bank buys 3-month CD money in the U.S. market and sells 3-month money at a higher rate in the

Eurodollar market. In the money market, often refers to: (a) a situation in which a trader buys one security and sells a similar security in the expectation that the spread in yields between the two instruments will narrow or widen to his profit, (b) a swap between two similar issues based on an anticipated change in yield spreads, and (c) situations where a higher return (or lower cost) can be achieved in the money market for one currency by utilizing another currency and swapping it on a fully hedged basis through the foreign exchange market.

ARTICLES OF INCORPORATION – A document that sets forth the basic terms of a corporation's existence, including its name, the authorized number and classes of shares and the purposes and duration of the corporation. In most states, the articles of incorporation are filed with the secretary of state as part of the process for forming the corporation. In some states, the articles serve as a certificate evidencing incorporation and are the official recognition of the corporation's existence. In other states, the government issues a separate certificate of incorporation after approving the articles and other required documents. Also called the "charter" or "certificate of incorporation".

AUDIT – An examination of financial accounts and statements with a possible adjustment thereof. One who conducts an audit is generally called an "auditor".

BALANCE SHEET – A financial statement showing, as of a specific date, a corporation's assets (what the company owns), its liabilities (what it owes), and the difference, called "net worth," "stockholders' equity" or "shareholders equity".

BASIS POINT – One one hundredth of 1%.

BEAR HUG LETTER – A letter sent by a prospective bidder or corporate raider making an unsolicited and often aggressive proposal for the bidder to acquire the target company at some premium price above the current market price for the target company's stock. Usually delivered in a fashion to generate the consideration by the management of the target company of an uncomfortable and unwanted early disclosure of the bid to the public. A device designed to squeeze the target company into acceptance of the bid.

BEAR MARKET – A declining market or a period of pessimism when declines in the market are anticipated. Usually represents at least a 20% overall decline in the market.

BID – Any proposal to acquire a company or its stock or assets. The maker of a bid is often called the bidder.

BLACK-SCHOLES FORMULA – A formula created by Messrs. Black and Scholes to value traded options. Also used in a corporate context to value stock options granted to officers and employees. Value depends upon such factors as volatility of underlying stock and terms of option. Many options have a Black-Scholes value of about 30% of their market capitalization (i.e., 30% of total of per share exercise price times number of shares issuable under the stock option).

BOARD OF DIRECTORS – A group of persons elected, usually annually, by the shareholders of a corporation to exercise powers granted by the corporation's charter and state law. These powers usually include management of the corporation's business and affairs, appointment of officers, issuance of shares, declaration of dividends, and similar matters.

BOOK VALUE – A company's total assets minus intangible assets and liabilities such as debt. Book value per share is the total book value divided by the average number of common shares. A company's book value may be higher or lower than the value of the company reflected by the trading value of its stock in the marketplace. Book value is often confused with inherent economic value, but it should not be since it only reflects the results of accounting principles and not necessarily an appraisal or a market valuation.

BULL MARKET – A period of optimism when increases in market prices are anticipated.

BUSINESS JUDGMENT RULE – A judicial presumption and defense that, in making a business decision, the directors of a corporation act on an informed basis, in good faith, and with the honest belief that the action taken is in the best interest of the corporation. Absent a abuse of discretion, ordinarily any director's judgment is respected by the court because courts ordinarily do not wish to interfere with business decisions and, absent that abuse, a director should not incur liability for that decision by way of a judicial judgment. In recent years, a good deal of emphasis has been placed in cases where the Rule has been invoked as a defense on such issues as whether a director is perceived to be interested in the subject matter of the business judgment and whether the director is well informed with respect to that subject matter.

BUYOUT – The purchase of all or a controlling percentage of the assets or shares of a corporation: *(a) Leveraged buyout.* The purchase of a publicly held corporation's outstanding stock by its management or outside investors, financed mainly with funds borrowed through investment bankers and usually secured by the corporation's

319

assets. – Abbr. LBO; *(b) Management buyout:* (1) A buyout of a corporation by its own directors and officers: (2) A leveraged buyout of a corporation by an outside entity in which the corporation's management has a material financial interest. – Abbr. MBO.

BYLAWS – Rules adopted by a corporation for its internal governance with permissible contents governed by state law. Bylaws often cover such matters as meetings of shareholders, the constituency of and procedures for the boards of directors, the nature of board committees, corporate officers, stock issuance and indemnification of directors and officers.

CALL – An option that gives the holder the right to buy the underlying security at a specified price during a fixed time period.

CALLABLE BOND – A bond that the issuer has the right to redeem prior to maturity by paying some specified call price.

CAPITAL – Money invested in a business is financial capital; generally a capital asset is one with a life of more than one year that is not bought and sold in the ordinary course of business; plant, equipment, and other physical resources that enable a business to produce goods and services are physical capital.

CAPITAL GAIN – A gain realized on the sale or exchange of securities, fixed property or similar "capital" assets. The term is used in the Internal Revenue Code. Any capital gain is taxed at substantially lower rates than those applicable to ordinary income.

CAPITALIZATION – All money that has been invested in a business, including equity capital (common stock and preferred stock), long term debt (bonds), retained earnings and other surplus funds.

CAPITALIZE – A procedure whereby certain expenditures are deemed to be payments for an asset and are therefore recorded on the books of the reporting company as an asset and later amortized over a number of years rather than being treated as a current expense in the period in which the payment is made. In the late 1990's, controversies arose as to whether certain outlays should be capitalized as apparently excessive capitalization practices were adopted by some companies thereby artificially increasing earnings by correspondingly reducing expenses accrued in the then current period.

CAPITAL LOSS – A loss realized on the sale or exchange of securities, fixed property or similar "capital" assets. The loss, in some cases, can be used to reduce taxes.

CASH FLOW – Reported net income of a corporation plus amounts charged off for deductions and not paid out in cash, such as depreciation, depletion, amortization, and extraordinary charges to reserves. Cash flow is a yardstick used for, among other things, the measurement of the ability of a company to pay dividends and finance expansion from self-generated cash: *(a) cash flow per common share.* The cash flow from operations minus preferred stock dividends divided by the number of outstanding common shares; *(b) discounted cash flow.* A method of evaluating a capital investment by comparing its projected cash outflow and cash costs with its current value. – Abbr. DCF; (c) *incremental cash flow.* The net increase in cash flow attributable to a particular capital investment; (d) n*egative cash flow.* A financial situation in which cash outflow exceeds cash inflow; (e) *net cash flow.* Cash inflow minus cash outflow.

CEO – The Chief Executive Officer of a corporation. Ordinarily, the senior-most corporate officer in management. Typically, in the United States, the Chief Executive Officer also serves as the Chairman of the Board, the senior officer of the Board of Directors. Ordinarily, an effective CEO must be a good manager and an outstanding leader. One business executive defined a leader as "someone who can take a group of people to a place they don't think they can go." (Daimler Chrysler CEO Bob Eaton)

CERTIFICATE OF INCORPORATION – A document issued by a state authority (usually the secretary of state) granting a corporation its legal existence and the right to function as a corporation. Also termed "charter" or "articles of incorporation".

CERTIFICATION – The process by which a CEO and CFO certify that the financial statements of a Company are adequate.

CFO – Stands for Chief Financial Officer. Usually the senior most officer in the financial area for a corporation. His or her responsibilities include financings, accounting, financial controls, investor relations and similar duties.

CHAIRMAN – The officer who presides over the Board of Directors. Often serves as the CEO as well. In addition, typically will preside at Annual Meeting of Shareholders.

CLOSING – The final meeting between the parties to a transaction, at which the transaction is consummated; especially, in real estate, the final transaction between the buyer and seller, whereby the conveyancing documents are concluded and the money and property transferred.

COLLATERALIZED BOND OBLIGATION (CBO) – A pool of bonds, usually through a trust consisting of high yield securities (both US high yield debt & emerging market debt). The trust is reduced to 2 or more portions or interests, varying in risk and yield. The Equity tranche is considered the most risky portion of the CBO because it bears the brunt of any default from the high yield trust. CBOs consist of a portfolio of many underlying securities where the cash flows from the securitization are derived from this portfolio.

COMMERCIAL PAPER – An unsecured promissory note with a fixed maturity of no more than 270 days. Commercial paper is normally sold by corporations with strong credit ratings.

COMMITTEE – A group of people appointed or elected to consider, determine, or manage a matter. A board committee usually consists of three or more directors.

Most Boards have some traditional committees described below: (a) *Audit Committee:* Selects or recommends to board the external auditor and reviews auditor compensation, reviews financial statements with management and auditors as well as certain SEC filings; meets with management to cover risk management; recommends inclusion of financial statements in annual SEC 10-K Report; (b) *Compensation Committee:* Reviews and recommends compensation for executive officers; reviews proposed executive incentive plans; often serves as a management succession and development committee as well; (c) *Nominating and Corporate Governance Committee:* Recommends to the board a slate of nominees to be proposed by the board for election at annual meeting of shareholders; develops board practices and policies through adoption of corporate governance guidelines.

COMMON LAW – The body of law derived from judicial decisions, rather than from statutes or constitutions.

CONFIDENTIALITY AGREEMENT – An agreement under which one party agrees to treat as confidential non-public information received from the other party.

CONFLICT OF INTEREST – In a corporate context, a real or seeming incompatibility or clash between one's personal interest and one's fiduciary duties.

CONSENT – Agreement, approval, or permission as to some act or purpose, especially given voluntarily by a competent person. A "Unanimous Written Consent" is a type of consent form signed by all members of a board or board committee which binds that group and is equivalent, in effect, to action taken at a face-to-face board meeting or committee meeting.

CONSOLIDATION – The process by which the financial statements of two or more companies in a parent-subsidiary relationship are combined into a single financial statement on a line by line basis.

CONTINGENT LIABILITY – An obligation which is not fixed and unconditional but which will become so in the event one or more future and uncertain events occur.

CONTROL PERSON – Someone having the power, through the ownership of shares of stock or through some other means (e.g., proxies to vote shares of stock of other parties) to direct the management or policies of a corporation.

CONVERSION PRICE – The effective price paid for common stock when the stock is obtained by converting either convertible preferred stocks or convertible bonds. For example, if a $1,000 bond is convertible into twenty shares of stock, the conversion price is $50 ($1,000/20).

CONVERSION RATIO OR CONVERSION RATE – Used to calculate the number of shares of common stock that may be obtained by converting a convertible bond or share of convertible preferred stock.

CONVERTIBLE BOND – A bond containing a provision that permits conversion to the issuer's common stock at some fixed exchange ratio.

CONVERTIBLE ISSUE – A bond, debenture or preferred share which may be exchanged, by the owner, for common stock or another security, usually of the same company, in accordance with the terms of the issue.

COO – The Chief Operating Officer of a corporation. Typically, the COO concentrates on day-to-day management matters, including operations, purchasing, marketing and similar functions. The COO also has the title of "president" of the corporation in many U.S. corporations. In certain cases, the COO may be an outstanding manager but may not have all of the required leadership skills to step up to the position of chief executive officer.

"COOKED BOOKS" OR "COOKING THE BOOKS" – A phrase frequently employed by the Securities and Exchange Commission to refer to financial records which have been intentionally prepared to distort financial condition and results of operation.

CORPORATE GOVERNANCE – The system by which business corporations are directed and controlled.

CORPORATE GOVERNANCE GUIDELINES – Are used to specify the distribution of rights and responsibilities among different participants in the control of the corporation and they spell out the principles (but not with hard and fast rules or legal requirements) for making decisions about corporate affairs. Typically these principles govern such matters as the size and structure of the board; board procedural matters; committee matters; board membership matters as well as such matters as those involving succession planning, management development, executive compensation and special issues, such as the use of a lead director concept.

CORPORATE OPPORTUNITY DOCTRINE – In general, a corporate opportunity is the opportunity to engage in a business activity of which a director or a senior executive may become aware, under circumstances that should reasonably lead that person to believe that it should be offered to the corporation because the corporation could be reasonably anticipated to have an interest in it. A director or senior executive officer may not take advantage of such an opportunity unless the person first offers the corporate opportunity to the corporation and makes full disclosure to the board members concerning the conflict of interest which he or she has encountered and the corporate opportunity. Then, in order to be lawfully available to the director or senior executive officer, the corporate opportunity must be rejected by the corporation and that rejection must be fair to the corporation with full disclosure to those authorizing the rejection.

CORPORATE SECRETARY – A corporate officer whose primary statutory duty is to record minutes of board and board committee meetings. In fact, this position usually has much broader responsibilities. They include making arrangements for timely and orderly meetings, handling travel arrangements for directors. This position is often held by the party overseeing the legal aspects of directors' duties (e.g., assuring time for proper diligence), preparing governance guidelines, resolutions, amendments to bylaws and coordinating SEC filings. The corporate secretary often provides the "glue" to effect governance proceedings in an orderly and stylish basis.

COVENANT – A detailed clause contained in loan agreements and debt securities. Covenants are designed to protect the lender and include such items as limits on total indebtedness, restrictions on dividends, minimum current ratio, and similar provisions.

CREDIT EVENT – A condition of contract termination relating to credit derivative structures. Credit events are typically defined to include failure to pay, bankruptcy, acceleration, repudiation, or debt restructuring for a specified reference asset that is incorporated within a credit derivative transaction.

CUMULATIVE VOTING – A method of voting for corporate directors which enables a shareholder to multiply the number of his shares by the number of directorships being voted on and cast the total for one director or a selected group of directors. For example, a holder of 10 shares of stock with cumulative voting rights would be able to cast 10 votes for each of, say 12 of 20 nominees to a board of 12 directors. He thus has 120 votes. Under the cumulative voting principle he may do that or he may cast 120 (10 x 12) votes for only one nominee, 60 for two, 40 for three, or any other distribution he chooses. Cumulative voting may be required in certain instances under the corporate laws of some states (e.g., California) and is permitted in most others.

CURRENT MATURITY – Current time to maturity on an outstanding note, bond, or other money market instrument; for example, a 5-year note 1 year after issue has a current maturity of 4 years.

CURRENT RATIO – This ratio is determined by dividing the amount of current assets by the amount of current liabilities. The more liquidity which a company has the higher its ratio. A ratio below 1 may give lenders and others concern as this ratio, in general, is a indicator of the ability to pay short-term debt.

CURRENT YIELD – Coupon payments on a security as a percentage of the security's market price. In many instances the price should be gross of accrued interest, particularly on instruments where no coupon is left to be paid until maturity.

DEBENTURES – An unsecured (without collateral) bond issued on the general credit of the borrower.

DERIVATIVE INSTRUMENT – A financial instrument for which its price or value is derived from the price of an underlying financial asset. Examples include an option or a futures contract, the value of which is based, in part, on the value of the underlying stock or commodity.

DILUTION – May result from the issuance of additional shares of stock. The dilution may be of voting power if shares are not issued proportionately to the holdings of existing shareholders. In the alternative it may be financial, if shares are issued disproportionately and the price at which the new shares are issued is less than the market value or book value of the outstanding shares prior to the issuance of the new shares. Typically in an initial public offering, dilution refers to the fact that the new shareholders are paying substantially more than existing shareholders paid on a per share basis.

DIRECTOR – A person appointed or elected to sit on a board that manages the affairs of a corporation or company by electing and exercising control over its officers: (a) *class director.* (1) A director whose term on a corporate board is staggered with those of the other directors; often used to make a hostile takeover more difficult. (2) A director elected or appointed to a corporate board to represent a special interest group, e.g., the preferred stockholders; (b) *dummy director.* A board member who is a mere figurehead and exercises no real control over the corporation's business. Also, may be referred to as a "dummy incorporator" who signs documents to initiate the corporation's existence; (c) *inside director.* A director who is also an employee or officer of the corporation; (d) *interlocking director.* A director who simultaneously serves on the boards of two or more corporations that deal with each other or have allied interests; (e) *outside or independent director.* A nonemployee director with little or no direct interest in the corporation. At this time, there is an active debate underway concerning what degree of personal interest in or involvement with a company causes a director to lose his or her independence. '

DIRECTORS' AND OFFICERS' INDEMNIFICATION INSURANCE – Insurance covering a corporation's officers and directors to indemnify or hold them harmless from judgments, settlements, and fines arising from negligence suits, shareholder actions and other business related suits. (Reference to this type of insurance is also termed "Directors' and Officers' Liability Insurance" and is often shortened to "D&O Insurance."

DISINTERMEDIATION – The investing of funds that would normally have been placed with a bank or other financial intermediary directly into debt securities issued by ultimate borrowers; e.g., into bills or bonds.

DIVIDEND – A payment ordinarily from earned surplus or retained earnings made on a periodic basis (usually quarterly) at a given rate to shareholders owning stock on a given record date (e.g., the corporation declared a cash dividend of.20 per share to shareholders of record on May 15, 2008.)

DUTCH AUCTION – Auction in which the lowest price necessary to sell the entire offering becomes the price at which all securities offered are sold. This technique has been used in Treasury auctions.

EARNINGS – The amount of profit a company realizes after all costs, expenses and taxes have been paid.

EARNINGS PER SHARE (EPS) – The earnings of the reporting company divided by the average number of outstanding shares or share equivalents. Earnings per share calculations are made on the basis of the weighted average number of shares outstanding during the accounting period and may take into consideration the rights of persons holding options, warrants or convertible securities to acquire shares of the reporting company's common stock.

EARNINGS REPORT – A financial statement – also called an income statement or profit and loss statement – issued by a company showing the details of sales or revenues, costs, expenses, losses for a given period.

EARNOUT AGREEMENT – An agreement for the sale of a business under which a buyer first pays an agreed amount at an initial closing, leaving the final purchase price to be determined by the business future profits with one or more successive payments if certain profit objectives are met by the seller on a post-closing basis.

EBIT – Abbreviation for "Earnings Before Interest and Taxes."

EBITDA – "Earnings Before Interest, Taxes, Depreciation and Amortization." A measure of a corporation's cash flow.

EDGAR – Electronic Data Gathering Analysis and Retrieval. An electronic filing system used by the Securities and Exchange Commission to permit companies to file SEC reports electronically.

ENTREPRENEUR – One who undertakes to start and conduct a business or enterprise, assuming full control and risk. Often used to describe a "high roller," one who looks for big returns but who is willing to assume big risks to achieve them.

EQUITY – This term is used to cover many concepts. The fundamental concept is that it is equivalent to the net worth of business, consisting of various line items in the balance sheet, including capital stock, capital (or paid in) surplus and earned surplus or retained earnings. Common equity is that part of the total net worth or total equity which is attributable to common shareholders. The total equity would include that amount also attributable to preferred shareholders. The terms "common stock," "net worth" and "common equity" are often used interchangeably. Equity may reference other concepts. For example, in the real estate area, equity is the dollar difference between what a property could be sold for and various debts or claims against that property. In a brokerage account, equity may equal the value of an account's securities reduced by any debit balance in a margin account.

EURO BONDS – Bonds issued in Europe outside the confines of any national capital market. A Euro bond may or may not be denominated in the currency of the issuer.

EURODOLLARS – U.S. dollars deposited in a U.S. bank branch or a foreign bank located outside the United States. The "Euro" is the currency used in the European Union.

EXEMPT SECURITIES – Instruments exempt from the registration requirements of the Securities Act of 1933 or the margin requirements of the Securities Exchange Act of 1934. Such securities include governments, agencies, municipal securities and commercial paper.

EXERCISE PRICE – The price at which an option holder may buy or sell the underlying security. Also called the strike price.

FAIRNESS OPINION – An opinion delivered by an expert, usually an investment banking firm, to a board of directors of a party to an acquisition that the transaction, or the consideration for that transaction, is fair to that party's shareholders from a financial point of view.

FASB – Financial Accounting Standards Board. An organization which promulgates standards for the preparation of financial statements.

FCPA – Foreign Corrupt Practices Act. A Federal law which generally prohibits the payment of bribes to foreign officials by United States companies.

FEDERAL FUNDS - Non-interest-bearing deposits held by member banks at the Federal Reserve; also Used to denote "immediately available" funds in the clearing sense.

FEDERAL FUNDS RATE – The rate of interest at which Federal Reserve Board funds are traded. This rate is currently pegged by the Federal Reserve through open market operations.

FIXED-RATE LOAN – A loan on which the rate paid by the borrower is fixed for the life of the loan.

FLIP-IN PLAN – Refers to a type of shareholder rights plan or "poison pill." Flip-in plans generally give the shareholders of a target corporation the right to acquire shares of the surviving corporation after the merger with the hostile offeror is complete (assuming the target corporation is the surviving corporation). A flip-in plan generally gives each target corporation's shareholder the right to acquire shares of the surviving corporation at an exercise price far below market value.

FLIP-OVER PLANS – Refers to a type of shareholder rights plan or "poison pill." Flipover plans generally give a shareholder of a target corporation the right to acquire shares of an acquiring corporation at an exercise price far below market value in the event of a takeover. Typically such rights are not exercised. The rights under a flip-in plan or a flip-over plan can be cancelled by the target corporation's board of directors if, after an initial offer, the prospective acquiror raises the offer sufficiently. See: Poison Pill.

FLOAT – Typically regarded as the number of shares of a corporation that are both outstanding and available for treating by the public, which typically excludes that number of shares attributable to insiders or shares that are restricted in their trading which are owned by those outside the company. In most respects, the volatility of a stock is inversely related to the size of its float. In other words, the smaller the float the more volatile a stock and its stock price are apt to be.

FREEZE OUT – (a) A process, usually in a closely held corporation, by which minority shareholders are prevented from receiving any direct or indirect financial return from the corporation in an effort to persuade them to liquidate their investment in the corporation on terms favorable to the controlling shareholder. (b) Refers to a type of merger in which an acquiror purchases or owns a controlling interest (i.e., a majority of shares) and then votes to merge the corporation with another corporation. The remaining shareholders can then be "frozen out," i.e., forced to accept cash or new stock for their shares.

GAAP – Generally Accepted Accounting Principles. A set of standards established to govern the preparation of financial statements. All GAAP financial statements use the same methods to compute financial data and therefore can be used to accurately compare the financial statements of different companies.

GAAS – This acronym references general accepted auditing standards. These are the standards and procedures which are used to define the duties of an accountant when conducting an audit.

GENERAL COUNSEL – A corporation's chief legal officer. Usually a corporate officer and an "insider," but not always. Term also can refer to an outside or independent lawyer or law firm.

GOLDEN PARACHUTE AGREEMENT – An agreement between a corporation and an executive under which he or she is entitled to terminate his employment and receive benefits in the event of a

329

change in control of the company (a single-trigger) or in the event of a change in control plus certain other actions by the company adversely affecting the executive (e.g., reduction in authority or compensation, alteration of duties) (a double-trigger). If the benefits under the agreement exceed certain levels, the company is denied a tax reduction and the executive is subject to a penalty or excise tax under Section 280G of the Internal Revenue Code. In some cases, the agreement contains a gross up benefit requiring the corporation to increase the benefits to make the executive whole for the penalty tax.

GOODWILL – A balance sheet account representing an intangible asset that may arise when business assets are purchased for a price above their individual current asset values. For example, the name and reputation of a particular company may add significantly to its value by attracting customers, but is not an asset which one could put his hands on, such as equipment or inventory.

HEDGE – To limit the financial risk of a financial position by a counterbalancing transaction.

INDEMNIFICATION – The action of compensating for or holding harmless from loss or damage sustained. Corporate bylaws often contain an indemnification provision that provides broad hold harmless protections to directors and officers for any loss or damage incurred from their conduct so long as it is within the scope of their duties and meets certain statutory standards. In an acquisition setting, a provision in an acquisition agreement giving one party post-closing claims against the other for the breach of the other's representations and/or covenants that survive the closing. Often subject to a "basket" (excluding the first immaterial amounts of claims, the size of which is measured by, say, 1% of the purchase price) or to provisions that permit so-called claims only during a certain period following the closing. See also **Directors' and Officers' Liability Insurance**.

INDENTURE – (or Bond Indenture) an agreement between a lender and borrower that details the specific terms and conditions of a bond. It specifies the legal obligations of the bond issuer and the rights of bondholders. It also often covers the roll of the indenture trustee which administers the terms of the bonds as between the issuer and the holders.

INITIAL PUBLIC OFFERING (ALSO CALLED "IPO") – The first public sale of securities by a company or a person controlling the company. Generally, any offering that is not exempt under the private offering exemptions of the federal securities laws or state blue sky laws is considered a public offering. Normally, a registration of the offering is required with the Securities and Exchange Commission and the offering is underwritten by investment bankers.

INSIDE DIRECTORS – Directors of a corporation who hold executive positions or who are otherwise affiliated with management.

INSIDER – Term of uncertain scope that refers to persons having some relationship to an issuer (e.g., an officer or director of an issuer corporation), and whose trading of securities on the basis of nonpublic information may be a violation of law.

INSIDER TRADING – Transactions in shares of publicly held corporations by persons with inside or advance information on which the trading is based. Usually the trader himself has an employment or other relation of trust and confidence with the corporation. Such a person is often called an Insider.

INSTITUTIONAL INVESTOR – A bank, mutual fund, pension fund, insurance company, university or other institution that invests in the securities markets with professional money managers or investment advisors usually providing advice to them. Also often advised by professional consulting firms concerning how to vote proxies on stock held by the institution. As a group, a formidable element influencing U.S. corporate governance policies and practices.

IN-THE-MONEY OPTION - An option where the differential between the exercise price and the market price of the underlying security represents a positive value to the option holder.

INVESTMENT ADVISOR (also spelled as "ADVISER") – A person or company which provides investment advice for compensation.

INVESTMENT BANKER – A title usually used to describe a registered broker-dealer involved in the underwriting of new issues. An investment banker is the intermediary between the issuer and the public. The usual practice is for one or more investment bankers to buy the subject securities outright from the issuer. The group forms a syndicate to sell the securities to individuals and institutions. Investment bankers also distribute very large blocks of stocks or bonds – perhaps held by an estate or institution. An investment banker may also provide other investment and advisory services to corporations, such as merger advice.

INVESTOR – A party who places money into a business through the acquisition of stock of debt securities who, in turn, is seeking a profit. A "growth investor" is an investor who is seeking principally appreciation from the party's investor as opposed to income. A "value investor" is a party who is seeking securities that are undervalued in terms of their fundamental economic value.

ISSUED SHARES – Shares a corporation has actually issued and has not cancelled. Issued shares should be contrasted with shares authorized, which are the total number of shares approved by shareholders for future issuance.

LBO – See Buyout.

LEAD DIRECTOR – A director who coordinates the activities of the independent or so-called "outside directors." The concept of "Lead Director" was developed by Martin Lipton and J.W. Lorsch and was first referenced in a November 1992 article in *The Business Lawyer*. According to Messrs. Lipton and Lorsch, if independent directors are to be effective, they need some form of leadership, and, if they do not use an independent or outside chairman, then it is recommended that each board select a leader from among the independent directors as the Lead Director. The CEO/Chairman should then consult with the Lead Director upon such matters as the selection of board committee members and chair persons; the board's meeting agenda; the adequacy of information that directors receive; and the effectiveness of the board meeting process. Additionally, the Lead Director also would play a leading role in CEO evaluation. Finally, if the independent directors face a crisis because of the incapacity of the CEO/chairman or a failure in top management performance, the Lead Director would be a designated leader in advance. When there are Lead Directors, they usually operate in a de facto leadership position without a formal title.

LETTER STOCK - (Also called investment letter stock) – Privately placed common stock using this terminology because SEC requires that a letter from the purchaser be obtained representing that the stock is being held for investment and not with a view to resale.

LEVERAGE – In effect, the relationship of a corporation's debt to its equity. Leverage may be advantageous when earnings are good, but may work against the common stock when earnings decline. When a company has common stock only, no leverage exists because all earnings are available for the common, although relatively large fixed charges may have an effect similar to that of the impact of interest payable on a bond issue.

LEVERAGED LEASE – The lessor provides only a minor portion of the cost of the leased equipment, borrowing the rest from another lender.

LIBOR – The London Interbank Offered Rate on Eurodollar deposits traded between banks. There is a different LIBOR rate for each deposit maturity. Different banks may quote slightly different LIBOR rates because they use different reference banks.

LINE OF CREDIT – An arrangement by which a bank agrees to lend to the line holder during some specified period any amount up to the full amount of the line.

LIQUIDITY – The ability to convert non-cash assets (stocks, bonds, options, real estate, and other assets) to cash. Assets that can be quickly converted to cash are said to have high liquidity.

LIQUIDITY RISK – In banking, liquidity risk refers to monies needed to fund assets but that may not be available in sufficient quantities at some future date. Implies an imbalance in committed maturities of assets and liabilities.

LISTED STOCK – The stock of a company which is traded on a national securities exchange, such as the New York Stock Exchange.

LOCK-UP OPTION – In a takeover context, when a target company gives an option to a "friendly" company to purchase certain specified (and often "crown jewel") assets of the target company or gives an option on a large block of stock at an advantageous price. A lock-up option is usually granted as a strategy to defend against a hostile tender offer made by another company.

MANIPULATION – Buying or selling a security for the purpose of creating false or misleading appearance of active trading or for the purpose of artificially raising or depressing the security's price to induce purchases or sales by others.

MARGIN – An arrangement which permits investors to purchase securities by borrowing money from a broker. The amount of the margin is typically the difference between the market value of the stock and the loan a broker makes on that stock. A margin account is an account which can be leveraged and through which stocks can be purchased using a combination of cash and a loan. Typically the loan in the margin account is collateralized by the stock itself. If the value of the stock drops sufficiently, the owner will be asked to either place more cash in the account or sell a portion of the stock.

MARGINAL TAX RATE – The tax rate that would have to be paid on any additional dollars of taxable income earned.

MARKET CAPITALIZATION – A valuation formula under which a company's total market price is computed by multiplying the total number of outstanding shares times the current market price per share. In general, the market capitalization, often called "market cap," is an approximate measure of corporate size. Certain investors focus on companies in various market capitalization categories, such as small cap, medium cap and large cap.

MARKET VALUE – The price at which a security is trading and could presumably be purchased or sold.

MARKETABILITY – A negotiable security is said to have good marketability if there is an active secondary market in which it can easily be resold.

MATERIAL ADVERSE CHANGE – A condition in an acquisition agreement which permits a bidder not to close or complete an acquisition in the event of a significant negative change in the financial condition or operations of the target company which occurs between the date of signing of the agreement and the closing date. Also refers to a representation which, if it survives the closing, can give the beneficiary of the representation a post-closing indemnity claim against the other party or its shareholders in the event of a significant negative adverse change in the other party or MAC.

M&A – Acronym for "merger and acquisition." Often precedes a reference to an expert in the field of mergers and acquisitions, such as an M&A lawyer.

MD&A – Management's Discussion and Analysis section of a reporting company's reports filed with the SEC (see "10-K Report" and "10-Q Report" below); a required category of disclosure (but not part of the financial statements) in certain documents required to be filed with the Securities and Exchange Commission.

MERGER – A combination of two corporations in accordance with statutory provisions in which one of the corporations survives and the other disappears. The acquiring company receives all of the assets of the acquired company and assumes all of its liabilities on the effective or closing date by operation of the law when the merger agreement is filed with the appropriate offices of the states of incorporation of the merging parties.

MEZZANINE INVESTMENT – A hybrid investment that is part debt and part equity. It is usually high coupon subordinated debt with an equity kicker. It is used for management buyouts, acquisitions, growth financings, and recapitalizations.

MONEY MARKET – The market in which short-term debt instruments (bills, commercial paper, bankers' acceptance, etc.) are issued and traded.

NASDAQ – Reference is to National Association of Securities Dealers Automated Quotation System. Shares traded under that system are also referenced as "OTC" or over the counter securities which are traded directly between buyers and sellers and not over a national securities exchange.

NOTE – Also called a promissory note; a written contract which represents a pledge by the obligor to pay a specified amount of principal and interest to the lender.

OFF-BALANCE SHEET FINANCING – A technique for obtaining financing not required to be reported on the debtor balance sheet. Often the off-balance-sheet financing has been done through so-called special purpose entities ("SPE's") which became infamous in the Enron matter.

OFFICER – In corporate law, the term refers especially to a person elected or appointed by the board of directors to manage the daily operations of a corporation, such as a CEO, COO, president, secretary, or treasurer.

OPPORTUNITY COST – The cost of pursuing one course of action measured in terms of the foregone return offered by the most attractive alternative.

OPTION – (a) Call option: A contract sold for a price that gives the holder the right to buy from the writer of the option, over a specified period, a specified amount of securities at a specified price. (b) Put option: A contract sold for a price that gives the holder the right to sell to the writer of the contract, over a specified period, specified amount of securities at a specified price.

OSHA – Abbreviation for the "Occupational Safety and Health Act of 1970". The act and regulations thereunder govern safety and health matters at many facilities operated by corporations, such as manufacturing plants.

POISON PILL – Also called a Shareholder Rights Plan. A device used to make a corporation unattractive to a hostile takeover. Typically, it involves a charter or bylaw provision, by which, in the event of an acquisition of a stated percentage of the outstanding shares of the company (often 15 to 20%) or certain types of asset sales or mergers, the shareholders would be entitled to certain rights or payments. Some poison pill plans allow shareholders to either acquire (a) shares of the acquiror at less than their market price (a "flip-over" pill) or (b) if the target corporation is the surviving corporation, after a merger, shares of the target corporation for less than their market price (a "flip-in" pill). Called a "poison pill" because to the bidder or raider, the implementation of the pill (while rarely triggered in fact) can be dilutive and be a "show stopper" or poison to achieving the closing of the proposed takeover on a successful basis.

PREFERRED STOCK – A class of stock with a claim on the company's earnings before payment may be made on the common stock and is usually entitled to priority over common stock if the company were to be liquidated.

PRIME RATE – Approximately but not always the rate at which banks lend to their best (prime) customers.

PRINCIPAL – (a) the face amount or par value of a debt security; (b) One who acts as a dealer buying and selling for his own account.

PRIVATE PLACEMENT – The sale of a stock, bond or other security directly to a limited number of investors. If done properly, the sale makes unnecessary any requirement for registration of the sale with the SEC. Just the opposite of a public offering transaction.

PROFIT MARGIN – The profitability of a company measured by relating profits to revenues. The three most common profit margin calculations are: operating profit margin, pretax profit margin and net profit margin.

PRO FORMA – A pro forma financial statement is one which shows how an actual financial statement would look if certain specified assumptions were to be realized. Pro forma financial statements may either be forward looking or involve past results. One example of a backward looking pro forma statement occurs when two companies are considering a merger and show what their consolidated financial statements would look like if they had been merged in preceding years. Another set of pro forma statements might reflect only the results from core operations and exclude special non-recurring items.

PROSPECTUS – A document issued by a corporation at the time securities are offered providing prospective buyers of the securities with relevant details and data on the corporation and the securities being issued. Often the preliminary prospectus is called a "red herring prospectus" as there are red colored notations in the margin of the cover page of the prospectus indicating that it is preliminary. It is rumored that the reference to "red herring" comes from the early use of similar documents when it was desired to warn the prospective investor that instead of buying high quality investments the investor may be buying a herring and something not altogether solid or something that might be weak or confusing.

PROXY – A document giving one person the authority or power to act for another. Typically, the authority in question is the power to vote shares of common stock.

PROXY AGENT – A person holding a proxy for another person, his or her principal.

PROXY CARD – The card issued by corporations, dissidents or other third parties to evidence, when signed, the authority of a shareholder to vote shares owned by him or her (the principal) at a shareholder meeting.

PROXY FIGHT – Two or more parties engaged in a struggle through the solicitation of signed proxy cards from stockholders to gain a voting majority. Usually a proxy fight is for the purpose of obtaining control of the corporation and to oust the incumbent management. It also can relate to seeking support for or opposition to a transaction which is being voted on by shareholders, such as is the case with a proposed merger. A famous proxy fight of this type was involved in the proposed merger of Hewlett-Packard and Compaq.

PROXY SOLICITATION – A request that a corporate shareholder authorize another person to cast the shareholder's vote at a corporate meeting.

PROXY STATEMENT – An informational document that accompanies a proxy solicitation and explains proposed actions by the corporation (such as the election of directors, approval of a stock option plan or a proposed merger).

PUBLIC OFFERING – Sale of securities by an issuing corporation (the "issuer") or a person controlling the issuer to members of the public. Generally, any offering that is not exempt under the private offering exemption of the Securities Act of 1933 and/or similar exemptions under state blue sky laws is considered a public offering. Normally, registration of a public offering under those statutes is required, though in some instances another exemption from registration may be available.

PUT – An option that gives the holder the right to sell the underlying security at a specified price during a fixed time period.

QUICK-ASSET RATIO – Current assets less inventories as a percent of current liabilities (i.e., current assets – inventories divided by current liabilities). Some accounting experts and lenders prefer dividing the sum of cash and marketable securities by current liabilities. A company's position is considered relatively healthy when its quick assets exceed its current liabilities by a comfortable margin.

QUORUM – The minimum number of people that must be present or must provide a proxy to vote at the meeting in order to make a valid decision. When there is a quorum for a board of directors meeting, the majority of the quorum may bind the entire board, including those directors who are absent from the meeting. In the absence of any law or rule fixing the number of members for a quorum, ordinarily it consists of a majority of those entitled to act. Under Delaware law unless the certificate of incorporation provides otherwise, the bylaws may provide that a number less than a majority shall constitute a quorum which in no case shall be less than one third of the total number of directors.

RATING – An evaluation given by Moody's, Standard & Poor's, Fitch, or other rating services of a security's credit worthiness.

RELATED PARTY TRANSACTION – A transaction between either an officer or a director of corporation, on the one hand, and the corporation, on the other. In effect, these transactions are "conflict of interest" transactions. Disclosure is required under the SEC Disclosure Rules for certain transactions in this category. If they are to be approved by a corporation's board or shareholders and qualify for a "safe harbor" from potential liability, they ordinarily must be approved under specific statutory requirements of various state corporations codes. (See "Conflict of Interest")

RESOLUTION – The evidence of a board action (e.g., a resolution to authorize the sale of stock), usually presented in relatively formal terms, preceded by a description of the board discussion leading up to the action item along with recitals (e.g., "Whereases") serving as factual predicates to the action item.

RESTRICTED SECURITIES – Securities which have been acquired directly or indirectly from the issuing company or from an affiliate of the issuer other than in a registered public offering and which have restrictions on resale (e.g., a required holding period).

RETURN ON EQUITY – The rate of return a company earns on shareholders' equity. Return on equity is calculated by dividing net earnings by average shareholders' equity. (Also called "ROE")

RETURN ON INVESTMENT – The rate of return a company earns on the total invested in a capital project. The return is calculated by dividing net earnings received from the project by the total investment. (Also called "ROI.")

REVOLVER – See Revolving Line of Credit.

REVOLVING LINE OF CREDIT – A bank line of credit on which the customer pays a commitment fee and can take down and repay funds according to his or her needs. Normally, the line involves a firm commitment from the bank for a period of several years.

RISK – Degree of uncertainty of return on an asset.

ROLL OVER – Reinvest funds received from a maturing security into a new issue of the same or a similar security.

RULE 10(b)-5 – Rule of the Securities and Exchange Commission governing insider trading and manipulation in buying and selling a security (see "Manipulation"). Under the rule, in connection with the trading of securities, generally it is unlawful for any person to employ any device, scheme or artifice to defraud; to make any untrue statement of a material fact or to omit the state of material fact necessary, in order to make the statements made, in light of the circumstances under which they were made, not misleading; or to engage in any act, practice or course of business which operates or would operate as a fraud or deceit upon any person in connection with the purchase or sale of any security. This rule became famous in the *Texas Gulf Sulphur* insider trading case.

SCHEDULE 13 D – Disclosure document required by the SEC to be filed with it by any party acquiring more than 5% of the stock of a publicly held corporation.

SEC – The Securities and Exchange Commission, established by Congress to help protect investors. The SEC administers the Securities Act of 1933, the Securities Exchange Act of 1934, the Trust Indenture Act, the Investment Company Act, the Investment Advisers Act, and the Public Utility Holding Company Act. Rumor has it that in the 1930s, the SEC was established to address many questionable or fraudulent practices. For example, it is alleged that some corporations would send a dividend check to shareholders. In the endorsement block on the reverse side of the check, the legend above the endorsement signature line would say: "*Your endorsement of this check also constitutes your vote in favor of the management slate of directors at the upcoming annual meeting.*"

SEC FORM 3 AND SEC FORM 4 – These are forms filed by insiders, usually directors, officers and 10% shareholders with the Securities and Exchange Commission. They are typically filed with the SEC within two days after the relevant event occurs (e.g., a party acquires more than 10% of the outstanding shares). The SEC Form 3 is used to establish what, in effect, is an initial registered status for a particular party with respect to insider trading and the Form 4 is used to show changes in that status (e.g., the purchase or sale of additional securities over and above what was reflected in the original Form 3).

James R. Ukropina

SECONDARY OFFERING – A public sale of previously issued securities, ordinarily those securities held by large investors (often institutional investors) as distinguished from a primary distribution where the seller of the stock is the issuing corporation.

SEVERANCE PAYMENT – A payment made to an officer or employee leaving a corporation. In some cases, paid because there is a dispute about whether the party's services were terminated for good cause or without adequate cause. Some employment agreements for corporate executives specify when such a payment will be made as well as the amount and the terms of payment. A severance payment can be part of a total severance "package" which can call for not only a cash payment but also the early acceleration of the vesting of stock options and the continuation of certain fringe benefits (e.g., the use of office space and secretarial assistance).

SHAREHOLDER – The owner of shares of stock of a corporation. This is the term used to describe an owner of stock under California statutory law. Another term used for an owner of corporate stock is "stockholder" and it is found in some state statutes, including Delaware's.

SHARES AUTHORIZED – The maximum number of shares allowed to be issued under a corporation's charter. Additional shares require a charter amendment.

SHARES OUTSTANDING – The number of authorized shares that have been issued and are now in the hands of owners.

SHARK REPELLANTS – Terms in a company's certificate or articles of incorporation or bylaws designed to deter or discourage a raider, including, for example, a poison pill (*supra*), certain advance notice bylaw provisions or supermajority vote requirements.

SHELF REGISTRATION – A Registration Statement filed in advance of any offering. It allows the issuer to take advantage of market conditions and issue securities immediately, instead of filing a registration statement and waiting for it to be declared effective or operative under the federal securities laws only at a specific opportune time.

SHORT SALE – The sales of securities not owned by the seller in the expectation that the price of these securities will fall or as part of an arbitrage. A short sale must eventually be covered by a purchase of the securities sold.

SHORT-SWING PROFITS – Profits made by a corporate insider on the purchase and sale (or sale and purchase) of company stock within a six-month period. Under Rule 16(b) of the Securities Exchange Act of 1934, these profits are subject to being returned to the company.

340

SOCIAL ISSUES – Issues concerning people and other matters that are negotiated in a friendly acquisition, such as board representation, name of surviving corporation on a post-closing basis, location of the principal headquarters office, executive officer positions, compensation and similar issues.

SPREAD – (a) Difference between bid and asked prices on a security; (b) difference between yields on or prices of two securities of differing sorts or differing maturities; (c) in underwriting, difference between price realized by the issuer and price paid by the investor; (d) difference between two prices or two rates.

SQUEEZEOUTS – Techniques by which a minority interest in a corporation is eliminated or reduced. Squeezeouts may occur in a variety of contexts, e.g., in a "going private" transaction in which minority shareholders are compelled to accept cash for their shares or the issuance of new shares to existing shareholders. Thus, minority shareholders may be given the unpleasant choice of having their proportionate interest in the corporation reduced significantly or of investing a large amount or additional or new capital over which they have no control and receive little or no return.

STAGGERED TERMS FOR BOARD OF DIRECTORS – A provision in the bylaws providing that a board of directors be elected under a system in which a fraction of the board is elected each year to serve for two or three year terms. Theoretically, if terms are staggered for directors, it will take more than a year for a raider to take control of the Board if only one meeting of shareholders is held each year.

STANDSTILL AGREEMENT – An agreement between a corporation and one or more of its prospective or actual substantial shareholders, pursuant to which such shareholder(s), in consideration of some acquiescence from management, agree(s) not to acquire additional securities of the corporation for a specified period of time.

STOCKHOLDER OF RECORD – A stockholder whose name is registered on the books of the issuing corporation.

STOCKHOLDERS' EQUITY – The difference between a company's total assets and total liabilities. Stockholders' equity, sometimes called "net worth," is the stockholders' ownership in the company. Also called "Shareholder Equity."

STOCK OPTION – The right to buy stock at a given price within a stated period of time, regardless of the market price.

STOCK SPLIT – The process of dividing a company's stock shares into a greater (or lesser) number. A 2-for-1 stock split means that two shares of stock will be issued for every one share that previously existed.

STREET – The financial community principally in the Wall Street area of New York. Term often used in the course of a board meeting in the context of measuring the effect a proposed transaction on the price of the stock, such as "How will the street react to a proposed merger or, say, a stock split?" A significant street reaction can have a substantial impact on a corporations' stock price, upward or downward – or sideways.

SUBORDINATED DEBENTURE – See Debenture. The claims of the holders of this type of debenture rank junior to or after those of the holders of other more unsecured debts incurred by the issuer. In other words, a debt instruments which is placed in a lower priority versus other debt instructions, the holders of which are in an inferior position in the event of a bankruptcy.

SWAP – (a) In securities, selling one issue and buying another; (b) In foreign exchange, buying a currency spot and simultaneously selling it forward: *Currency Swap*: An agreement between two parties to exchange future payments in one currency for payments in another currency. These agreements are used to transform the currency denomination of assets or liabilities. Unlike interest rate swaps, currency swaps must include an exchange of principal at maturity. This exchange ensures that neither party is subject to currency risk because exchange rates are predetermined; *Interest Rate Swap*: An exchange between two parties of interest rate exposures from floating to fixed rate or vice versa. Each thereby gains indirect access to the fixed or floating capital markets.

TARGET CORPORATION – A corporation, the control of which is sought by an aggressor corporation.

TENDER OFFER – An offer to purchase the securities of another corporation (the "target corporation") made directly to the shareholders of the target corporation. Usually the tender offer is made at a higher price than the prevailing market price. If there ever was a phenomenon that is not tender, soft or subtle, this often is it.

10-K REPORT – A report filed annually with the SEC by a registered corporation, traditionally within 90 days of the end of each year. It typically includes audited financial statements, description of the corporation's business and financial condition, summary of other financial data and an MD&A section (see "MD&A").

10-Q REPORT – A report filed quarterly with the SEC by a registered corporation, traditionally within 45 days of the end of each quarter. It typically includes unaudited quarterly financial statements, statements concerning financial condition and an MD&A section. (Note, at the time of the preparation of this book, the SEC law was changed shortening the period for filing of 10-K and 10Q reports.) Also note that in addition to 10-K and 10-Q reports, corporations may have to file so-called 8-K reports describing special material events which may occur between the filing dates for K and Q reports.

TIME VALUE – (a) A part of a stock option contract's premium that shows how much time is left before the contract expires, thereby indicating how much the premium exceeds the contract's intrinsic value; (b) the value associated with the amount of time an investor has to wait for an investment to mature, represented by the present value at maturity; (c) difference between the price paid to acquire a company and its value before the takeover.

TREASURY BILL – A non-interest-bearing discount security issued by the U.S. Treasury to finance the national debt. Most bills are issued to mature in 3 months, 6 months, or 1 year.

ULTRA VIRES – Unauthorized; beyond the scope of power allowed or granted by a corporate charter or bylaw (e.g., the officer was liable for the firm's ultra vires actions).

UNDERWRITERS – A person, group of persons, company or syndicate which either purchases new securities from the issuer or government entity at a stated price (on a firm commitment basis) and guarantees its sale and distribution to investors, or promises to use its "best efforts" to sell the securities of the issuer, but does not have an obligation to purchase the unsold securities of the issuer: (a) In a "firm commitment" underwriting, the issuer sells its securities to the underwriting firm, which then resells to dealers and/or the general public. The underwriter bears the risk of loss if it cannot sell the securities to the public. The way most underwritten deals are run, by the time the Underwriting Agreement is signed, there is little risk of a non-sale, but there can be a real risk of a soft aftermarket; (b) In a "best efforts" underwriting, the underwriter undertakes to use its best efforts to sell the issuer's securities on a commission basis. The issuer is paid only for what the underwriter is able to sell.

UNDERWRITING SYNDICATE – A syndicate of investment firms formed to spread the risk associated with the purchase and distribution of a new issue of securities. The larger the issue, the more firms typically are involved in the syndicate.

VENTURE CAPITAL – Risk money; money invested in a company, particularly for a new or start-up business, for greater than average profit, but with greater than average risk.

VENTURE CAPITAL INVESTMENTS – New and early-stage companies whose securities are not publicly traded. Venture capital investments may present significant opportunities for capital appreciation, but involve a high degree of business and financial risk that can result in substantial losses.

VOTING RIGHT – The shareholder's right to vote his stock in the affairs of his or her company. Most common shares have one vote each. Preferred stock usually has the right to vote when preferred dividends are in default for a specified period. The right to vote may be delegated by the stockholder to another person. See: Cumulative Voting, Proxy.

WARRANT – A warrant confers upon its holder the right to purchase an amount of securities at a particular time and price. Because a warrant does not carry with it the right to dividends or voting rights with respect to the securities which it entitles a holder to purchase, and because it does not represent any rights in the assets of the issuer, warrants may be considered more speculative than certain other types of investment. A warrant ceases to have value if it is not exercised prior to its expiration date.

WHITE KNIGHT – In a hostile takeover situation, a white knight refers to one who comes to the rescue of a target corporation at the request of the target company's management. The white knight often fends off the hostile tender offer by purchasing a large amount of the securities of the target entity. Management benefits because the white knight allows them to continue running the corporation.

WORKING CAPITAL OR NET WORKING CAPITAL – The excess of current assets over current liabilities.

WORKING CONTROL – Theoretically, ownership of more than 50 percent of a company's voting stock is necessary to exercise control. In practice – and this is particularly true in the case of a large corporation – effective control sometimes can be exerted through ownership, individually or by a group action in concert, of far less than 50 percent (e.g., in some cases far less than 20%).

WRITE-DOWN – To transfer a portion of the cost of an asset to an expense account because the asset's value has been decreased.

WRITE-OFF – To remove an asset from the books, usually through taking a loss or an expense.

YIELD TO MATURITY – The rate of return yielded by a debt security held to maturity when both interest payments and the investor's capital gain or loss on the security are taken into account.

James R. Ukropina

FINAL COMMENTS

Before I finish, I have a few final comments about governance critics, Enron and a few other matters.

The Critics

It is fascinating that a few – fortunately, very few – corporate activists seem to maintain they have all the answers as to how every board should operate because, in my experience, there is no one "model" or "template" for good board governance, nor is there one pattern for benign board conduct. It is increasingly true, however, that many important institutional investors will pay some premium for the stock of a company that has board governance processes that at least look good, and they seem to hold stock much longer if the board appears to be a strong rudder for the corporate ship. Nonetheless, good governance practices do not necessarily ensure profitability (but they can help a lot). Like many directors, I have seen bad boards for good companies (i.e., profitable ones) and good boards for marginal-to-poor corporate performers. Also, keep in mind – a board can *never* be a good one until it has a leader (usually the Chairman-CEO) who has integrity and character and who will, within reason, embrace inquiry and constructive criticism.

In recent years, U.S. boards have come under a lot of criticism. After one notorious corporate debacle, Stanley Sporkin, former head of the Division of Enforcement for the SEC and now a federal judge, asked, "Where were the directors?" Even more intense questions are being posed following the Enron meltdown and similar recent experiences that are leading to the largest bankruptcies in U.S. history. With the decline in the economy in the early part of the 21st century and the slump in various business sectors – including the high-tech and dot-com industries – companies failed and boards were beaten up by critics. In numerous instances, however, those declines appear to have had little or nothing to do with the performance of boards. Instead, they turned on more systemic economic and operating issues that affected those industries.

While boards can do good work in preserving capital in a severe business downturn, few can reverse cascading broadscale negative industrial dynamics. Even so, damage control may be possible. It is noteworthy that, in a few cases, some boards of dot-com companies decided, relatively early in the game of the descending business cycle, that a company was better "dead" than "alive." Those boards terminated ventures far earlier than others did in order to preserve some of the remaining seed capital for the benefit of anxious investors.

Enron

Comments are in order about the Enron controversy. Since I personally know various parties connected with Enron, including large investors, officers and directors, let me cite the remarks of another party, a Congressman, in order to place the matter in context. They come from Congressional hearings held on March 14, 2002. At that hearing, the Chairman of the Oversight and Investigations Subcommittee of the House Energy and Commerce Committee, U.S. Rep. James C. Greenwood, said the following in connection with corporate governance and boards of directors:

> The words "corporate governance" describe the entire architecture of how a modern corporation is managed on behalf of its investors and stockholders, its customers and its employees. This encompasses executives at every level, corporate accounting teams, corporate counsel, senior managers and the board of directors. It also includes the outside expert advice, often from consultants, attorneys and accountants, that senior management, the board of directors or the audit committee of the board retain to provide advice on a wide array of issues. These issues range from human resources to tax analyses to producing an audited financial statement.

Up to this point, [the work of the Greenwood subcommittee] has focused primarily on what went wrong at Enron. Through our work, we have been able to cast a considerable amount of light on the people and transactions behind this company's unparalleled failure. As a result of this effort, we have been able to slowly parse the complex of self-dealing transactions that contributed to Enron's dramatic descent into bankruptcy. We have acquired a more complete understanding of how these highly irregular transactions were cloaked behind a curtain of nearly impenetrable financial arrangements.

Many have suggested to me that this book focus exclusively on Enron-type issues and lodge sharp criticism at all members of the corporate governance teams for excesses and improprieties. While it is tempting to do so because the book might be more widely read, I have chosen not to take that road for one reason. Before one can understand the complexities of corporate governance – only a few of which are described in the material above – one first needs to understand how boards operate on a more traditional and customary basis. This book illustrates that boards, even in routine circumstances, are confronted with complex and challenging issues and suggests that the fictional board here, like most boards I know, tries to do the right thing in the right way.

Commentators and others have criticized Enron's board of directors and senior management. While the issues concerning that matter had not yet been litigated when this book was written, this book should serve to illustrate that a board – and perhaps the Enron Board – is only as good as the information provided to board members. As noted in the above quotations from Congressman Greenwood, some corporate problems can be virtually impenetrable, because they are hidden behind complex financial arrangements and they can be difficult to pierce, even for the most conscientious fiduciary.

Actions or preparation for action cannot be taken to prevent corporate disasters unless a board has some early warning signals that a disaster is on its way. The art of being a good director, however, is to try to work with management and "see around corners," to hear soft noises or even minor indicia that a tornado aimed at a corporation will soon turn and come up its street.

Corporate Governance Changes, New Constituencies

The face of corporate governance has changed significantly in the past few decades, and I expect further similar changes. In this book, I tried to use my crystal ball along with input from Norman Augustine, to speculate about the evolving shape of governance practices in the 21st century. The type of issues depicted here, however, probably will be with us for most of this century.

People have asked me about specific changes in corporate governance. Perhaps the most dramatic change in board duties has been the *de facto* need for management and directors to address multiple corporate constituencies. With my first directorship in the early 1970s, the only constituency I was concerned about was the shareholders. Current statutory and case law continue to underscore the need to focus on them, but, in fact, a director who only looks at shareholder interests without evaluating the impact of decisions on other constituencies probably is not doing his or her job effectively. More specifically, he or she is not performing their duty of care.

The non-shareholder constituencies include employees, lenders, vendors, various community interest groups that attempt to influence corporate behavior and organizations for institutional investors that take public positions on corporate governance and management issues. (One sophisticated CEO said his job was to serve as a conductor of a symphony orchestra consisting of musicians using atonal instruments and to try to harmonize the end result.) While significant case law requires directors to focus only on shareholder interests, certain state statutes expressly permit consideration of other constituencies in fiduciary decision-making. In any event, reality may dictate consideration of other constituencies in certain instances. For example, under case law, in those situations where a company starts to face severe cash liquidity problems and approaches the so-called "vicinity of insolvency," then the fiduciary duties of a board shift from focusing primarily on the shareholders to focusing, at least in part, on the interests of lenders.

One interest group or constituency that is far more active than it was 30 years ago is the plaintiffs' bar. Certain plaintiffs' counsel play an extremely constructive role in shaping corporate governance, while, in my opinion, others may be far less responsible and have relatively narrow selfish economic interest in filing litigation against the boards.

In one acquisition proceeding in which I was involved, in a disturbing, post-closing scenario, a plaintiffs' law firm filed a lawsuit against the board of the selling corporation for selling the corporation at far too low a price. At the same time, a firm that appeared to me to be closely related to the first law firm filed a lawsuit against the buyer corporation for paying too high a price. Shortly thereafter, one of those law firms was disciplined on grounds that did not relate to the specific litigation but reflected a highly questionable type of conduct as also evidenced by the totally irreconcilable litigation positions taken in the courts.

What This Book Is and Is Not

This book was not intended as a scholarly work. Instead, it is a loose compendium of the many experiences I have had as a director while attending more than a thousand board and committee meetings. I have done so both as a lawyer and as a director for more than 30 years and, as such, in most instances, I continue to face ongoing duties of confidentiality as to what went on in each boardroom. Therefore, I decided to write about a fictional company, "DFP, Inc.," and the equally fictional DFP board. As a result, this book is fictional and does not breach those confidences. At the same time, it is also a semi-

351

"docudrama," as it represents an amalgam of actual fact settings in which I have found myself at varying times, many of them encouraging, some of them disappointing, and, a few, even poignant and humorous. The use of descriptions about fictional, but near life-like, corporate board proceedings should help apply numerous "how-to-do-it" principles in a realistic setting. As such, this book provides a *context* against which principles of good corporate governance can be applied.

I also have included a chapter in this book (Chapter 19) with a short profile on how one nonprofit board for the fictional "Dakota Foundation" operates. In my experience, the board of a *smaller* foundation typically operates quite differently from the board of a large for-profit company inasmuch as the non-profit board is not driven by near-term factors. In addition, the board constituency usually is more mixed in terms of backgrounds, technical competence and sophistication. Even so, many of the observations outlined in this book relating to for-profit boards and to how they operate would, if applied, significantly benefit many nonprofit institutions (e.g., close monitoring of financial performance, especially cash flow; management succession; and a sharp focus on the specific purpose of the non-profit institution and whether its activities are furthering that purpose). Further, one distinguished governance commentator, Dr. William G. Bowen, notes that external, market-driven forces and constraints are far less circumscribing for non-profit entities than those imposed on for-profits. Therefore, he submits that effective internal governance may be more important for the former than for the latter. For these reasons, I thought a chapter on non-profit governance was appropriate.

Given my legal background (more than 25 years in a large multi-national corporate law firm which now has more than 800 attorneys, and about eight years as a general counsel of two large NYSE companies), I also wanted to include in this book references to general legal principles. In this book, most of them are ones applicable in the fictional jurisdiction of "Dakota." Dakota is the home state for DFP's headquarters and the state of incorporation. While Dakota's corporate laws are intended to be similar to those of Delaware's, they are not identical. As a result, the reader may become a student of the fictional law of Dakota but not the laws of a real jurisdiction. In most (though not all) cases, however, the legal principles described are intended to bear some resemblance to corporate common law in the United States. Even so, this book is not intended to convey legal advice – nor does it.

In writing this book, I have drawn from my experiences in the boardrooms of more than 20 companies and institutions for which I have had the privilege of engaging in board service. These have ranged from a local Little League board to the board of a large university to the boards of two Fortune 100 companies. (I remember my Little League board experience vividly as one week after I became the president of the Little League, we received a notice that our League was about to be audited by the IRS!)

For a short time, I served as the chairman and chief executive officer of a large public company – an experience that also taught me about the value of boards. I have served on boards for companies in the following major industries, among others: aerospace, banking, financial services, energy, insurance, petroleum, real estate development, retail and public utility. And guess what: even though the industries mentioned are disparate in an operating sense, the governance issues confronted by the boards of companies in these industries are similar.

Therefore, this book is one that is at least designed to help others better understand or more effectively deal with future governance issues that I, my board colleagues, and other directors have confronted under often difficult, but in many cases repeated, circumstances.

Before coming to my conclusion, there are some important caveats I'd like to add:

- This book does not pretend to cover the gamut of all issues faced by boards – even a fictional board for a fictional company. Among the topics not included here, for example, are the often puzzling and always complex issues of derivative litigation, as well as the nuts-and-bolts of conducting an initial public offering. Still, there are a lot of episodic experiences that should make at least some of the narrative compelling – just like actual countless boardroom experiences that often take a volatile path.

- In order to more heavily "dramatize" the relationship between DFP's board and the company's CEO, the conflicts between them – as well as the manner in which some issues arise – are much more sharply drawn and occur far more repetitively than they might in real life, if they did, in fact, ever occur. In fact, most good boards confront few surprises and many board meetings can be a little slow-paced. Also, this book contains both parody and satire to make a few points more intensely. If these approaches trouble corporate representatives, I apologize, but counsel you not to take yourselves so seriously. After all, this book *is* fiction.

- This book may not be as politically correct as it should be because masculine terms are used in some instances where other terms could be used, such as referring to the board "Chair" to describe the senior officer of the board. On the other hand it is hard to say "the Chair sat in the chair at the head of the table" and, further, using masculine terminology is how most directors talk in board rooms. At the same time, I have tried to use masculine and feminine pronouns where appropriate. It is noteworthy that boardroom jargon may change as more than 90 percent of the boards of large public companies have one or more women directors in their ranks.

A few veteran directors who read this book may not take much away from it other than to conclude that corporate life in the boardroom repeats itself. On the other hand, the rookie director, the "wannabe," and the student – as well as corporate managers and some investors – should be able to take away a decent roadmap of the "who" and "how" of corporate boardrooms in the U.S.

Conclusion

I began by saying that this book will provide answers to questions from many parties about the nature of board service. Others who may find this book of interest include executives who are thrust into the position of serving as the chairman of the board when they have been in few, if any, corporate boardrooms; new directors who want a quick overview of what they can expect in board meetings during routine and less routine settings; members of the corporate staff who are scheduled to make a report to a board and never have done so; students, particularly those in business schools and law schools; others who are generally interested in or curious about corporate governance; and, importantly, investors in public companies – especially since more than half of the U.S. population holds stock in public companies either directly or indirectly through mutual funds.

Some of the book's potential readers may not be familiar with many of the issues and terms discussed in this book, so I included a Glossary of Terms. It explains more than 200 terms and concepts either used in the book or often dealt with in the boardroom. Hint: if you are to become a director, keep this book and the glossary in your file. I guarantee you will find the glossary a handy reference tool.

This Closing Commentary section was requested by a number of those who reviewed early drafts of this book. A short bibliography is also provided.

Finally, I hope this is a book all can enjoy, while learning how other directors have addressed issues they confronted – up to now – behind closed doors.

James R. Ukropina

BIBLIOGRAPHY

Books:

American Bar Association Section of Business Law, *Corporate Director Guidebook*, 56 *The Business Lawyer, 1575, August 2001.*

American Bar Association (Securities Law Committee of the Young Law Division), *Securities Law Glossary, 1991.*

The American Law Institute, *Principles of Corporate Governance: Analysis and Recommendations, 1994.*

Lorne, Simon M., *A Director's Handbook of Cases*, CCH, Incorporated, 2001.

Cases:

In re *Caremark International Inc. Derivative Litigation*, 698 A.2d. 959 (Del. Ch. 1996).

In re *The Walt Disney Company Derivative Litigation*, 731 A.2d 342 (Del. Ch 1998).

Revlon, Inc. v. Mac Andrews and Forbes Holdings, Inc., 506 A.2d. 173 (Del. 1986).

Securities and Exchange Commission v. Texas Gulf Sulphur Co. 401 F.2d 833 (2d Cir. 1968).

Smith v. Van Gorkom, 488 A.2d858 (Del. 1985)

"A lifetime's experience in the boardroom - but without the scar tissue! A <u>must</u> read…"

-Norman Augustine,
Former CEO of NYSE company, veteran of
numerous boards and author of *Augustine's Laws*

"*The Board* should be read by every investor and student of the American economic system."

-Edward L. Felton, Jr., Business School Professor

"A revealing look at boardroom experiences from the inside out. An essential tool for anyone who expects to successfully navigate the turbulent waters of corporate America."

-Richard Koppes,
Distinguished Corporate Lawyer and
former Senior Officer and General Counsel of one of
the country's largest public employee retirement systems

"Jim Ukropina has distilled in *The Board* his years of experience as a director, leader of directors and counselor to directors. Directors will find in this book not only experiences they have had but that they soon will have. Investors will learn of the complex challenges directors confront in representing shareholder interests."

-John Lillie,
Former CEO of two NYSE companies and
member of numerous corporate and nonprofit boards

"Over a decade of experiences in the life of a corporate boardroom: *The Board* is a riveting blend of fact and fiction, weaving a labyrinth of crisis and intrigue, hitting close to home for anyone involved in corporate America."

-Harold Messmer, CEO of NYSE
company and Author of *Managing Your Career*

ABOUT THE AUTHOR

Jim Ukropina's board experiences range from a Little League board to the board of a national university to the boards of Fortune 500 companies. Currently an independent strategic consultant and Of Counsel for a multinational law firm, Ukropina is regarded as an expert in corporate governance. Ukropina received his AB from Stanford University, his MBA from Stanford and his J.D. from the University of Southern California Law School. He lives in Pasadena, California.

Printed in the United States
957300002BA